Marxism and
the Philosophy of Language

MARXISM
AND
THE PHILOSOPHY OF LANGUAGE

V. N. Vološinov

Translated by
LADISLAV MATEJKA and I. R. TITUNIK

Harvard University Press
Cambridge, Massachusetts
London, England

This Harvard University Press paperback is published by
arrangement with Academic Press, Inc.

LIBRARY OF CONGRESS CATALOGING IN PUBLICATION DATA

Voloshinov, V. N.
   Marxism and the philosophy of language.
   Translation of: Marksizm i filosofiĩa ĩazyka.
   Bibliography: p.
   1. Dialectical materialism. 2. Languages—
Philosophy. I. Title.
B809.8.V59413 1986   401   85-27163
ISBN 0-674-55098-6

Contents

Translators' Preface, 1986

In the early 1970s, when V. N. Vološinov's book of 1929, *Marksizm i filosofija jazyka,* was translated into English and published as *Marxism and the Philosophy of Language,* both the book and its author were virtually unknown. Very few scholars possessed any knowledge of Vološinov's work and even fewer made any use of it. Among those rare exceptions, fortunately, was that coryphaeus of modern thought in the humanities, Professor Roman Jakobson. For Jakobson, Vološinov was first and foremost an insightful linguist who skillfully used a semiotic framework for the study of utterances and their dialogical exchange in verbal communication. In a letter of 1931 to Nikolaj Trubetzkoy, Jakobson praised Vološinov's "superb interpretation of linguistic problems" and, in the spirit of Vološinov's book, emphasized the dialectic method as a prerequisite for an adequate understanding of historical philology.[1]

While Vološinov's work went largely ignored in the Soviet Union, it played an important role, thanks to Jakobson, in shaping the theories of the Prague Linguistic Circle. It also influenced Jakobson's model of the incessant interaction between the variability of utterances and the systematic provisions of language, as developed in his trail-blazing treatise *Shifters, Verbal Categories, and the Russian Verb.* In that study, Jakobson prominently cited Vološinov's key concept of the nature of reported speech, the topic to which the entire third part of *Marxism and the Philosophy of Language* had been devoted. Furthermore, it was Jakobson's good offices that brought

---

1. Roman Jakobson to Nikolaj Trubetzkoy, *N. S. Trubetzkoy's Letters and Notes* (The Hague-Paris, 1975), p. 222.

about the selection of that book in 1972 by Seminar Press for translation as the first volume in its series *Studies in Language*. In honor of the role he played, the translators wish to dedicate the present Harvard University Press edition of *Marxism and the Philosophy of Language* to the memory of Roman Osipovič Jakobson.

With its appearance in English in 1973, *Marxism and the Philosophy of Language* began to attract considerable interest. Indeed, for many of its new readers it had the impact of a major discovery. It provided, to speak in its own terms, a welcome synthesis to replace the Humboldtian / Vosslerian thesis and the Saussurean antithesis in the theory and study of language. Vološinov is concerned above all with the social role of verbal utterances. He regards verbal utterances as social interaction, which is most typically displayed in dialogical exchanges and, by means of internalization, in inner speech and thoughts. In his view, the refraction of existence in the human consciousness originates solely in verbal communication which, by its nature, is anchored in social interaction. Consequently, for Vološinov, the study of human language cannot be detached from social existence in time and space and from the impact of socioeconomic conditions. The conceptualization of dialogue in the dialectical method is regarded by Vološinov as the only way of understanding the fundamental significance of language for all aspects of human civilization.

It was precisely the suggestive ramifications of dialectics for all fields of the humanities that made the resurrected *Marxism and the Philosophy of Language* an important book for modern trends not only in linguistics but also in anthropology, psychology, and the studies of literature and culture. In his comprehensive review of Vološinov's book (in its English translation), Fredric Jameson called *Marxism and the Philosophy of Language* "the best general introduction to linguistic study as a whole."[2] According to Aram Yemgoyan, Vološinov's book "is a must for anthropological linguists for it moves beyond all traditional linguistic concerns and virtually predates all contemporary interests ranging from semiotics to speech act theory."[3] And in the view of the British "neo-formalist" Ann Shukman, "Vološinov's extreme contextualism leads him to a semiotic theory that is primarily sociological, and to a theory of language that emphasizes process rather than system, function rather than essence."[4]

2. Fredric Jameson, review of *Marxism and the Philosophy of Language, Style,* **1** (Fall 1974), p. 535.

3. Aram Yemgoyan, review of *Marxism and the Philosophy of Language, American Anthropologist,* **79**, no. 3 (1977), p. 701.

4. Ann Shukman, review of *Marxism and the Philosophy of Language, Language and Style,* **12**, no. 1 (1979), p. 54.

There can be no doubt that a paramount factor in the promotion of *Marxism and the Philosophy of Language* to international prominence was the association of this book with the name of M. M. Baxtin, whose reputation among students of the humanities around the world has reached prodigious proportions. Undoubtedly instrumental in this development was V. V. Ivanov, the distinguished Soviet semiotician and linguist who, in his contribution to the celebration of Baxtin's 75th birthday in 1973, publicly declared that certain works signed by P. N. Medvedev and V. N. Vološinov, including *Marxism and the Philosophy of Language,* actually belonged to the pen of M. M. Baxtin. Although he provided no proof whatsoever, many scholars accepted Ivanov's claim as fact. Baxtin himself, then still alive, of course, had the opportunity to accept Ivanov's assertion or to deny it, but he remained silent and never made a public statement. It is known, however, that he refused to sign an affidavit concerning the alleged authorship when, shortly before his death, the official Soviet publishing agency (VAAP) urged him to sign for the sake of the copyright law.

The effect of Ivanov's declaration and its wide acceptance has been to draw into one integral and magisterial oeuvre works previously understood to have belonged to different writers and thinkers. Thus, works like *Marxism and the Philosophy of Language*—and indeed that work prominently among them—came to share the limelight of international attention along with the signed works of Baxtin, such as his books on Dostoevskij and Rabelais. In fact, *Marxism and the Philosophy of Language* became a focal point as the fundamental and most systematic exposition of the "Bakhtinian" conception of sign and language.

The merging of all the various writings into a single unified Bakhtinian recension is problematic, however. To this day, for example, no one has convincingly explained why Baxtin in 1929 would have used the name of his friend Vološinov for *Marxism and the Philosophy of Language* when that very same year Baxtin's book on Dostoevskij was published under his own name and was acclaimed by the Soviet critics, including the cultural commissar Lunačarskij. The seemingly simple question as to what actually happened remains unanswered, despite considerable research and inquiry, and despite the fact that some participants and witnesses—among them Baxtin himself—remained alive until fairly recently; indeed, a few are still alive today. Instead of being clarified by concrete evidence, the problem of authorship has turned into a mystery compounded by the special Soviet penchant for secrecy.

There are also the conceptual and ideological divergencies and even contradictions among writings signed by Baxtin, Vološinov, and Medvedev. The books and articles by Vološinov and Medvedev explicitly declare and implement a Marxist orientation. If Baxtin is to be regarded their author, then his relationship to Marxism must be defined—an issue of considerable controversy in itself. Some critics have explicitly denied Baxtin's Marxist sympathies or, at least, tried to minimize the Marxist character of the writings signed by Vološinov and Medvedev as "editorial re-touches," mere "expedience," "window-dressing" meant to insure publication in the Soviet Union. Among the holders of this view are Katerina Clark and Michael Holquist, the authors of the most ambitious and, in many respects, the most fascinating work on Baxtin yet published (*Mikhail Bakhtin*). Others, however, have hailed Baxtin precisely as an outstanding Marxist writer and thinker; this is the opinion of such authors as Frederic Jameson, Marina Yaguello, and Radovan Matijašević, among others. Quite a different tack is taken by the German Marxist scholar Helmut Glück, who assigns Marxist credentials only to Vološinov and Medvedev, denying them to Baxtin, and on that basis rejecting Ivanov's claim of Baxtin's authorship of their writings. Still other scholars, most notably Tzvetan Todorov, are inclined to see all the writings in question as belonging to one unified system whose author is Baxtin, but do, nevertheless, admit that the question of Marxism is a serious moot point. Such a variety and contradiction of informed expert opinion must give one pause, especially since identification of the overall conceptual and ideological framework is by no means a trivial matter: similar ideas in different systems of thought may well possess different values and pursue different aims.

Another point that deserves, but has not received, attention concerns what V. V. Ivanov apparently meant when he claimed that the "technical aspect" of his approach had always been "a secondary matter" for Baxtin.[5] Indeed, there have been many critics who have claimed that the loose, ambiguous, and contradictory nature of Baxtin's "technical aspect" has been exonerated by the "profundity of his ideas." Such a strategy, however, flagrantly ignores the fact that there are among the works attributed to Baxtin at least two in which the technical aspect is highly developed and skillfully deployed: they are *The Formal Method in Literary Scholarship* (Medvedev) and the very work presented in this volume, *Marxism and the Philosophy of Language*. The first documents the technical expertise of the practicing professional literary critic, polemicist, and theorist in its detailed, closely argued analysis of formalism and in its elaboration of a program for "sociological poetics." The second brings to bear, especially in its third part, the professional linguist's technical concern with "theory of the utterance" and "problems of syntax," specifically with the problem of "reported speech." That these two works,

5. V. V. Ivanov, "The Significance of M. M. Bakhtin's Ideas on Sign, Utterance and Dialogue for Modern Semiotics," in *Semiotics and Structuralism: Readings from the Soviet Union,* ed. H. Baran (White Plains, N.Y., 1976), p. 332.

technically and stylistically so different from Baxtin's signed writings, are at the same time attributed to him inevitably makes for something of a poser: if Baxtin did write these works in the technical register of their signatories as well as in their conceptual and ideological code, then the result may be viewed as an extreme case of stylization or even as a sort of intellectual forgery.

Thus there are serious grounds for reservations regarding the attribution to Baxtin of works signed by Vološinov and Medvedev. This has been acknowledged by the occasional use of the ambiguous slash in the designation of author of the works in question, that is, Voloshinov / Bakhtin, Medvedev / Bakhtin, allowing, to paraphrase Tzvetan Todorov, for the possibilities of collaboration and / or substitution and / or discussion.

We, the translators of this English version of *Marxism and the Philosophy of Language,* aware of the new materials and information that have come to light since its first publication and aware of the arguments in the controversy over attribution, understand that certain assumptions we made and certain conclusions we drew in 1973 are now open to question. To help the reader acquaint himself with other, more recent assumptions and conclusions, we append below a selected list of titles from the current literature on the Baxtin problem in addition to the works already cited. At the same time, we stand by the main content of our analyses and arguments. Furthermore, we believe that fair-mindedness and scholarly integrity dictate that the author of *Marxism and the Philosophy of Language* continue to be identified as Valentin Nikolaevič Vološinov since it has not been conclusively proved otherwise. It is a common practice in countries like the Soviet Union to remake the past by fiat; we see no reason to follow suit.

RECENT LITERATURE

Bahtin, Mihail, *Marksizam i filozofija jezika,* translated and introduced by Radovan Matijašević (Belgrade, 1980).

Bakhtin, M. M. / P. N. Medvedev, *Formal Method in Literary Scholarship: A Critical Introduction to Sociological Poetics,* translated by Albert J. Wehrle with a new introduction by Wlad Godzich (Cambridge, Mass., 1985).

Bakhtine, Mikhail (V. N. Volochinov), *Le marxisme et la philosophie du language,* translated and presented by M. Yaguello with a preface by Roman Jakobson (Paris, 1977).

Baxtin, M. M., *Èstetika slovesnogo tvorčestva,* ed. with commentaries S. G. Bočarov and S. S. Averincev (Moscow, 1979).

Baxtin, M. M., V. N. Vološinov, *Frejdizm: kritičeskij očerk,* reprint of 1927 original edition with new afterword by Anna Tamarchenko (New York, 1983).

Clark, Katerina, and Michael Holquist, *Mikhail Bakhtin* (Cambridge, Mass., 1984).

Holquist, Michael, "The Politics of Representation," in *Allegory and Representation*, ed. S. J. Greenblatt, Selected Papers from the English Institute, vol. 5 (Baltimore, 1979–80), pp. 163–182.

Kožinov, V., and S. Konkin, "Mixail Baxtin, kratkij očerk žizni i dejatel'nosti," in *Problemy poetiki i istorii literatury* (Saransk, 1973), pp. 5–35.

Matejka, Ladislav, "The Roots of Russian Semiotics of Art," in *The Sign: Semiotics around the World*, ed. R. Bailey et al. (Ann Arbor, Mich., 1978), pp. 146–169.

Medvedev, Pavel, *Die formale Methode in der Literaturwissenschaft*, presented and translated by Helmut Glück (Stuttgart, 1976).

Perlina, Nina, "Bakhtin-Medvedev-Voloshinov: An Apple of Discourse," *Revue de l'Université d'Ottawa / Ottawa University Quarterly*, **53**, no. 1 (1983), pp. 35–47.

Segal, D., *Aspects of Structuralism in Soviet Philology*, Papers on Poetics and Semiotics, vol. 2 (Tel-Aviv, 1974), pp. 120–132.

Titunik, I. R., "Bachtin and Soviet Semiotics (A Case Study: Boris Uspenskij's Poètika kompozicii)," *Russian Literature*, **10** (1981), pp. 1–16.

"Bakhtin & / or Vološinov & / or Medvedev: Dialogue & / or Doubletalk?" in *Language and Literature*, ed. B. A. Stolz et al. (Ann Arbor, Mich., 1984), pp. 535–564.

Todorov, Tzvetan, *Mikhail Bakhtin: The Dialogical Principle* (Minneapolis, 1984).

Vološinov, V. N., *Freudianism: A Marxist Critique*, translated by I. R. Titunik and ed. in collaboration with Neal H. Bruss (New York, 1976).

Marxismus und Sprachphilosophie, translated and introduced by Samuel M. Weber (Frankfurt, 1975).

Author's Introduction, 1929

To date, there is not as yet a single Marxist work on the philosophy of language. What is more, nothing of a definitive or elaborated nature has been said about language in Marxist works devoted to other, related fields.[1] For completely understandable reasons, then, our work, which is essentially the first of its kind, can set itself only the most modest of objectives. Nothing like a systematic and conclusive Marxist analysis even of only the basic issues in philosophy of language is feasible here. Such an analysis could only come about as the product of long and collaborative effort. Here we have had to limit ourselves to the modest task of delineating the *basic directions* that genuine Marxist thinking about language must take and the *methodological guidelines* on which that thinking must rely in approaching the concrete problems of linguistics.

Our task has been made especially difficult by the fact that Marxist literature as yet contains no conclusive and commonly accepted definitions as to the specific nature of the reality of ideological phenomena.[2] In the majority

1. The sole Marxist work touching on language—the recently published little book by I. Present, *The Origin of Speech and Thought*—has little, if anything, to do with the philosophy of language. The book examines problems of the genesis of speech and thought, where speech is understood not in terms of language as a certain specific ideological system but in terms of "signal" in the reflexological sense. Language as a phenomenon of a specific type cannot under any circumstances be reduced to "signal," and for that reason I. Present's investigations do not engage language at all. There is no direct route from his investigations to the concrete issues of linguistics and the philosophy of language.

2. Definition of the place of ideology in the unity of social life was provided by the founders of Marxism: ideology as superstructure, the relation of the superstructure to the basis, and so on. But as far as questions connected with the material of ideological creativity and the conditions of ideological communication are concerned, those questions, as secondary matters for the overall theory of historical materialism, did not receive concrete or conclusive resolution.

of cases, ideological phenomena are understood as phenomena of consciousness; that is, they are understood psychologistically. Such a conception is detrimental in the extreme to a correct approach to the specific characteristics of ideological phenomena, which under no circumstances are reducible to the characteristic features of the subjective consciousness and psyche. This also explains why the role of language as the specific material reality of ideological creativity has failed to be adequately appreciated.

Furthermore, it must be added that mechanistic categories are firmly entrenched in all those fields of knowledge untouched, or only perfunctorily touched upon, by the hands of Marxism's founders—Marx and Engels. All those fields of knowledge are still, in a fundamental sense, arrested at a stage of predialectical mechanistic materialism. An expression of this is the continued dominance, to the present day, of the category of mechanistic causality in all fields in the study of ideology. Along with mechanistic causality is the still unsurmounted positivistic conception of empirical data—a reverence for "fact" understood not in a dialectical sense but as something fixed and stable.[3] The philosophical spirit of Marxism has hardly yet made itself felt in those fields.

As a consequence of this state of affairs, we find ourselves virtually unable in the field of philosophy of language to derive support from any definitive, positive achievements in other fields of ideological studies. Even literary scholarship, the most advanced field of ideological study thanks to Plexanov, provides us with practically nothing relevant to our topic.

The work presented here basically pursues purely scientific investigative aims. However, we have made efforts to give it as popular a character as we could.[4]

In the first part of our work, we attempt to substantiate the significance of the philosophy of language for Marxism as a whole. That significance, as we said, has yet to be adequately appreciated. The fact is that *the concerns of the philosophy of language stand squarely at the juncture of several paramount domains in the Marxist worldview*—domains, moreover, that today enjoy wide interest at the leading edge of our society.[5]

In addition, issues concerning the philosophy of language have recently taken on extraordinary acuteness and fundamentality, in Western Europe as well as the U.S.S.R.[6] Contemporary bourgeois philosophy may be said to

3. Positivism is essentially a transfer of the basic categories and habits of substantialistic thought from the region of "essences," "ideas," "the general," etc. to the region of individual facts.

4. Of course, in addition to a general background in Marxism, the reader will need some familiarity with the basics of linguistics.

5. These are such fields as literary criticism and psychology.

6. But not at all in Marxist circles. We have in mind here the awakening of interest in the word brought about by the "formalists" and by such books as those of G. Spett (*Esthetic Fragments, The Inner Form of the Word*) and also Losev's book, *The Philosphy of Name*.

have begun developing under *the sign of the word,* this new trend in the philosophical thought of the West still being in its very earliest stage. A vehement struggle is going on over "the word" and its place in the system, a struggle for which analogy can be found only in the medieval debates involving realism, nominalism, and conceptualism. And indeed, the traditions of those philosophical trends of the Middle Ages have, to some degree, begun to be revived in the realism of the phenomenologists and the conceptualism of the neo-Kantians.

In linguistics itself, once its positivistic aversion to the theoretical aspect of posing scientific questions had passed and with it the enmity (typical for latter-day positivism) toward all demands for taking account of the worldview, an acute awareness of the discipline's own general-philosophical presuppositions and of its ties with other fields of knowledge awakened. Together with that awareness has come a sense of crisis which linguistics is experiencing due to its inability to meet all those new challenges.

To bring out the position that the philosophy of language occupies in the Marxist worldview — that is the objective of the first part of our book. Therefore, we do not in the first part attempt to prove anything and do not offer final solutions to any of the questions raised; what interests us here is not so much the connections between phenomena as the connections between problems.

In the second part of the book we attempt to resolve the basic problem of the philosophy of language, that of the *actual mode of existence of linguistic phenomena.* This problem is the axis around which turn all the major issues in modern thought on philosophy of language. Such basic problems as those of *the generation of language,* of *verbal interaction,* of *understanding,* and of *meaning,* as well as others, all converge on this one problem at their common center. Of course, as regards the solution of this problem itself, we have been able merely to map out its basic routes. Numerous questions remain barely touched upon; numerous lines of inquiry brought out in our exposition are left without being followed through to the end. But that could not be otherwise in a book of small size, which attempts virtually for the first time to approach these problems from a Marxist point of view.

The final part of our work is a concrete investigation of one of the problems of syntax. The fundamental idea of our entire work — *the productive role and social nature of the utterance* — needs concretization; its significance needs to be shown not only on the plane of general worldview and of theoretical issues in the philosophy of language but also in issues particular and peculiar to the science of language. After all, if an idea is correct and productive, then that productivity must manifest itself from top to bottom. But the topic of the third part — *the problem of the reported utterance* — has in itself broad significance extending beyond the confines of syntax. The fact is that a number of paramount literary phenomena—character speech (the construction of character in general), *skaz*, stylization, and parody—are nothing but different varieties of refraction of "another's speech." An understanding of this kind of speech and its sociological governance is an essential condition for the productive treatment of all the literary phenomena mentioned.[7]

Moreover, the very question dealt with in the third part has been totally neglected in the Russian linguistic literature. For instance, no one has yet pointed out and described the phenomenon of *quasi-direct discourse in Russian* (found already in Puškin). The considerable variety of modifications of direct and indirect discourse have been left entirely unstudied.

Thus, our work moves in the direction from the general and abstract to the particular and concrete: from the concerns of general philosophy we turn to general linguistic concerns and from there, finally, to an issue of a more specialized nature that lies on the boundary between grammar (syntax) and stylistics.

7. As a matter of fact, precisely these phenomena are attracting the attention of literary scholars at the present time. Of course, other points of view would also have to be applied to gain a full understanding of all the phenomena we have mentioned. However, without analysis of the forms of reported speech no productive work is possible here.

Marxism and
the Philosophy of Language

Guide to Transliteration

Russian names and words in the translated text and footnotes and in the appendices are transliterated in accordance with the standard scholarly system in which the following special signs have the approximate values indicated below:

'   *soft sign,*   indicating that the preceding consonant is "softened" (i.e., palatalized)

''   *hard sign,* indicating that the preceding consonant is not palatalized

c   *ts*

č   *ch*

è   *e,* as in *egg*

e   *e,* as in *egg,* preceded by "j" as explained below

j   *y* initially (before a vowel), terminally (after a vowel), medially between vowels or between hard or soft sign and a vowel; elsewhere indicates that the preceding consonant is palatalized

š   *sh*

šč   *shch*

x   *h*

y   *i,* as in *bill*

ž   *zh*

Compare the following examples of certain Russian names in their common English spellings and their transliterated equivalents: Chekhov = Čexov, Dostoyevsky = Dostoevskij, Gogol = Gogol', Pushkin = Puškin, Tolstoy = Tolstoj, etc.

Translators' Introduction

In his retrospective observations about the early stages of American structural linguistics, Zellig Harris found it relevant to recall the impact Karl Marx's *Das Kapital* had made on Leonard Bloomfield, the most powerful leader of the structuralist school in the United States. Writes Harris:

> In the late Depression years, when neither admiration of Russia nor war preparations in America had yet obscured the scientific and social results of Karl Marx, Leonard Bloomfield remarked to me that in studying *Das Kapital* he was impressed above all with the similarity between Marx's treatment of social behavior and that of linguistics.[1]

In curious contrast, Bloomfield's Russian contemporary, Valentin Nikolaevič Vološinov (1895-?), whose *Marxism and the Philosophy of Language* was written in the late twenties in the U.S.S.R., makes no reference to *Das Kapital* at all. Instead, in the brief introduction to his work,[2] Vološinov openly declares that the study of language was one of those fields of knowledge "untouched or only perfunctorily touched upon by the hands of Marxism's founders" and that such fields of knowledge were still, at that time, under the domination of a "predialectical, mechanistic materialism" wherein the "philosophical spirit of Marxism had hardly yet made itself felt." Indeed, Vološinov considered *Marxism and the Philosophy of Language* to be a pioneering venture, a first of its kind having no *direct*, substantive, positive support in Marxian or Marxist writings.

1. *Language*, 27 (1951), p. 297.
2. That introduction is included in this edition as "Author's Introduction, 1929."

1

Lacking sources in Marxism itself, as he claimed, and eschewing the common exegetical technique of speciously coaxing needed principles from canonical dicta, Vološinov found his inspiration in the von Humboldtian concept of the creative aspects of human language and proposed analyzing language as "a continuous generative process implemented in the social-verbal interaction of speakers." At the same time, he cautions linguists against mere descriptive cataloguing of forms and patterns, against mechanistic systematization and, in general, against the temptations of a superficial empiricism which, he avers, are very powerful in linguistic science. "The study of the sound aspect of language," he says, "occupies a disproportionately large place in linguistics, often setting the tone for the field, and in most cases carried on outside any connection with the real essence of language as a meaningful sign." From this basic position, he vehemently attacks reflexology, which was preoccupied with investigation of responses of the animal organism to signals (stimuli). "The grievous misconceptions and ingrained habits of mechanistic thought," Vološinov asserts, "are alone responsible for the attempt to take these 'signals' and very nearly make of them the key to the understanding of language and the human psyche."

In the 1920s, according to Vološinov's account, the most influential book among the leading Russian linguists was Ferdinand de Saussure's *Course in General Linguistics*. It is obvious that Vološinov himself was strongly impressed by Saussure, although he approaches him critically and often uses lengthy quotations from the *Course* as antitheses to his own views. He is particularly challenge by the Saussurian dichotomy between *la langue* (language system) and *la parole* (speech act/utterance), and he seriously questions the conceptual separation of synchrony from diachrony in the investigation of verbal communication. In Vološinov's view, the very foundations of the Saussure school represent an intellectual heritage originating from Leibniz's conception of universal grammar and, above all, from the Cartesianism and rationalism of the 17th and 18th centuries.

Here are his own words:

> The idea of the conventionality, the arbitrariness, of language is a typical one for rationalism as a whole; and no less typical is the comparison of language to the system of mathematical signs. What interests the mathematically minded rationalists is not the relationship of the sign to the actual reality it reflects or to the individual who is its originator, but the relationship of sign to sign within a closed system already accepted and authorized. In other words, they are interested only in the inner logic of the system of signs itself, taken, as in algebra, completely independently of the meanings that give signs their content.

According to Vološinov's interpretation, a verbal sign is a speech act that necessarily includes as inseparable components the active participation of the speaker (writer) on the one hand, and the hearer (reader) on the other. "Its specificity," as he puts it, "consists precisely in its being located between organized individuals, in its being the medium of their communication." Convinced that the verbal sign is the purest and most sensitive medium of social intercourse, Vološinov promotes the study of signs to the primary task of linguistic investigation. Consequently, in spite of its title, Vološinov's book is chiefly concerned with the sign and with the laws governing the systems of signs in their deployment within human society. In certain respects, therefore, Vološinov's pivotal interests overlap with questions that had challenged the profound inquisitiveness of Charles Sanders Peirce and had stimulated his epoch-making contribution to the general theory of signs.

Among various sign systems, Vološinov considers human language the most fundamental and the most characteristic of that which is human about man.as a species. For that reason, Vološinov suggests that the analysis of the speech act as a verbal interaction can illuminate not only the mysteries of the human psyche, but also that complex phenomenon called "social psychology" in Marxism and considered by the majority of Marxists as the link between the material basis and the mental creativity of man. He does not hesitate to assert that the Marxist "social psychology," removed from the actual process of verbal interaction, risks turning into the metaphysical or mythic concept of "collective soul," "collective inner psyche," or "spirit of the people." In short, the speech act and the rules that govern its systematic usage in society were recognized by Vološinov as the dominant characteristic of human behavior and assigned a central role in the framework of Marxism itself. In this way, the science of signs, which could be traced back to the ancient philosophers, which had inspired St. Augustine, and which, in the Middle Ages, had challenged the scholastics, became an important issue of dialectical materialism as conceived by Vološinov. The most decisive impulses for such a revision of Marxism came, no doubt, from Saussure, from the American pragmatists, and from the Vosslerian reinterpretation of von Humboldt, all critically transformed in the intellectual climate of Leningrad in the late 1920s.

The philosophy of language, for Vološinov, is the philosophy of sign. Among numerous systems of signs, he held the verbal sign, implemented in an utterance, to be the most revealing object of semiotic studies. Vološinov views every sign operation, including the utterance, as a binary arrangement inseparably associating the physical properties with the meaning they stand for and necessarily involving the binary participation of those who enter into the meaningful process of communication. "Utterance," as Vološinov puts it, "is constructed between two socially organized persons and, in the absence of a real addressee, an addressee is presupposed in the representative of the social group to which the speaker belongs." Vološinov, of course, recognizes the fact that every word as a sign has to be selected from the inventory of available signs, but he emphasizes that the individual manipulation of this social sign in a concrete utterance is regulated by social relations. In his words, "The immediate social situation and the broader social milieu wholly determine—and determine from within, so to speak—the structure of an utterance."

It follows naturally that, for Vološinov, dialogue is the basic model of reciprocal relations in verbal communication. "Dialogue," Vološinov asserts, "can be understood in a broader sense, meaning not only direct, face-to-face, vocalized verbal communication between persons, but also verbal communication of any type whatsoever." He implies that actually every cultural pattern can be derived from the conceptual framework of human dialogue; hence dialogue assumes the character of a primordial source of social creativity in general. In striking parallel to the Peircian interpretation of inner speech, Vološinov suggests that closer analysis reveals that the units of inner speech join and alternate in a way that resembles an exchange in dialogue. "The understanding of a sign," Vološinov claims, "is an act of reference between the sign apprehended and other already known signs: understanding is a response to a sign with signs." Thus the underlying operation is viewed as a creative activity matching another creative activity and understandable only in that relationship; since, "a generative process can only be grasped with the aid of another generative process."

In his book on psychoanalysis, published in 1928 under the title *Freudianism*, Vološinov was even inclined to recognize the therapeutic effects of dialogue in its role of verbalization of hidden mental complexes. As a matter of fact, Vološinov felt that Freud's attention to the role of language in psychoanalysis was a major asset, while, at the same time, fundamentally disagreeing with the ideological aspects of Freudianism.

In connection with dialogue, Vološinov brings into focus the problem of defining the elementary linguistic units in their relationship to the form of the utterance as a whole. He seems to be convinced that linguistic analysis, which proceeds from the constitutive parts to the structural whole and not vice versa, cannot adequately handle the structural characteristics of dialogue and their relevance to semiotic communication. "As long as the utterance in its wholeness remains *terra incognita* for the linguist," Vološinov asserts, "it is out of the question to speak of a genuine, concrete, and not a scholastic kind of understanding of syntactic forms." According to Vološinov, most linguists, being still under the impact of 19th-century comparative Indo-European studies, have continued to think in terms of phonetic and morphological categories and have tried to approach syntax by morphologization of syntactic problems. In Vološinov's view, syntactic forms come closer to the real conditions of discourse than do phonetic and morphological ones. "Therefore," he insists, "our point of view, which deals with the living phenomena of language, must give precedence to syntactic forms over morphological or phonetic ones."

To illustrate his approach to syntax, Vološinov devotes a third of his book to the problem of reported speech conceived as "speech within speech, utterance within utterance and, at the same time, as speech about speech and utterance about utterance." In this crucial verbal operation, an utterance, removed from its original context, becomes a part of another utterance within another context, so that two different contexts, implying two different time-space positions, appear in an interaction within a single unifying syntactic structure. Such a structure has to provide for two sets of speech participants and, consequently, for two sets of grammatical and stylistic rules. In this way, two distinct dialects, whether cultural or regional, or two distinct stylistic variants of the same dialect, can interact within a single sentence.

In such an arrangement, one utterance reports while the other utterance is reported, either as a citation (repetition), a paraphrase (transformation), or as an interaction of repetition and transformation. Thus the resulting construction brings into contrast the products of two distinct speech acts and their contextual implications. Actually, each reported utterance can be at the same time a reporting utterance so that, theoretically, the resulting structure can consist of the interaction of an unlimited number of dialects or dialectal variants; it appears as a system of systems integrated by the structural properties of the syntactic whole. Since the usage of reported speech, as Vološinov shows, is very typical for verbal communication, the problems of citation and of paraphrase are revealed as crucial operations in the generative processes of verbal sign. Vološinov suggestively indicates that an adequate analysis of reported speech, which he considers intrinsically related to the problems of dialogue, can illuminate all aspects of verbal communication, including verbal art. His book, in effect, implies that such an analysis can be directly relevant to the study of ideological values and of the human mind in general.

Although V. N. Vološinov professed himself to be a Marxist theorist of the philosophy of language and set himself the task, as he specifies in the introduction to *Marxism and the Philosophy of Language,* of "marking out the basic direction which genuine Marxist thinking about language must take . . . in approaching the concrete problems of linguistics," his work ran afoul of the Party line version of Marxism then in force in the U.S.S.R. Along with a great many other outstanding intellectual and creative personalities, he became the victim of the Stalinist purges of the 1930s, and he and his work were consigned to oblivion. For decades no mention of Vološinov was to be found. His own personal fate remains a mystery to the present day.

Only outside the Soviet Union did Vološinov's ideas find acknowledgment and productive treatment. In the 1930s and 1940s, members of the Prague Linguistic Circle openly continued to develop various aspects of Vološinov's stimulating outline of the philosophy of language. Vološinov's suggestions contributed greatly to the semiotic studies of Petr Bogatyrev, Jan Mukařovský, and Roman Jakobson.

trail-blazing treatise, *Shifters, Verbal Categories, and the Russian Verb* (first published by the Harvard University Slavic Department in 1957).

Recently, thanks to the current phenomenal renaissance of semiotics in the Soviet Union, new and intriguing information has come to light concerning a whole school of semioticians operating during the period of the late 1920s and early 1930s. M. M. Baxtin, whose masterworks on Dostoevskij and Rabelais have now achieved international acclaim, has been identified as the leader of this school and V. N. Vološinov as his closest follower and collaborator.[3]

The Russian original, *Marksizm i filosofija jazyka: osnovnye problemy sociologičeskogo metoda v nauke o jazyke* [Marxism and the Philosophy of Language: Basic Problems of the Sociological Method in the Study of Language], appeared in Leningrad in two editions, 1929 and 1930 respectively, in the series *Voprosy metodologii i teorii jazyka i literatury* [Problems of the Methodology and Theory of Language and Literature]. The translation presented here is based on the second edition. Insofar as could be ascertained by comparing the two editions, they differ only with respect to a few minor discrepancies. The translators willingly acknowledge the difficulty of the translated text and their frequent recourse to English locutions and terms whose special technical meanings have to be grasped from the context of the argument itself. While not wishing to excuse errors and misunderstandings of which they may well be guilty, the translators should like to bring to the reader's attention the fact that Vološinov himself had to contend with the formidable problem of finding suitable expression for ideas and concepts that lacked any established vocabulary in Russian.

In an appendix following the translated text, the reader will find essays by the translators that attempt to clarify and comment on certain key aspects of the intellectual trend in Russia represented by V. N. Vološinov with regard to the studies of language and literature.

Thanks are due to the Editors of the MIT Press for permission to utilize the Translators' earlier version of Part III, Chapters 2 and 3, of *Marxism and the Philosophy of Language*, which appeared in *Readings in Russian Poetics (Formalist and Structuralist Views)*, edited by Ladislav Matejka, and Krystyna Pomorska, MIT Press, Cambridge, Massachusetts, 1971, pp. 149-179. Omissions in the earlier translation have been restored in the present one and a few minor changes and corrections made.

3. *Voprosy jazykoznanija*, 2 (1971), p. 160.

PART I

PHILOSOPHY OF LANGUAGE AND ITS SIGNIFICANCE FOR MARXISM

CHAPTER 1

The Study of Ideologies
and Philosophy of Language

*The problem of the ideological sign. The ideological sign and
consciousness. The word as an ideological sign par excellence.
The ideological neutrality of the word. The capacity of the
word to be an inner sign. Summary.*

Problems of the philosophy of language have in recent times acquired exceptional pertinence and importance for Marxism. Over a wide range of the most
vital sectors in its scientific advance, the Marxist method bears directly upon
these problems and cannot continue to move ahead productively without special
provision for their investigation and solution.

First and foremost, the very foundations of a Marxist theory of ideologies—
the bases for the studies of scientific knowledge, literature, religion, ethics, and
so forth—are closely bound up with problems of the philosophy of language.

Any ideological product is not only itself a part of a reality (natural or social),
just as is any physical body, any instrument of production, or any product for
consumption, it also, in contradistinction to these other phenomena, reflects and
refracts another reality outside itself. Everything ideological possesses *meaning:*
it represents, depicts, or stands for something lying outside itself. In other words,
it is a *sign. Without signs there is no ideology.* A physical body equals itself, so
to speak; it does not signify anything but wholly coincides with its particular,
given nature. In this case there is no question of ideology.

However, any physical body may be perceived as an image; for instance, the
image of natural inertia and necessity embodied in that particular thing. Any
such artistic-symbolic image to which a particular physical object gives rise is
already an ideological product. The physical object is converted into a sign. Without ceasing to be a part of material reality, such an object, to some degree, reflects and refracts another reality.

9

The same is true of any instrument of production. A tool by itself is devoid of any special meaning; it commands only some designated function—to serve this or that purpose in production. The tool serves that purpose as the particular, given thing that it is, without reflecting or standing for anything else. However, a tool also may be converted into an ideological sign. Such, for instance, is the hammer and sickle insignia of the Soviet Union. In this case, hammer and sickle possess a purely ideological meaning. Additionally, any instrument of production may be ideologically decorated. Tools used by prehistoric man are covered with pictures or designs—that is, with signs. So treated, a tool still does not, of course, itself become a sign.

It is further possible to enhance a tool artistically, and in such a way that its artistic shapeliness harmonizes with the purpose it is meant to serve in production. In this case, something like maximal approximation, almost a coalescence, of sign and tool comes about. But even here we still detect a distinct conceptual dividing line: the tool, as such, does not become a sign; the sign, as such, does not become an instrument of production.

Any consumer good can likewise be made an ideological sign. For instance, bread and wine become religious symbols in the Christian sacrament of communion. But the consumer good, as such, is not at all a sign. Consumer goods, just as tools, may be combined with ideological signs, but the distinct conceptual dividing line between them is not erased by the combination. Bread is made in some particular shape; this shape is not warranted solely by the bread's function as a consumer good; it also has a certain, if primitive, value as an ideological sign (e.g., bread in the shape of a figure eight *(krendel)* or a rosette).

Thus, side by side with the natural phenomena, with the equipment of technology, and with articles for consumption, there exists a special world—the *world of signs.*

Signs also are particular, material things; and, as we have seen, any item of nature, technology, or consumption can become a sign, acquiring in the process a meaning that goes beyond its given particularity. A sign does not simply exist as a part of a reality—it reflects and refracts another reality. Therefore, it may distort that reality or be true to it, or may perceive it from a special point of view, and so forth. Every sign is subject to the criteria of ideological evaluation (i.e., whether it is true, false, correct, fair, good, etc.). The domain of ideology coincides with the domain of signs. They equate with one another. Wherever a sign is present, ideology is present, too. *Everything ideological possesses semiotic value.*

Within the domain of signs—i.e., within the ideological sphere—profound differences exist: it is, after all, the domain of the artistic image, the religious symbol, the scientific formula, and the judicial ruling, etc. Each field of ideological creativity has its own kind of orientation toward reality and each refracts reality in its own way. Each field commands its own special function within the unity of social life. *But it is their semiotic character that places all ideological phenomena under the same general definition.*

Every ideological sign is not only a reflection, a shadow, of reality, but is also itself a material segment of that very reality. Every phenomenon functioning as an ideological sign has some kind of material embodiment, whether in sound, physical mass, color, movements of the body, or the like. In this sense, the reality of the sign is fully objective and lends itself to a unitary, monistic, objective method of study. A sign is a phenomenon of the external world. Both the sign itself and all the effects it produces (all those actions, reactions, and new signs it elicits in the surrounding social milieu) occur in outer experience.

This is a point of extreme importance. Yet, elementary and self-evident as it may seem, the study of ideologies has still not drawn all the conclusions that follow from it.

The idealistic philosophy of culture and psychologistic cultural studies locate ideology in the consciousness.[1] Ideology, they assert, is a fact of consciousness; the external body of the sign is merely a coating, merely a technical means for the realization of the inner effect, which is understanding.

Idealism and psychologism alike overlook the fact that understanding itself can come about only within some kind of semiotic material (e.g., inner speech), that sign bears upon sign, that *consciousness itself can arise and become a viable fact only in the material embodiment of signs.* The understanding of a sign is, after all, an act of reference between the sign apprehended and other, already known signs; in other words, understanding is a response to a sign with signs. And this chain of ideological creativity and understanding, moving from sign to sign and then to a new sign, is perfectly consistent and continuous: from one link of a semiotic nature (hence, also of a material nature) we proceed uninterruptedly to another link of exactly the same nature. And nowhere is there a break in the chain, nowhere does the chain plunge into inner being, nonmaterial in nature and unembodied in signs.

This ideological chain stretches from individual consciousness to individual consciousness, connecting them together. Signs emerge, after all, only in the process of interaction between one individual consciousness and another. And the individual consciousness itself is filled with signs. Consciousness becomes consciousness only once it has been filled with ideological (semiotic) content, consequently, only in the process of social interaction.

1. It should be noted that a change of outlook in this regard can be detected in modern neo-Kantianism. We have in mind the latest book by Ernst Cassirer, *Philosophie der symbolischen Formen*, Vol. 1, 1923. While remaining on the grounds of consciousness, Cassirer considers its dominant trait to be representation. Each element of consciousness represents something, bears a symbolic function. The whole exists in its parts, but a part is comprehensible only in the whole. According to Cassirer, an idea is just as sensory as matter; the sensoriness involved, however, is that of the symbolic sign, it is representative sensoriness.

Despite the deep methodological differences between them, the idealistic philosophy of culture and psychologistic cultural studies both commit the same fundamental error. By localizing ideology in the consciousness, they transform the study of ideologies into a study of consciousness and its laws; it makes no difference whether this is done in transcendental or in empirical-psychological terms. This error is responsible not only for methodological confusion regarding the interrelation of disparate fields of knowledge, but for a radical distortion of the very reality under study as well. Ideological creativity—a material and social fact—is forced into the framework of the individual consciousness. The individual consciousness, for its part, is deprived of any support in reality. It becomes either all or nothing.

For idealism it has become all: its locus is somewhere above existence and it determines the latter. In actual fact, however, this sovereign of the universe is merely the hypostatization in idealism of an abstract bond among the most general forms and categories of ideological creativity.

For psychological positivism, on the contrary, consciousness amounts to nothing: it is just a conglomeration of fortuitous, psychophysiological reactions which, by some miracle, results in meaningful and unified ideological creativity.

The objective social regulatedness of ideological creativity, once misconstrued as a conformity with laws of the individual consciousness, must inevitably forfeit its real place in existence and depart either up into the superexistential empyrean of transcendentalism or down into the presocial recesses of the psychophysical, biological organism.

However, the ideological, as such, cannot possibly be explained in terms of either of these superhuman or subhuman, animalian, roots. Its real place in existence is in the special, social material of signs created by man. Its specificity consists precisely in its being located between organized individuals, in its being the medium of their communication.

Signs can arise only on *interindividual territory*. It is territory that cannot be called "natural" in the direct sense of the word:[2] signs do not arise between any two members of the species *Homo sapiens*. It is essential that the two individuals be *organized socially,* that they compose a group (a social unit); only then can the medium of signs take shape between them. The individual consciousness not only cannot be used to explain anything, but, on the contrary, is itself in need of explanation from the vantage point of the social, ideological medium.

The individual consciousness is a social-ideological fact. Not until this point is recognized with due provision for all the consequences that follow from it will it be possible to construct either an objective psychology or an objective study of ideologies.

2. Society, of course, is also a *part of nature*, but a part that is qualitatively separate and distinct and possesses its own *specific* systems of laws.

It is precisely the problem of consciousness that has created the major difficulties and generated the formidable confusion encountered in all issues associated with psychology and the study of ideologies alike. By and large, consciousness has become the *asylum ignorantiae* for all philosophical constructs. It has been made the place where all unresolved problems, all objectively irreducible residues are stored away. Instead of trying to find an objective definition of consciousness, thinkers have begun using it as a means for rendering all hard and fast objective definitions subjective and fluid.

The only possible objective definition of consciousness is a sociological one. Consciousness cannot be derived directly from nature, as has been and still is being attempted by naive mechanistic materialism and contemporary objective psychology (of the biological, behavioristic, and reflexological varieties). Ideology cannot be derived from consciousness, as is the practice of idealism and psychologistic positivism. Consciousness takes shape and being in the material of signs created by an organized group in the process of its social intercourse. The individual consciousness is nurtured on signs; it derives its growth from them; it reflects their logic and laws. The logic of consciousness is the logic of ideological communication, of the semiotic interaction of a social group. If we deprive consciousness of its semiotic, ideological content, it would have absolutely nothing left. Consciousness can harbor only in the image, the word, the meaningful gesture, and so forth. Outside such material, there remains the sheer physiological act unilluminated by consciousness, i.e., without having light shed on it, without having meaning given to it, by signs.

All that has been said above leads to the following methodological conclusion: *the study of ideologies does not depend on psychology to any extent and need not be grounded in it.* As we shall see in greater detail in a later chapter, it is rather the reverse: *objective psychology must be grounded in the study of ideologies.* The reality of ideological phenomena is the objective reality of social signs. The laws of this reality are the laws of semiotic communication and are directly determined by the total aggregate of social and economic laws. Ideological reality is the immediate superstructure over the economic basis. Individual consciousness is not the architect of the ideological superstructure, but only a tenant lodging in the social edifice of ideological signs.

With our preliminary argument disengaging ideological phenomena and their regulatedness from individual consciousness, we tie them in all the more firmly with conditions and forms of social communication. The reality of the sign is wholly a matter determined by that communication. After all, the existence of the sign is nothing but the materialization of that communication. Such is the nature of all ideological signs.

But nowhere does this semiotic quality and the continuous, comprehensive role of social communication as conditioning factor appear so clearly and fully expressed as in language. *The word is the ideological phenomenon par excellence.*

The entire reality of the word is wholly absorbed in its function of being a sign. A word contains nothing that is indifferent to this function, nothing that would not have been engendered by it. A word is the purest and most sensitive medium of social intercourse.

This indicatory, representative power of the word as an ideological phenomenon and the exceptional distinctiveness of its semiotic structure would already furnish reason enough for advancing the word to a prime position in the study of ideologies. It is precisely in the material of the word that the basic, general-ideological forms of semiotic communication could best be revealed.

But that is by no means all. The word is not only the purest, most indicatory sign but is, in addition, *a neutral sign.* Every other kind of semiotic material is specialized for some particular field of ideological creativity. Each field possesses its own ideological material and formulates signs and symbols specific to itself and not applicable in other fields. In these instances, a sign is created by some specific ideological function and remains inseparable from it. A word, in contrast, is neutral with respect to any specific ideological function. It can carry out ideological functions of *any* kind—scientific, aesthetic, ethical, religious.

Moreover, there is that immense area of ideological communication that cannot be pinned down to any one ideological sphere: the area of *communication in human life, human behavior.* This kind of communication is extraordinarily rich and important. On one side, it links up directly with the processes of production; on the other, it is tangent to the spheres of the various specialized and fully fledged ideologies. In the following chapter, we shall speak in greater detail of this special area of behavioral, or life, ideology. For the time being, we shall take note of the fact that the material of behavioral communication is preeminently the *word.* The locale of so-called conversational language and its forms is precisely here, in the area of behavioral ideology.

One other property belongs to the word that is of the highest order of importance and is what makes the word the primary medium of the individual consciousness. Although the reality of the word, as is true of any sign, resides between individuals, a word, at the same time, is produced by the individual organism's own means without recourse to any equipment or any other kind of extracorporeal material. This has determined the role of word as *the semiotic material of inner life—of consciousness* (inner speech). Indeed, the consciousness could have developed only by having at its disposal material that was pliable and expressible by bodily means. And the word was exactly that kind of material. The word is available as the sign for, so to speak, inner employment: it can function as a sign in a state short of outward expression. For this reason, the problem of individual consciousness as the *inner word* (as an *inner sign* in general) becomes one of the most vital problems in philosophy of language.

It is clear, from the very start, that this problem cannot be properly approached by resorting to the usual concept of word and language as worked out in nonsociological linguistics and philosophy of language. What is needed is profound and acute analysis of the word as social sign before its function as the medium of consciousness can be understood.

It is owing to this exclusive role of the word as the medium of consciousness that *the word functions as an essential ingredient accompanying all ideological creativity whatsoever.* The word accompanies and comments on each and every ideological act. The processes of understanding any ideological phenomenon at all (be it a picture, a piece of music, a ritual, or an act of human conduct) cannot operate without the participation of inner speech. All manifestations of ideological creativity—all other nonverbal signs—are bathed by, suspended in, and cannot be entirely segregated or divorced from the element of speech.

This does not mean, of course, that the word may supplant any other ideological sign. None of the fundamental, specific ideological signs is replacable wholly by words. It is ultimately impossible to convey a musical composition or pictorial image adequately in words. Words cannot wholly substitute for a religious ritual; not is there any really adequate verbal substitute for even the simplest gesture in human behavior. To deny this would lead to the most banal rationalism and simplisticism. Nonetheless, at the very same time, every single one of these ideological signs, though not supplantable by words, has support in and is accompanied by words, just as is the case with singing and its musical accompaniment.

No cultural sign, once taken in and given meaning, remains in isolation: it becomes part of the *unity of the verbally constituted consciousness.* It is in the capacity of the consciousness to find verbal access to it. Thus, as it were, spreading ripples of verbal responses and resonances form around each and every ideological sign. Every *ideological refraction of existence in process of generation,* no matter what the nature of its significant material, *is accompanied by ideological refraction in word* as an obligatory concominant phenomenon. Word is present in each and every act of understanding and in each and every act of interpretation.

All of the properties of word we have examined—*its semiotic purity, its ideological neutrality, its involvement in behavioral communication, its ability to become an inner word and, finally, its obligatory presence, as an accompanying phenomenon, in any conscious act*—all these properties make the word the fundamental object of the study of ideologies. The laws of the ideological refraction of existence in signs and in consciousness, its forms and mechanics, must be studied in the material of the word, first of all. The only possible way of bringing the Marxist sociological method to bear on all the profundities and subtleties of "immanent" ideological structures is to operate from the basis of the philosophy of language as the *philosophy of the ideological sign.* And that basis must be devised and elaborated by Marxism itself.

CHAPTER 2

Concerning the Relationship of the Basis and Superstructures

Inadmissibility of the category of mechanistic causality in the study of ideologies. The generative process of society and the generative process of the word. The semiotic expression of social psychology. The problem of behavioral speech genres. Forms of social intercourse and forms of signs. The theme of a sign. The class struggle and the dialectics of signs. Conclusions.

The problem of the *relationship of basis and superstructures*—one of the fundamental problems of Marxism—is closely linked with questions of philosophy of language at a number of crucial points and could benefit considerably from a solution to those questions or even just from treatment of them to some appreciable extent and depth.

When the question is posed as to how the basis determines ideology, the answer given is: *causally;* which is true enough, but also far too general and therefore ambiguous.

If what is meant by causality is mechanical causality (as causality has been and still is understood and defined by the positivistic representatives of natural scientific thought), then this answer would be essentially incorrect and contradictory to the very fundaments of dialectal materialism.

The range of application for the categories of mechanical causality is extremely narrow, and even within the natural sciences themselves it grows constantly narrower the further and more deeply dialectics takes hold in the basic principles of these sciences. As regards the fundamental problems of historical materialism and of the study of ideologies altogether, the applicability of so inert a category as that of mechanical causality is simply out of the question.

No cognitive value whatever adheres to the establishment of a connection between the basis and some isolated fact torn from the unity and integrity of its

17

ideological context. It is essential above all to determine the *meaning of any,* *given ideological change in the context of ideology appropriate to it,* seeing that every domain of ideology is a unified whole which reacts with its entire consti- tution to a change in the basis. Therefore, any explanation must preserve *all the* *qualitative differences* between interacting domains and must trace all the vari- ous stages through which a change travels. Only on this condition will analysis result, not in a mere outward conjunction of two adventitious facts belonging to different levels of things, but in the process of the actual dialectical genera- tion of society, a process which emerges from the basis and comes to completion in the superstructures.

If the specific nature of the semiotic-ideological material is ignored, the ideo- logical phenomenon studied undergoes simplification. Either only its rational- istic aspect, its content side, is noted and explained (for example, the direct, referential sense of an artistic image, such as "Rudin as superflous man"), and then that aspect is correlated with the basis (e.g., the gentry class degenerates; hence the "superflous man" in literature); or, oppositely, only the outward, technical aspect of the ideological phenomenon is singled out (e.g., some tech- nicality in building construction or in the chemistry of coloring materials) and then this aspect is derived directly from the technological level of production.

Both these ways of deriving ideology from the basis miss the real essence of an ideological phenomenon. Even if the correspondence established is correct, even if it is true that "superfluous men" did appear in literature in connection with the breakdown of the economic structure of the gentry, still, for one thing, it does not at all follow that related economic upsets mechanically cause "super- fluous men" to be produced on the pages of a novel (the absurdity of such a claim is perfectly obvious); for another thing, the correspondence established itself remains without any cognitive value until both the specific role of the "superfluous man" in the artistic structure of the novel and the specific role of the novel in social life as a whole are elucidated.

Surely it must be clear that between changes in the economic state of affairs and the appearance of the "superfluous man" in the novel stretches a long, long road that crosses a number of qualitatively different domains, each with its own specific set of laws and its own specific characteristics. Surely it must be clear that the "superfluous man" did not appear in the novel in any way independent of and unconnected with other elements of the novel, but that, on the contrary, the whole novel, as a single organic unity subject to its own specific laws, under- went restructuring, and that, consequently, all its other elements—its composi- tion, style, etc.—also underwent restructuring. And what is more, this organic restructuring of the novel came about in close connection with changes in the whole field of literature, as well.

The problem of the interrelationship of the basis and superstructures—a prob- lem of exceptional complexity, requiring enormous amounts of preliminary data for its productive treatment—can be elucidated to a significant degree through the material of the word.

Looked at from the angle of our concerns, the essence of this problem comes down to *how* actual existence (the basis) determines sign and *how* sign reflects and refracts existence in its process of generation.

The properties of the word as an ideological sign (properties discussed in the preceding chapter) are what make the word the most suitable material for viewing the whole of this problem in basic terms. What is important about the word in this regard is not so much its sign purity as its *social ubiquity*. The word is implicated in literally each and every act or contact between people—in collaboration on the job, in ideological exchanges, in the chance contacts of ordinary life, in political relationships, and so on. Countless ideological threads running through all areas of social intercourse register effect in the word. It stands to reason, then, that the word is the most sensitive *index of social changes*, and what is more, of changes still in the process of growth, still without definitive shape and not as yet accomodated into already regularized and fully defined ideological systems. The word is the medium in which occur the slow quantitative accretions of those changes which have not yet achieved the status of a new ideological quality, not yet produced a new and fully-fledged ideological form. The word has the capacity to register all the transitory, delicate, momentary phases of social change.

That which has been termed "social psychology" and is considered, according to Plexanov's theory and by the majority of Marxists, as the transitional link between the sociopolitical order and ideology in the narrow sense (science, art, and the like), is, in its actual, material existence, *verbal interaction*. Removed from this actual process of verbal communication and interaction (of semiotic communication and interaction in general), social psychology would assume the guise of a metaphysical or mythic concept—the "collective soul" or "collective inner psyche," the "spirit of the people," etc.

Social psychology in fact is not located anywhere within (in the "souls" of communicating subjects) but entirely and completely *without*—in the word, the gesture, the act. There is nothing left unexpressed in it, nothing "inner" about it—it is wholly on the outside, wholly brought out in exchanges, wholly taken up in material, above all in the material of the word.

Production relations and the sociopolitical order shaped by those relations determine the full range of verbal contacts between people, all the forms and means of their verbal communication—at work, in political life, in ideological creativity. In turn, from the conditions, forms, and types of verbal communication derive not only the forms but also the themes of speech performances.

Social psychology is first and foremost an atmosphere made up of multifarious *speech performances* that engulf and wash over all persistent forms and kinds of ideological creativity: unofficial discussions, exchanges of opinion at the theater or a concert or at various types of social gatherings, purely chance exchanges of words, one's manner of verbal reaction to happenings in one's life and daily existence, one's inner-word manner of identifying oneself and identifying one's position in society, and so on. Social psychology exists primarily in a wide variety of forms of the "utterance," of little *speech genres* of internal and external kinds—things left completely unstudied to the present day. All these speech performances, are, of course, joined with other types of semiotic manifestation and interchange—with miming, gesturing, acting out, and the like.

All these forms of speech interchange operate in extremely close connection with the conditions of the social situation in which they occur and exhibit an extraordinary sensitivity to all fluctuations in the social atmosphere. And it is here, in the inner workings of this verbally materialized social psychology, that the barely noticeable shifts and changes that will later find expression in fully fledged ideological products accumulate.

From what has been said, it follows that social psychology must be studied from two different viewpoints: first, from the viewpoint of content, i.e., the themes pertinent to it at this or that moment in time; and second, from the viewpoint of the forms and types of verbal communication in which the themes in question are implemented (i.e., discussed, expressed, questioned, pondered over, etc.)

Up till now the study of social psychology has restricted its task to the first viewpoint only, concerning itself exclusively with definition of its thematic makeup. Such being the case, the very question as to where documentation—the concrete expressions—of this social psychology could be sought was not posed with full clarity. Here, too, concepts of "consciousness," "psyche," and "inner life" played the sorry role of relieving one of the necessity to try to discover clearly delineated material forms of expression of social psychology.

Meanwhile, this issue of concrete forms has significance of the highest order. The point here has to do, of course, not with the sources of our knowledge about social psychology at some particular period (e.g., memoirs, letters, literary works), nor with the sources for our understanding of the "spirit of the age"—the point here has to do with the forms of concrete implementation of this spirit, that is, precisely with the very forms of semiotic communication in human behavior.

A typology of these forms is one of the urgent tasks of Marxism. Later on, in connection with the problem of the utterance and dialogue, we shall again touch upon the problem of speech genres. For the time being, let us take note at least of the following.

Each period and each social group has had and has its own repertoire of speech forms for ideological communication in human behavior. Each set of cognate forms, i.e., each behavioral speech genre, has its own corresponding set of themes.

An interlocking organic unity joins the form of communication (for example, on-the-job communication of the strictly technical kind), the form of the utterance (the concise, businesslike statement) and its theme. Therefore, *classification of the forms of utterance must rely upon classification of the forms of verbal communication.* The latter are entirely determined by production relations and the sociopolitical order. Were we to apply a more detailed analysis, we would see what enormous significance belongs to *the hierarchical factor* in the processes of verbal interchange and what a powerful influence is exerted on forms of utterance by the hierarchical organization of communication. Language etiquette, speech tact, and other forms of adjusting an utterance to the hierarchical organization of society have tremendous importance in the process of devising the basic behavioral genres.[1]

Every sign, as we know, is a construct between socially organized persons in the process of their interaction. Therefore, *the forms of signs are conditioned above all by the social organization of the participants involved and also by the immediate conditions of their interaction.* When these forms change, so does sign. And it should be one of the tasks of the study of ideologies to trace this social life of the verbal sign. Only so approached can the *problem of the relationship between sign and existence* find its concrete expression; only then will the process of the causal shaping of the sign by existence stand out as a process of genuine existence-to-sign transit, of genuine dialectical refraction of existence in the sign.

To accomplish this task certain basic, methodological prerequisites must be respected:

1. *Ideology may not be divorced from the material reality of sign* (i.e., by locating it in the "consciousness" or other vague and elusive regions);

2. *The sign may not be divorced from the concrete forms of social intercourse* (seeing that the sign is part of organized social intercourse and cannot exist, as such, outside it, reverting to a mere physical artifact);

3. *Communication and the forms of communication may not be divorced from the material basis.*

Every ideological sign—the verbal sign included—in coming about through the process of social intercourse, is defined by the *social purview* of the given time period and the given social group. So far, we have been speaking about the form of the sign as shaped by the forms of social interaction. Now we shall deal with its other aspect—the *content* of the sign and the evaluative accentuation that accompanies all content.

Every stage in the development of a society has its own special and restricted circle of items which alone have access to that society's attention and which are

---

1. The problem of behavioral speech genres has only very recently become a topic of discussion in linguistic and philosophical scholarship. One of the first serious attempts to deal with these genres, though, to be sure, without any clearly defined sociological orientation, is Leo Spitzer's *Italienische Umgangssprache*, 1922. More will be said about Spitzer, his predecessors, and colleagues later on.

endowed with evaluative accentuation by that attention. Only items within that circle will achieve sign formation and become objects in semiotic communication. What determines this circle of items endowed with value accents?

In order for any item, from whatever domain of reality it may come, to enter the social purview of the group and elicit ideological semiotic reaction, it must be associated with the vital socioeconomic prerequisites of the particular group's existence; it must somehow, even if only obliquely, make contact with the bases of the group's material life.

Individual choice under these circumstances, of course, can have no meaning at all. The sign is a creation between individuals, a creation within a social milieu. Therefore the item in question must first acquire interindividual significance, and only then can it become an object for sign formation. In other words, *only that which has acquired social value can enter the world of ideology, take shape, and establish itself there.*

For this reason, all ideological accents, despite their being produced by the individual voice (as in the case of word) or, in any event, by the individual organism—all ideological accents are social accents, ones with claim to *social recognition* and, only thanks to that recognition, are made outward use of in ideological material.

Let us agree to call the entity which becomes the object of a sign the *theme* of the sign. Each fully fledged sign has its theme. And so, every verbal performance has its theme.[2]

An ideological theme is always socially accentuated. Of course, all the social accents of ideological themes make their way also into the individual consciousness (which, as we know, is ideological through and through) and there take on the semblance of individual accents, since the individual consciousness assimilates them as its own. However, the source of these accents is not the individual consciousness. Accent, as such, is interindividual. The animal cry, the pure response to pain in the organism, is bereft of accent; it is a purely natural phenomenon. For such a cry, the social atmosphere is irrelevant, and therefore it does not contain even the germ of sign formation.

The theme of an ideological sign and the form of an ideological sign are inextricably bound together and are separable only in the abstract. Ultimately, the same set of forces and the same material prerequisites bring both the one and the other to life.

Indeed, the economic conditions that inaugurate a new element of reality into the social purview, that make it socially meaningful and "interesting," are exactly the same conditions that create the forms of ideological communication

---

2. The relationship of theme to the semantics of individual words shall be dealt with in greater detail in a later section of our study.

(the cognitive, the artistic, the religious, and so on), which in turn shape the forms of semiotic expression.

Thus, the themes and forms of ideological creativity emerge from the same matrix and are in essence two sides of the same thing.

The process of incorporation into ideology—the birth of theme and birth of form—is best followed out in the material of the word. This process of ideological generation is reflected two ways in language: both in its large-scale, universal-historical dimensions as studied by semantic paleontology, which has disclosed the incorporation of undifferentiated chunks of reality into the social purview of prehistoric man, and in its small-scale dimensions as constituted within the framework of contemporaneity, since, as we know, the word sensitively reflects the slightest variations in social existence.

Existence reflected in sign is not merely reflected but *refracted.* How is this refraction of existence in the ideological sign determined? By an intersecting of differently oriented social interests within one and the same sign community, i.e., *by the class struggle.*

Class does not coincide with the sign community, i.e., with the community which is the totality of users of the same set of signs for ideological communication. Thus various different classes will use one and the same language. As a result, differently oriented accents intersect in every ideological sign. Sign becomes an arena of the class struggle.

This social *multiaccentuality* of the ideological sign is a very crucial aspect. By and large, it is thanks to this intersecting of accents that a sign maintains its vitality and dynamism and the capacity for further development. A sign that has been withdrawn from the pressures of the social struggle—which, so to speak, crosses beyond the pale of the class struggle—inevitably loses force, degenerating into allegory and becoming the object not of live social intelligibility but of philological comprehension. The historical memory of mankind is full of such worn out ideological signs incapable of serving as arenas for the clash of live social accents. However, inasmuch as they are remembered by the philologist and the historian, they may be said to retain the last glimmers of life.

The very same thing that makes the ideological sign vital and mutable is also, however, that which makes it a refracting and distorting medium. The ruling class strives to impart a supraclass, eternal character to the ideological sign, to extinguish or drive inward the struggle between social value judgments which occurs in it, to make the sign uniaccentual.

In actual fact, each living ideological sign has two faces, like Janus. Any current curse word can become a word of praise, any current truth must inevitably sound to many other people as the greatest lie. This *inner dialectic quality* of the sign comes out fully in the open only in times of social crises or revolutionary changes. In the ordinary conditions of life, the contradiction embedded in every ideological sign cannot emerge fully because the ideological sign in an established, dominant ideology is always somewhat reactionary and tries, as it were, to stabilize the preceding factor in the dialectical flux of the social generative process, so accentuating yesterday's truth as to make it appear today's. And that is what is responsible for the refracting and distorting peculiarity of the ideological sign within the dominant ideology.

This, then, is the picture of the problem of the relation of the basis to superstructures. Our concern with it has been limited to concretization of certain of its aspects and elucidation of the direction and routes to be followed in a productive treatment of it. We made a special point of the place philosophy of language has in that treatment. The material of the verbal sign allows one most fully and easily to follow out the continuity of the dialectical process of change, a process which goes from the basis to superstructures. The category of mechanical causality in explanations of ideological phenomena can most easily be surmounted on the grounds of philosophy of language.

CHAPTER 3
Philosophy of Language and Objective Psychology

The task of defining the psyche objectively. Dilthey's notion of an "understanding and interpreting" psychology. The semiotic reality of the psyche. The point of view of functional psychology. Psychologism and antipsychologism. The distinctive quality of inner sign (inner speech). The problem of introspection. The socioideological nature of the psyche. Summary and conclusions.

One of Marxism's fundamental and most urgent tasks is to construct a genuinely objective psychology, which means a psychology based on *sociological*, not physiological or biological, principles. As part and parcel of that task, Marxism faces the difficult problem of finding an objective—but also subtle and flexible—approach to the conscious, subjective human psyche over which, ordinarily, methods of introspection claim jurisdiction.

This is a task which neither biology or physiology is equipped to cope with: the conscious psyche is a socioideological fact and, as such, beyond the scope of physiological methods or the methods of any other of the natural sciences. The subjective psyche is not something that can be reduced to processes occurring within the confines of the natural, animalian organism. The processes that basically define the content of the psyche occur not inside but outside the individual organism, although they involve its participation.

The subjective psyche of the human being is not an object for natural-scientific analysis, as would be any item or process in the natural world; *the subjective psyche is an object for ideological understanding and socioideological interpretation via understanding.* Once understood and interpreted, a psychic phenomenon becomes explainable solely in terms of the social factors that shape the concrete life of the individual in the conditions of his social environment.[1]

The first issue of fundamental importance that arises once we move in this direction is that of defining "inner experience" objectively. Such a definition must include inner experience within the unity of objective, outer experience.

What sort of reality pertains to the subjective psyche? *The reality of the inner psyche is the same reality as that of the sign.* Outside the material of signs there is no psyche; there are physiological processes, processes in the nervous system, but no subjective psyche as a special existential quality fundamentally distinct from both the physiological processes occurring within the organism and the reality encompassing the organism from outside, to which the psyche reacts and which one way or another it reflects. By its very existential nature, the subjective psyche is to be localized somewhere between the organism and the outside world, on the *borderline* separating these two spheres of reality. It is here that an encounter between the organism and the outside world takes place, but the encounter is not a physical one: *the organism and the outside world meet here in the sign.* Psychic experience is the semiotic expression of the contact between the organism and the outside environment. That is why *the inner psyche is not analyzable as a thing but can only be understood and interpreted as a sign.*

The idea of an "understanding and interpreting" psychology is a very old one and has an instructive history. Symptomatically, in modern times it has found its greatest substantiation in connection with the methodological requirements of the humanities, i.e., the ideological sciences.

The most astute and well-grounded advocate of this idea in modern times was Wilhelm Dilthey. For Dilthey, it was not so much a matter that subjective psychic experience existed, the way a thing may be said to exist, as that it *had meaning.* When disregarding this meaning in the attempt to arrive at the pure reality of experience, we find ourselves, according to Dilthey, confronting in actual fact a physiological process in the organism and losing sight of the experience in the meantime—just as, when disregarding the meaning of a word, we lose the word itself and confront its sheer physical sound and the physiological process of its articulation. What makes a word a word is its meaning. What makes an experience an experience is also its meaning. And only at the expense of losing the very essence of inner, psychic life can meaning be disregarded. Therefore, psychology cannot pursue tasks of explaining experiences causally, as if they were analogous to physical or physiological processes. Psychology must pursue the task of understanding, describing, segmenting, and interpreting psychic life, just as if it were a document under philological analysis. Only that kind of des-

---

1. A popular sketch of the modern problems of psychology is given in our book *Frejdizm (kritičeskij očerk)* [Freudianism (A Critical Outline)] (Leningrad, 1927). See Chapter 2, "Two Trends in Contemporary Psychology."

criptive and interpretive psychology is capable, according to Dilthey, of serving as the basis for the humanities, or as he calls them, the "spiritual sciences" *(Geisteswissenschaften).*[2]

Dilthey's ideas have proved to be very fecund and, to the present day, continue to find many supporters among representatives of the humanities. It could be claimed that virtually all contemporary German humanist scholars with a philosophical bent are to a greater or lesser degree dependent upon the ideas of Wilhelm Dilthey.[3]

Dilthey's conception grew from idealistic grounds and it is on these same grounds that his followers remain. The idea of an understanding and interpreting psychology is very closely connected with certain presuppositions of idealistic thought and in many respects may be said to be a specifically idealistic idea.

Indeed, in the form in which it was first established and has continued to develop to the present day, interpretive psychology *is* idealistic and untenable from the standpoint of dialectical materialism.

What is untenable above all is *the methodological precedence of psychology over ideology.* After all, Dilthey and other representatives of interpretive psychology would have it that their psychology must provide the basis for the humanities. Ideology is explained in terms of psychology—as the expression and incarnation of psychology—and not the other way around. True, the psyche and ideology are said to coincide, to share a common denominator—meaning—by virtue of which both the one and the other are alike distinguished from all the rest of reality. But it is psychology, not ideology, that sets the tone.

Furthermore, the ideas of Dilthey and his followers *make no provision for the social character of meaning.*

Finally—and this is the *proton pseudos* of their whole conception—*they have no notion of the essential bond between meaning and sign,* no notion of the specific nature of the sign.

In point of fact, the comparison Dilthey makes between experience and word means nothing more to him than a simple analogy, an explanatory figure—a rather rare occurrence in Dilthey's works, at that. He is far from drawing the conclusions that should follow from that comparison. What is more, he is interested in explaining not the psyche through the agency of the ideological sign but, just like any other idealist, the sign through the agency of the psyche: a sign becomes a sign for Dilthey only insofar as it serves as the means of expression for inner life. And the latter, he maintains, confers its own proper meaning upon the sign. In this respect Dilthey's postulation carries on the common tendency of all idealism:

2. An account of Dilthey in Russian can be found in Frišejzen-Keler's article in *Logos,* I-II, 1912-1913.

3. Dilthey's trend-setting influence has been acknowledged by (to mention only names of the most distinguished members of the humanities in present-day Germany) Oskar Walzel, Wilhelm Gundolf, Emil Ermatinger, and others.

to remove all sense, all meaning from the material world and to locate it in a-temporal, a-spatial Spirit.

If experience does have meaning and is not merely a particular piece of reality (and in this contention Dilthey is correct), then surely experience could hardly come about other than in the material of signs. After all, meaning can belong only to a sign; meaning outside a sign is a fiction. Meaning is the expression of a semiotic relationship between a particular piece of reality and another kind of reality that it stands for, represents, or depicts. Meaning is a function of the sign and is therefore inconceivable (since meaning is pure relation, or function) outside the sign as some particular, independently existing thing. It would be just as absurd to maintain such a notion as to take the meaning of the word "horse" to be this particular, live animal I am pointing to. Why, if that were so, then I could claim, for instance, that having eaten an apple, I have consumed not an apple but the meaning of the word "apple." A sign is a particular material thing, but meaning is not a thing and cannot be isolated from the sign as if it were a piece of reality existing on its own apart from the sign. Therefore, if experience does have meaning, if it is susceptible of being understood and interpreted, then it must have its existence in the material of actual, real signs.

Let us emphasize this point: *not only can experience be outwardly expressed through the agency of the sign* (an experience can be expressed to others variously— by word, by facial expression, or by some other means), but also, aside from this outward expression (for others), *experience exists even for the person undergoing it only in the material of signs.* Outside that material there is no experience as such. In this sense *any experience is expressible,* i.e., is potential expression. Any thought, any emotion, any willed activity is expressible. This factor of expressivity cannot be argued away from experience without forfeiting the very nature of experience.[4]

Thus there is no leap involved between inner experience and its expression, no crossing over from one qualitative realm of reality to another. The transit from experience to its outward expression occurs within the scope of the same qualitative realm and is *quantitative* in nature. True, it often happens that in the process of outward expression a transit from one type of semiotic material (e.g., mimetic) to another (e.g., verbal) occurs, but nowhere in its entire course does the process go outside the material of signs.

What, then, is the sign material of the psyche? Any organic activity or process: breathing, blood circulation, movements of the body, articulation, inner speech, mimetic motions, reaction to external stimuli (e.g., light stimuli) and so forth.

4. The notion of the expressivity of all phenomena of consciousness is not foreign to neo-Kantianism. Besides the book by Cassirer already cited, Herman Cohen, in the third section of his system, *Aesthetik des reinen Gefühls,* has written on the expressive character of consciousness. However, the idea as expounded there least of all allows of the proper conclusions. The essence of consciousness continues to remain beyond the pale of existence.

In short, *anything and everything occurring within the organism can become the material of experience,* since everything can acquire semiotic significance, can become expressive.

To be sure, all this material is far from standing on the same level of importance. Any psyche that has reached any degree of development and differentiation must have subtle and pliable semiotic material at its disposal, and semiotic material of a kind that can be shaped, refined, and differentiated in the extracorporeal social milieu in the process of outward expression. Therefore, the semiotic material of the psyche is preeminently the word—*inner speech.* Inner speech, it is true, is intertwined with a mass of other motor reactions having semiotic value. But all the same, it is the word that constitutes the foundation, the skeleton of inner life. Were it to be deprived of the word, the psyche would shrink to an extreme degree; deprived of all other expressive activities, it would die out altogether.

If we disregard the sign function of inner speech and of all the other expressive activities that together make up the psyche, we would turn out to be confronting a sheerly physiological process taking place within the confines of the individual organism. Abstraction of that kind is perfectly legitimate and necessary for the physiologist: all he needs is the physiological process and its mechanics.

Yet, even for the physiologist, in his capacity as biologist, there is good reason to take into account the expressive sign function (i.e., social function) of the various physiological processes involved. Otherwise he will not grasp their biological position in the overall economy of the organism. The biologist, too, in this respect, cannot afford to ignore the sociological point of view, cannot afford to discount the fact that the human organism does not belong to the abstract realm of nature but forms part of a specifically social realm. But when he has taken into account the sign function of the various physiological processes involved, the physiologist proceeds to investigate their purely physiological mechanism (for example, the mechanism of the conditioned reflex) and completely disregards the ideological values inherent in these processes that are variable and subject to their own sociohistorical laws. In a word, the content of the psyche does not concern him.

But it is precisely this content of the psyche, taken with regard to the individual organism, that is the object for psychology. No science worthy of the name psychology has or can have any object of interest other than this.

It has been asserted that the content of the psyche is not the object of psychology but, rather, only the function that this content has in the individual psyche. Such is the point of view of so-called *functional psychology.*[5]

5. The major representatives of functional psychology are Stumpf, Meinong, *et al.* The foundations for functional psychology were laid down by Franz Brentano. Functional psychology is unquestionably at this moment the dominant movement in German psychological thought, although not, to be sure, in its pure, classical form.

According to the doctrine of this school, "experience" is composed of two factors. One factor is the *content of experience.* It is not *psychic* in nature. What is involved is either a physical phenomenon on which the experience focuses (e.g., an object of perception) or a cognitive concept having its own logical governance or an ethical value, etc. This content-oriented, referential aspect of experience is a property of nature, culture, or history and, consequently, pertains to the competence of the appropriate scientific disciplines and is of no concern to the psychologist.

The other factor in experience is *the function of any particular referential content within the closed system of individual psychic life.* And it is precisely this *experienced-ness* or *experientiality* of any content outside the psyche that is in fact the object of psychology. Or, to put it another way, the object of functional psychology is not the *what* of experience but its *how.* So, for example, the content of any thought process—its what—is nonpsychic and pertains to the competence of the logician, epistemologist, or mathematician (if the kind of thinking involved is mathematical thinking). The psychologist, in contrast, studies only *how* thought processes with various objective contents (logical, mathematical, or other) come about under conditions supplied by any given individual subjective psyche.

We shall not delve into the details of this psychological conception, and we shall skip certain, sometimes very apposite, distinctions regarding psychic function such as can be found in the writings of representatives of this school and of other related movements in psychology. For our purposes, the basic principle of functional psychology, already set forth, will be sufficient. It will help us to express in more precise terms our own conception of the psyche and of the significance that belongs to the philosophy of the sign (or the philosophy of language) in the solution of the problem of psychology.

Functional psychology also grew and took shape on the grounds of idealism. Yet, in certain respects, it exhibits a tendency diametrically opposite to the interpretive psychology of the Dilthey type.

In point of fact, while Dilthey would seem intent on bringing the psyche and ideology down to one common denominator—meaning—functional psychology makes the opposite effort of drawing a fundamental and rigorous *borderline between the psyche and ideology,* a borderline that seems to cut *through the psyche itself.* As a result, everything regarded as meaning ends up being excluded without a trace from the scope of the psyche, while everything regarded as pertaining to the psyche ends up amounting to the sheer functioning of separate referential contents arranged in some sort of individual constellation called the "individual soul." Thus functional psychology, as distinguished from interpretive psychology, gives precedence to ideology over the psyche.

One may ask at this point: How does the psyche function, and what is the nature of its existence? This is a question for which we cannot find a clear-cut, satisfactory answer in the writings of the representatives of functional psychology. There is no clear idea, no agreement, no unanimity among them on this issue. However, there is one point on which they all agree: the functioning of the psyche is not to be identified with any physiological process. Thus the psychic is sharply delimited from the physiological. But what sort of entity this new quality, the psychic, is—that remains unclarified.

Similarly, the problem of the reality of an ideological phenomenon remains equally unclear in functional psychology.

The only instance where the functionalists provide a clear answer is the case of an experience directed toward some object in nature. Here they draw an opposition between psychic functioning and natural, physical being—this tree, earth, stone, and the like.

But what sort of opposition obtains between psychic functioning and ideological being—a logical concept, an ethical value, an artistic image, etc.?

On this issue the majority of representatives of functional psychology adhere to commonly held idealistic, mainly Kantian, views.[6] In addition to the individual psyche and the individual subjective consciousness, they make a provision for a "transcendental consciousness," "consciousness per se," or "pure epistemological subject," and the like. And into that transcendental realm they place the ideological phenomenon in its opposition with individual psychic function.[7]

Thus the problem of the reality of ideology remains without a solution on the grounds of functional psychology.

Failure to understand the ideological sign and its specific mode of being is, consequently, what is responsible, both in this and in all other instances, for the insolubility of the problem of the psyche.

The problem of the psyche will never find a solution until the problem of ideology is solved. These two problems are inextricably bound together. The whole history of psychology and the whole history of the ideological sciences—logic, epistemology, aesthetics, the humanities, etc.—is a history of incessant struggle involving mutual delimitation and mutual assimilation between these two cognitive disciplines.

A sort of peculiar periodic alternation seems to take place between an elemental psychologism, which subjects all the ideological sciences to inundation, and a sharply reacting antipsychologism, which deprives the psyche of all its content, relegating it to some empty, formal status (as in functional psychology) or to sheer physiologism. As for ideology, once a consistent antipsychologism has taken away its normal place in existence (which place is precisely the psyche),

6. At the present time, the *phenomenologists*, too, take their stand on the grounds of functional psychology, associated, as they are, with Franz Brentano (an association that extends to their overall philosophical outlook).

7. As for the phenomenologists, they ontologize ideological notions, providing them with an autonomous sphere of ideal being.

it is left with no place at all and is obliged to exit from reality and to take to the transcendental, or even literally ascend to the transcendent.

At the beginning of the 20th century, we experienced one of those strong waves of antipsychologism (by no means the first in history, to be sure). The trend-setting works of Husserl,[8] the main representative of modern antipsychologism; the works of his followers, the *intentionalists* ("phenomenologists"); the sharply antipsychologistic turn taken by representatives of modern neo-Kantianism of the Marburg and Freiburg school;[9] and the banishment of psychologism from all fields of knowledge and even from psychology itself!—all these things constituted an event of paramount philosophical and methodological importance in the first two decades of our century.

Now, in the third decade of the century, the wave of antipsychologism has begun to abate. A new and evidently very powerful wave of psychologism is coming to take its place. A fashionable form of psychologism is the "philosophy of life." Under that trade name, psychologism of the most unbridled kind once again, with extraordinary speed, has occupied all the positions in all the branches of philosophy and ideological study that it had so recently abandoned.[10]

The approaching wave of psychologism carries with it no fresh ideas about the fundamentals of psychic reality. In contrast to the preceding wave of psychologism (the positivistic-empirical psychologism of the second half of the 19th century whose most typical representative was Wundt), the new psychologism is inclined to interpret inner being, the "elemental phenomenon of experience," in metaphysical terms.

Thus no dialectical synthesis has resulted from this dialectical flux of psychologism and antipsychologism. Neither the problem of psychology nor the prob-

8. See Volume 1 of his *Logische Untersuchungen* (a Russian translation was made in 1910). The work has become something of a bible of contemporary antipsychologism. See, also, his article (Russian translation), "Philosophy as an Exact Science," *Logos*, I, 1911-1912.

9. See, for example, the instructive study by Heinrich Rickert, the head of the Freiburg school, (Russian translation) "Two Paths in the Theory of Knowledge," *Novye idei v filosofii* [New Ideas in Philosophy], VII, 1913. In this study, Rickert, under Husserl's influence, translates his originally somewhat psychologistic concept of theory of knowledge into antipsychologistic terms. The article is very characteristic for the attitude taken by neo-Kantianism toward the antipsychologistic movement.

10. A general survey of contemporary philosophy of life, though a tendentious and somewhat out-dated one, can be found in Rickert's book, (Russian translation) *The philosophy of Life,* "Academia," 1921. Very considerable influence on the humanities was exerted by E. Spranger's book, *Lebensformen.* All the major representatives of the fields of literary and linguistic studies in Germany are to greater or lesser degrees under the influence of the philosophy of life at the present time. Let us mention: Ermatinger *(Das dichterische Kunstwerk,* 1921), Gundolf (books about Goethe and George, 1916-1925), Hefele *(Das Wesen der Dichtung,* 1923), Walzel *(Gehalt und Gestalt im dichterischen Kunstwerk,* 1923), Vossler and the Vosslerites, and many others. About certain of these scholars we shall have something to say later on.

lem of ideology has to this very day found its proper solution in bourgeois philosophy.

The bases for the treatment of both problems must be established simultaneously and interconnectedly. We are suggesting that one and the same key opens objective access to both spheres. That key is the *philosophy of sign* (the philosophy of the word as the ideological sign par excellence). The ideological sign is the common territory for both the psyche and for ideology, a territory that is material, sociological, and meaningful. It is on this very territory that a delimitation between psychology and ideology should be worked out. The psyche need not be a duplicate of the rest of the world (the ideological world above all), and the rest of the world need not be a mere material remark to the monologue of the psyche.

But if the nature of the psyche's reality is the same as that of the sign's reality, how can one draw a dividing line between the individual subjective psyche and ideology, in the exact sense of the word, which is likewise a semiotic entity? We have so far only pointed out the general territory; now we must draw the appropriate boundary within it.

The kernel of this issue amounts to a definition of inner (intracorporeal) sign which, in its immediate reality, is accessible to introspection.

Between the psyche and ideology no boundaries do or can exist from the point of view of ideological content itself. All ideological content, without exception, no matter what the semiotic material embodying it may be, is susceptible of being understood and, consequently, of being taken into the psyche, i.e., of being reproduced in the material of inner signs. On the other hand, any ideological phenomenon in the process of creation passes through the psyche as an essential stage of that process. We repeat: every outer ideological sign, of whatever kind, is engulfed in and washed over by inner signs—by the consciousness. The outer sign originates from this sea of inner signs and continues to abide there, since its life is a process of renewal as something to be understood, experienced, and assimilated, i.e., its life consists in its being engaged ever anew into the inner context.

Therefore, *from the standpoint of content, there is no basic division between the psyche and ideology; the difference is one of degree only.* The ideologeme is a vague entity at that stage of its inner development when it is not yet embodied in outer ideological material; it can acquire definition, differentiation, fixity only in the process of ideological embodiment. Intention is always a lesser thing than creation—even unsuccessful creation. A thought that as yet exists only in the context of my consciousness, without embodiment in the context of a discipline constituting some unified ideological system, remains a dim, unprocessed thought. But that thought had come into existence in my consciousness already with an orientation toward an ideological system, and it itself had been engendered by the ideological signs that I had absorbed earlier. We repeat, there is no qualitative difference here in any fundamental sense. Cognition with respect to books and to other people's words and cognition inside one's head belong to the same sphere of reality, and such differences as do exist between the head and book do not affect the content of cognition.

What mostly complicates our problem of delimiting psyche and ideology is the concept of "individuality." The "social" is usually thought of in binary opposition with the "individual," and hence we have the notion that the psyche is individual while ideology is social.

Notions of that sort are fundamentally false. The correlate of the social is the "natural" and thus "individual" is not meant in the sense of a person, but "individual" as natural, biological specimen. The individual, as possessor of the contents of his own consciousness, as author of his own thoughts, as the personality responsible for his thoughts and feelings,—such an individual is a purely socioideological phenomenon. Therefore, the content of the "individual" psyche is by its very nature just as social as is ideology, and the very degree of consciousness of one's individuality and its inner rights and privileges is ideological, historical, and wholly conditioned by sociological factors.[11] Every sign *as* sign is social, and this is no less true for the inner sign than for the outer sign.

To avoid misunderstandings, a rigorous distinction must always be made between the concept of the individual as natural specimen without reference to the social world (i.e., the individual as object of the biologist's knowledge and study) and the concept of individuality which has the status of an ideological-semiotic superstructure over the natural individual and which, therefore, is a social concept. These two meanings of the word "individual" (the natural specimen and the person) are commonly confused, with the result that the arguments of most philosophers and psychologists constantly exhibit *quaternio terminorum:* now one concept is in force, now the other takes its place.

If the content of the individual psyche is just as social as is ideology, then, on the other hand, ideological phenomena are just as individual (in the ideological meaning of the word) as are psychological phenomena. Every ideological product bears the imprint of the individuality of its creator or creators, but even this imprint is just as social as are all the other properties and attributes of ideological phenomena.

Thus every sign, even the sign of individuality, is social. In what, then, does the difference between inner and outer sign, between psyche and ideology, consist?

Meaning implemented in the material of inner activity is meaning turned toward the organism, toward the particular individual's self, and is determined

11. In the last section of our study, we shall see how relative and ideological the concept of verbal authorship, of "property right to the word," really is and how late in appearance is the development in language of a distinct sense of individual prerequisites of speech.

first of all in the context of that self's particular life. In this respect, a certain element of truth does adhere to the views held by representatives of the functional school. The psyche does possess a special unity distinguishable from the unity of ideological systems, and to ignore that unity is inadmissable. The special nature of this psychic unity is completely compatible with the ideological and sociological conception of the psyche.

In point of fact, any cognitive thought whatever, even one in my consciousness, in my psyche, comes into existence, as we have said, with an orientation toward an ideological system of knowledge where that thought will find its place. My thought, in this sense, from the very start belongs to an ideological system and is governed by its set of laws. But, at the same time, it belongs to another system that is just as much a unity and just as much in possession of its own set of laws—the system of my psyche. The unity of this second system is determined not only by the unity of my biological organism but also by the whole aggregate of conditions of life and society in which that organism has been set. It is along the lines of this organic unity of my self and these specific conditions of my existence that the psychologist will study my thought. This same thought will interest the ideologist only in terms of its objective contribution to a system of knowledge.

The system of the psychic, a system determined by organic and, in the broad sense of the word, biographical factors, is by no means merely the result of the psychologist's "point of view." It is indeed a real unity, as real as the biological self with its particular constitution, on which the psyche is founded, and as real as the whole set of conditions of life that determines the life of this self. The more closely the inner sign is interwoven with the unity of this psychic system and the more strongly marked by biological and biographical factors, the further away will the inner sign be from fully fledged ideological expression. Conversely, as it approaches closer to its ideological formulation and embodiment, the inner sign may be said to cast off the bonds of the psychic context in which it had been held.

This is what also determines the difference in the processes of understanding the inner sign (i.e., experience) on the one hand, and the outer, purely ideological sign, on the other. In the first instance, *to understand* means to refer a particular inner sign to a unity consisting of other inner signs, to perceive it in the context of a particular psyche. In the second instance, to understand is to perceive the sign in the system of ideology appropriate to it. True, the first instance must also include consideration of the purely ideological meaning of the experience—after all, if the psychologist does not understand the purely cognitive sense of some thought, he will not be able to understand its place in his subject's psyche either. If he disregards the cognitive meaning of the thought, he will be confronting what is not a thought, not a sign, but the sheer physiological process of implementing the thought or sign in the organism. That is why psychology of cognition must be grounded in epistemology and logic; why, in general, psychology must be grounded in ideological science and not the other way around.

It should be noted that any outer sign expression, an utterance, for instance, can also be organized in either one of two directions: either toward the subject himself or away from him toward ideology. In the first instance, the utterance aims at giving outer sign expression to inner signs, as such, and requires the receiver of the utterance to refer them to an inner context, i.e., requires a purely psychological kind of understanding. In the second instance, a purely ideological, objective-referential understanding of the utterance is required.[12]

It is in this way that a delimitation between the psyche and ideology takes shape.[13]

Now, in what form do we receive the psyche, receive inner signs, for observation and study? In its pure form, the inner sign, i.e., experience, is receivable only by self-observation (introspection). Does introspection contravene the unity of outer, objective experience? Given a proper understanding of the psyche and of introspection itself, nothing of the sort occurs.[14]

The fact is, after all, that inner sign is the object of introspection and inner sign, as such, can also be outer sign. Inner speech could indeed be given voice. The results of introspection in its process of self-clarification must necessarily be expressed outwardly or, at the very least, be brought up to the stage of outer expression. Introspection, functioning as such, follows a course from inner to outer signs. Introspection itself, then, has an expressive character.

Self-observation (introspection) is the understanding of one's own inner sign. In this respect it is distinguished from observation of a physical object or some physical process. We do not see or feel an experience—we understand it. This means that in the process of introspection we engage our experience into a context made up of other signs we understand. A sign can be illuminated only with the help of another sign.

---

12. It should be noted that utterances of the first kind can have a dual character: they can inform about experiences ("I feel joy"), or they can express them directly ("Hurray!"). Transitional forms are possible ("I'm so happy!"—with a strong expressive intonation of joy). The distinction between these two types is of enormous importance for both the psychologist and the ideologist. In the first case, there is no expression of the experience and, therefore, no actualization of inner sign. What is expressed is the result of introspection (the sign of a sign is given, so to speak). In the second case, introspection in inner experience erupts to the surface and becomes an object for external observation (granted, having been altered somewhat in erupting to the surface). In the third—transitional—case, the result of introspection is colored by the erupting inner sign (the initial sign).

13. An exposition of our view on the content of the psyche as ideology is given in our book cited above, *Frejdizm.* See the chapter, "The Content of the Psyche as Ideology."

14. Such a contravention would have taken place if the reality of the psyche were the reality of a thing and not that of a sign.

Introspection is a kind of *understanding* and, therefore, inevitably proceeds in some specific ideological direction. Thus it can be carried out in the interests of psychology, and, in that case, it becomes understanding of a particular experience within the context of other inner signs, with focus on the unity of psychic life.

In this instance, introspection illuminates inner signs with the help of the cognitive system of psychological signs; it subjects the experience to clarification and differentiation, aiming toward an exact psychological account of it. This is just the sort of thing, for instance, that a subject in a psychological experiment is asked to do. The subject's response is a psychological account, or the roughing out of such an account.

But introspection can proceed in a different direction, gravitating toward ethical or moral self-objectification. Here the inner sign is drawn into a system of ethical values and norms, and is understood and elucidated from their point of view.

Other directions are also possible. But always and everywhere introspection aims at elucidating inner sign, at advancing it to the highest degree of semiotic definitiveness. This process reaches its limit when the object of introspection becomes fully *understood,* i.e., when it can become an object not of introspection only but also of ordinary, objective, ideological (semiotic) observation.

Thus introspection, as ideological understanding, is included within the unity of objective experience. To this we must append the qualification that in concrete instances it is impossible to draw a clear dividing line between inner and outer signs, between internal introspection and external observation, the latter supplying a steady stream of both semiotic and empirical commentaries to the inner signs being understood.

Empirical commentary is always present. The understanding of any sign, whether inner or outer, occurs inextricably tied in with the *situation in which the sign is implemented.* This situation, even in the case of introspection, exists as an aggregate of facts from external experience, the latter commentating upon and illuminating a particular inner sign. It is always a *social situation.* Orientation in one's own soul (introspection) is in actuality inseparable from orientation in the particular social situation in which the experience occurs. Thus, any deepening of introspection can come about only in unremitting conjunction with a deepened understanding of the social orientation. Complete disregard of social orientation leads to a complete extinguishment of experience, just as also happens when its semiotic nature is disregarded. As we shall see in greater detail later on, *the sign and its social situation are inextricably fused together.* The sign cannot be separated from the social situation without relinquishing its nature as sign.

The problem of the inner sign is one of the most crucial problems of philosophy of language. Inner sign is, after all, preeminently the word, or inner speech.

The problem of inner speech is a philosophical problem, as are all the problems treated in this chapter. It lies at the juncture between psychology and the concerns of the ideological sciences. A fundamental, methodological solution to this problem can be arrived at only on the grounds of the philosophy of language as the philosophy of sign. What is the nature of the word in its role as inner sign? In what form is inner speech implemented? How does it tie in with the social situation? What is its relation to the external utterance? What are the procedures for uncovering, for seizing hold, so to speak, of inner speech? The answers to all these questions can only be given by a fully elaborated philosophy of language.

Let us take a look at just the second of these questions—the question of the forms in which inner speech is implemented.

It is clear from the outset that, without exception, all categories worked out by linguistics for the analysis of the forms of external language (the lexicological, the grammatical, the phonetic) are inapplicable to the analysis of inner speech or, if applicable, are applicable only in thoroughly and radically revised versions.

Closer analysis would show that the units of which inner speech is constituted are certain *whole entities* somewhat resembling a passage of monologic speech or whole utterances. But most of all, they resemble the *alternating lines of a dialogue.* There was good reason why thinkers in ancient times should have conceived of inner speech as *inner dialogue.* These whole entities of inner speech are not resolvable into grammatical elements (or are resolvable only with considerable qualifications) and have in force between them, just as in the case of the alternating lines of dialogue, not grammatical connections but connections of a different kind. These units of inner speech, these *total impressions*[15] *of utterances,* are joined with one another and alternate with one another not according to the laws of grammar or logic but according to the laws of *evaluative* (emotive) *correspondence, dialogical deployment,* etc., in close dependence on the historical conditions of the social situation and the whole pragmatic run of life.[16]

Only by ascertaining the forms of whole utterances and, especially, the forms of dialogic speech, can light be shed on the forms of inner speech, as well, and on the peculiar logic of their concatenation in the stream of inner speech.

15. The term is borrowed from Gompertz, *Weltanschauungslehre.* It appears that the term was first used by Otto Weininger. Total impression means the still undifferentiated impression of the totality of an object—the aroma of its totality, as it were, which precedes and underlies knowing the object distinctly. So, for example, we sometimes cannot remember a name or a word, though "it is on the tip of our tongue," i.e., we already have a total impression of the name or word but the impression cannot develop into its concrete differentiated image. According to Gompertz, total impressions have great epistemological significance. They are the psychic equivalents of the forms of the whole and endow the whole with its unity.

16. The common distinction made among types of inner speech—visual, aural, and motor—is not relevant to our considerations here. Within each type, speech proceeds in terms of total impressions, whether visual, aural, or motor.

All the problems of inner speech we have noted here far exceed the bounds of our study. Their productive treatment is still an impossibility at the present time. It is essential to have huge amounts of preliminary factual material beforehand and an elucidation of the more elementary and basic issues of the philosophy of language, for example, the problem of the utterance in particular.

In conclusion, then, we believe that the problem of the mutual delimitation of the psyche and ideology can be solved on the unitary territory of the ideological sign which embraces both.

By means of this solution, the contradiction between psychologism and antipsychologism would be done away with, dialectically, as well.

Antipsychologism is correct in refusing to derive ideology from the psyche. But even more than that is needed: the psyche must be derived from ideology. Psychology must be grounded in ideological science. Speech had first to come into being and develop in the process of the social intercourse of organisms so that afterward it could enter within the organism and become inner speech.

Psychologism is also correct, however. There is no outer sign without an inner sign. An outer sign incapable of entering the context of inner signs, i.e., incapable of being understood and experienced, ceases to be a sign and reverts to the status of a physical object.

The ideological sign is made viable by its psychic implementation just as much as psychic implementation is made viable by its ideological impletion. Psychic experience is something inner that becomes outer and the ideological sign, something outer that becomes inner. The psyche enjoys extraterritorial status in the organism. It is a social entity that penetrates inside the organism of the individual person. Everything ideological is likewise extraterritorial in the socioeconomic sphere, since the ideological sign, whose locus is outside the organism, must enter the inner world in order to implement its meaning as sign.

Between the psyche and ideology there exists, then, a continuous dialectical interplay: *the psyche effaces itself, or is obliterated, in the process of becoming ideology, and ideology effaces itself in the process of becoming the psyche.* The inner sign must free itself from its absorption by the psychic context (the biological-biographical context), must cease being a subjective experience, in order to become an ideological sign. The ideological sign must immerse itself in the element of inner, subjective signs; it must ring with subjective tones in order to remain a living sign and not be relegated to the honorary status of an incomprehensible museum piece.

This dialectical interplay between inner and outer signs—between the psyche and ideology—has attracted the attention of thinkers many a time, but it has never found proper understanding or adequate expression.

In recent times the most profound and interesting analysis of this interplay was given by the philosopher and sociologist Georg Simmel.

Simmel perceived this interplay in a form typical for contemporary bourgeois speculation—that of the "tragedy of culture" or, more accurately, the tragedy of the subjective personality creating culture. This creative personality, according to Simmel, obliterates itself, its subjectivity, and its very "personality" in the objective product it itself creates. The birth of an objective cultural value entails the death of the subjective soul.

We shall not go into the details of Simmel's analysis of this whole problem (an analysis which contains no small number of acute and interesting observations).[17] But let us take note of the basic deficiency in Simmel's conception.

For Simmel, an irreconcilable discrepancy exists between the psyche and ideology: *he does not know the sign of a form of reality common to both psyche and ideology.* Moreover, though a sociologist, he utterly *fails to appreciate the thoroughgoing social nature of the reality of ideology, as well as the reality of the psyche.* Both the one and the other kind of reality are, after all, a refraction of one and the same socioeconomic existence. As a result, the vital dialectical contradiction between the psyche and existence assumes for Simmel the shape of an inert, fixed antinomy—a "tragedy," and he endeavors in vain to surmount that inevitable antinomy by resorting to a metaphysically colored dynamics of the life process.

Only on the grounds of a materialistic monism can a dialectical resolution of all such contradictions be achieved. Any other grounds would necessarily entail either closing one's eyes to these contradictions and ignoring them or transformating them into a hopeless antinomy, a tragic dead end.[18]

In the verbal medium, in each utterance, however trivial it may be, this living dialectical synthesis is constantly taking place again and again between the psyche and ideology, between the inner and the outer. In each speech act, subjective experience perishes in the objective fact of the enunciated word-

17. Two studies of Simmel's, devoted to this issue, have been translated into Russian: "The Tragedy of Culture," *Logos*, II-III, 1911-1912, and "The Conflicts of Contemporary Culture," published separately and with a preface by Professor Svjatlovskij under the title, *Načatki znanij* ["Rudiments of Knowledge"] (Petrograd, 1923). Simmel's most recent book, *Lebensanschauung*, 1919, is a treatment of the same problem from the philosophy-of-life point of view. The very same idea is the leitmotif of Simmel's life of Goethe and to some degree also of his books on Nietzsche and Schopenhauer and his studies of Rembrandt and Michelangelo (the latter appeared in Russian translation in *Logos*, I, 1911-1912). The various means for overcoming this conflict between psyche and its creative objectification in an external product of culture underlie Simmel's typology of creative personalities.

18. In Russian philosophical literature, Fedor Steppun has dealt and continues to deal with the problem of the objectification of the subjective psyche in ideological products and the contradictions and conflicts that result therefrom. See his studies in *Logos*, II-III, 1911-1912, and II-IV, 1913. Steppun, too, presents these problems in a tragic and even mystical light. He is incapable of examining them in the framework of objective material reality. Only in that framework can the problem find productive and sober dialectical solution.

utterance, and the enunciated word is subjectified in the act of responsive understanding in order to generate, sooner or later, a counter statement. Each word, as we know, is a little arena for the clash and criss-crossing of differently oriented social accents. A word in the mouth of a particular individual person is a product of the living interaction of social forces.

Thus, the psyche and ideology dialectically interpenetrate in the unitary and objective process of social intercourse.

PART II

TOWARD A MARXIST
PHILOSOPHY OF LANGUAGE

CHAPTER 1

Two Trends of Thought
in Philosophy of Language

The problem of the actual mode of existence of language. The basic principles of the first trend of thought in the philosophy of language (individualistic subjectivism). Representatives of the first trend. The second trend of thought in philosophy of language: abstract objectivism. The historical roots of the second trend. Contemporary representatives of abstract objectivism. Conclusions.

What, in fact, is the subject matter of the philosophy of language? Where are we to find it? What is its concrete, material existence like? By what method or methods can we come to grips with its mode of existence?

In the first—the introductory—section of our study, we completely eschewed these concrete issues. We addressed ourselves to the philosophy of language, the philosophy of the word. But what is language, and what is word?

We do not, of course, have in mind anything like a conclusive definition of these concepts. Such a definition (insofar as any scientific definition may be called conclusive) might come at the end of a study, but not at its beginning. When beginning an investigation, one needs to construct methodological guidelines, not definitions. It is essential above all to get the feel of the actual subject matter—the object under investigation; it is essential to separate it from the reality surrounding it and to make a preliminary delimitation of it. At the outset of an investigation, it is not so much the intellectual faculty for making formulas and definitions that leads the way, but rather it is the eyes and hands attempting to get the feel of the actual presence of the subject matter.

But when we turn to our particular case, the eyes and hands find themselves in a quandary: the eyes see nothing and there is nothing for the hands to touch. The ear, it would seem, is at an advantage because it can claim to hear a word, to hear language. And indeed, the temptations of a *superficial phonetic empiricism* are very powerful in linguistic science. The study of the sound aspect of language occupies a disproportionately large place in linguistics, often setting the tone for the field, and in most cases is carried on outside any connection with the real essence of language as ideological sign.[1]

The task of identifying the real object of study in the philosophy of language is by no means an easy one. With each attempt to delimit the object of investigation, to reduce it to a compact subject-matter complex of definitive and inspectable dimensions, we forfeit the very essence of the thing we are studying—its semiotic and ideological nature. If we isolate sound as a purely *acoustic phenomenon,* we will not have language as our specific object. Sound pertains wholly to the competence of physics. If we add the *physiological process of sound production* and the process of sound *reception,* we still come no closer to our object. If we join onto this the *experience* (inner signs) of the speaker and listener, we obtain two psychophysical processes, taking place in two different psychophysiological beings, and one physical sound complex whose natural manifestation is governed by the laws of physics. Language as the specific object of study keeps eluding us. Yet we have already encompassed three spheres of reality—the physical, the physiological, and the psychological, and we have obtained a fairly elaborate composite complex. What this complex lacks is a "soul"; its component parts are a collection of separate entities not joined together to form a unity by some inner, pervasive governance that would transform that complex into precisely the phenomenon of language.

What, then, needs to be added to our already elaborate complex? First of all, this complex needs to be included into a much wider and more comprehensive complex—into the unified sphere of organized social intercourse. In order to observe the process of combustion, a substance must be placed into the air. In order to observe the phenomenon of language, both the producer and the receiver of sound and the sound itself must be placed into the social atmosphere. After all, the speaker and listener must belong to the same language community— to a society organized along certain particular lines. Furthermore, our two individuals must be encompassed by unity of the immediate social situation, i.e., they must make contact, as one person to another, on a specific basis. Only on a specific basis is a verbal exchange possible, however impersonal and however much dictated, so to speak, by the occasion that shared basis may be.

---

1. This concerns primarily experimental phonetics, which, in fact, does not study sounds in a language but sounds as produced by the vocal organs and received by the ear, completely without regard for the position those sounds occupy in the system of a language or in the construction of an utterance. Other branches of phonetics also employ huge masses of factual material, laboriously and meticulously collected, which are in no way methodologically positioned in language.

So, we may say that the *unity of the social milieu and the unity of the imme-diate social event of communication* are conditions absolutely essential for bringing our physico-psycho-physiological complex into relation with language, with speech, so that it can become a language-speech fact. Two biological organisms under purely natural conditions will not produce the fact of speech.

But the results of our analysis, instead of providing us the desired delimitation of our object of investigation, have brought us to an extreme expansion and to a further complication of it. For the fact of the matter is that the organized social milieu into which we have included our complex and the immediate social communicative situation are in themselves extremely complicated and involve hosts of multifaceted and multifarious connections, not all of which are equally important for the understanding of linguistic facts, and not all of which are constituents of language. What is needed, finally, is to bring this whole multifarious system of features and relations, of processes and artifacts, to one common denominator: all its various lines must be channeled to one center—to the focal point of the language process.

Above we gave an exposition of the problem of language, that is to say, we unfolded the problem itself and revealed the difficulties inherent in it. What, then, are the attempts that have been made by philosophy of language and by general linguistics to solve this problem? What are the signposts already placed along the road to its solution by which we may take our bearings?

A detailed survey of the history of philosophy of language and general linguistics or even only of their contemporary states is not our aim. We shall limit ourselves here to a general analysis of the main arteries of philosophical and linguistic thought in modern times.[2]

In the philosophy of language and in the related methodological sectors of general linguistics, we observe *two basic trends* in the solution of our problem,

2. Up to the present moment, no studies specially devoted to the philosophy of language have appeared. Basic research is available only on the subject of the philosophy of language in antiquity, e.g., Steinthal, *Geschichte der Sprachwissenschaft bei den Griechen und Römern* (1890). As regards its European history, we possess only monographs on individual thinkers and linguists (Humboldt, Wundt, Marty, and others). We shall refer to them in their proper place. The reader will find an outline of the history of the philosophy of language and linguistics, so far the only substantive one of its kind, in Ernst Cassirer's book, *Philosophie der symbolischen Formen: Die Sprache* (1923). See Chapter 1, "Das Sprachproblem in der Geschichte der Philosophie," pp. 55-121.

In Russian scholarly literature, a brief but solid sketch of the contemporary state of affairs in linguistics and the philosophy of language is provided by R. Šor in her article, "Krizis sovremennoj lingvistiki" [The Crisis in Contemporary Linguistics], *Jafetičeskij sbornik*, V (1927), pp. 32-71. A general, though far from complete, survey of sociological studies in linguistics is given in an article by M. N. Peterson, "Jazyk kak social'noe javlenie" [Language as a Social Phenomenon], *Učenye zapiski instituta jazyka i literatury*, Ranion (Moscow, 1927), pp. 3-21. Works on the history of linguistics shall be left unmentioned here.

i.e., the *problem of the identification and the delimitation of language as a specific object of study.* Differences over this issue also imply, of course, fundamental differences between these two trends over all other issues concerning the study of language.

The first trend can be termed *individualistic subjectivism* in the study of language, and the second, *abstract objectivism.*[3]

The first trend considers the basis of language (language meaning all linguistic manifestations without exception) to be the individual creative act of speech. The source of language is the individual psyche. The laws of language creativity— and language is, it assumes, a continuous process, an unceasing creativity—are the laws of individual psychology, and these laws are just what the linguist and the philosopher of language are supposed to study. To elucidate a linguistic phenomenon means to bring it in line with a meaningful (often even discursive) individual act of creativity. Everything else the linguist does has only a preliminary, delineatory, descriptive, or classifactory character; it is meant only to prepare the ground for the true explanation of the linguistic phenomenon in terms of the individual creative act or to serve the practical aims of language teaching. Language, so viewed, is analogous to other ideological phenomena, in particular, to art—to aesthetic activity.

The fundamental outlook on language of the first trend amounts, therefore, to these four basic principles:

1. *Language is activity, an unceasing process of creation* (energeia) *realized in individual speech acts;*
2. *The laws of language creativity are the laws of individual psychology;*
3. *Creativity of language is meaningful creativity, analogous to creative art;*
4. *Language as a ready-made product* (ergon), *as a stable system (lexicon, grammar, phonetics), is, so to speak, the inert crust,* the hardened lava of language creativity, *of which linguistics makes an abstract construct in the interests of the practical teaching of language as a ready-made instrument.*

The most important representative of the first trend, the one who laid its foundations, was Wilhelm von Humboldt.[4]

Humboldt's powerful thought has exercised an influence far exceeding the scope of the trend we have just characterized. It can be claimed that all post-Humboldtian linguistics, to the present day, has experienced his determinative influence. The whole of Humboldt's thought in its totality does not, needless to say, fall within the four-principle framework we have adduced; it is broader,

3. Neither term, as always happens with terms of this sort, fully covers the breadth and complexity of the trend denoted. As we shall see, the designation of the first trend is particularly inadequate. We were unable to devise better ones, however.
4. Hamann and Herder were Humboldt's predecessors so far as this trend is concerned.

more complex, and more contradictory, which explains how it was possible for Humboldt to become the preceptor for widely divergent trends and movements.[5] Yet, the kernel of Humboldt's ideas may be taken as the most powerful and most profound expression of the basic tendencies exemplified by the first trend.

A. A. Potebnja and his circle of followers are the most important representatives of this trend in Russian linguistic scholarship.[6]

The representatives of the first trend, who came after Humboldt, did not reach the scale of his philosophical synthesis and profundity. The trend became decidedly narrower especially as part and parcel of its adopting positivistic and quasi-empiricistic ways. Already in Steinthal's case, the Humboldtian sweep is missing. As compensation, however, greater methodological precision and systematization came to the fore. Steinthal, too, viewed the individual psyche as the source for language and considered the laws of linguistic development to be psychological laws.[7]

The basic principles of the first trend were drastically reduced in scale by the empiricistic psychologism of Wundt and his followers.[8] Wundt's position amounts to the notion that all the facts of language without exception are amenable to explanation in terms of individual psychology on a voluntaristic basis.[9] True, Wundt considers language, as does Steinthal, a fact of the "psychology of nations"

---

5. Humboldt exposited his ideas on philosophy of language in his study, "Ueber die Verschiedenheiten des menschlichen Sprachbaues," *Gesammelte Werke*, **VI**, (Berlin, 1841-1852); a Russian translation was made a long time ago, in 1859, by P. Biljarskij under the title, *O različii organizmov čelovečeskogo jazyka* [On the Distinction among Organisms of Human Language]. There is a vast literature about Humboldt. We might mention the book by R. Haym, *Wilhelm von Humboldt*, which is available in Russian translation. Among more recent studies, we might mention Edward Spranger, *Wilhelm von Humboldt*, (Berlin, 1909).

Russian commentary on Humboldt and his role in Russian linguistic thought can be found in the book by B. M. Èngel'gart, *A. N. Veselovskij* (Petrograd, 1922). Recently G. Špett published a provocative and interesting book entitled: *Vnutrennjaja forma slova (ètjudy i variacii na temu Gumbol'dta)* [The Inner Form of the Word (Etudes and Variations on a Theme of Humboldt)]. In it, Špett tries to restore the original, authentic Humboldt from under successive overlays of traditional interpretations. Špett's very subjective concept of Humboldt once again proves how complex and contradictory Humboldt is; the "variations" prove to be very free indeed.

6. Potebnja's basic philosophical study is: *Mysl' i jazyk* [Thought and Language]. His followers, the so-called Xar'kov school (Ovsjaniko-Kulikovskij, Lezin, Xarciev, *et al.*), published a nonperiodical series, *Voprosy teorii i psixologii tvorčestva*, which included Potebnja's posthumous works and articles about him by his students. In Potebnja's volume of basic writings, there is an exposition of Humboldt's ideas.

7. Behind Steinthal's conception stands Herbart's psychology, which is an attempt to construct the whole edifice of the human psyche out of elements of ideas bound together by association.

8. At this point, the connection with Humboldt becomes very slight.

9. Voluntarism places the element of will at the basis of the psyche.

(Volkerpsychologie) or "ethnic psychology."[10] However, Wundt's national psychology is made up of the psyches of individual persons; only they, for him, possess a full measure of reality.

In the final analysis, all his explanations of the acts of language, myth, and religion amount to purely psychological explanations. A purely sociological regulatedness, which is a property of all signs and which cannot be reduced to laws of individual psychology, is beyond his ken.

In recent times, the first trend in the philosophy of language, having cast off the bonds of positivism, has once again achieved powerful growth and wide scope in the conception of its tasks through the Vossler school.

The Vossler school (the so-called "Idealistische Neuphilologie") is beyond question one of the most potent movements in contemporary philosophical-linguistic thought. And the positive, specialized contribution its adherents have made to linguistics (in Romance and Germanic philology) is also exceptionally great. One need only name, in addition to Vossler himself, such of his followers as Leo Spitzer, Lorck, Lerch, among others. About each of these scholars we shall have occasion to speak later on.

The general philosophical-linguistic view held by Vossler and the Vossler school is fully characterized by the four basic principles we have adduced for the first trend. The Vossler school is defined first and foremost by its decisive and theoretically grounded *rejection of linguistic positivism* with its inability to see anything beyond the linguistic form (primarily, the phonetic form as the most "positive" kind) and the elementary psychophysiological act of its generation.[11] In connection with this, the *meaningful ideological* factor in language has been advanced to the fore. The main impetus to linguistic creativity is said to be "linguistic taste," a special variety of artistic taste. Linguistic taste is that linguistic truth by which language lives and which the linguist must ascertain in every manifestation of language in order genuinely to understand and explain the manifestation in question. Writes Vossler:

> The only history of language that can claim the status of a science is the one that can run the whole gamut of the practical, causal order of things so as to arrive at the aesthetic order, so that thereby linguistic thought, linguistic truth, linguistic taste, and

10. It was G. Špett who proposed using the term "ethnic psychology" instead of the literal translation of the German term, "Volkerpsychologie." The original term is indeed completely unsatisfactory and Špett's alternative seems to us very apt. See G. Špett, *Vvedenie v ètničeskuju psixologiju* [Introduction to Ethnic Psychology], Gosudarstvennaja Akademija Xudožestv i Nauk (Moscow, 1927). The book contains substantive criticism of Wundt's outlook, but G. Špett's own system is completely unacceptable.

11. Vossler's first, trend-setting philosophical study, *Positivismus und Idealismus in der Sprachwissenschaft* (Heidelberg, 1904), set out to criticize linguistic positivism.

linguistic sensibility or, as Wilhelm Humboldt has called it, the inner form of language, in its physically, psychically, politically, economically and, in general, its culturally conditioned transformations, may be made clear and understandable.[12]

Thus we see that all factors having a determinative effect on a linguistic phenomenon (physical, political, economic, and other factors) have no direct relevance for the linguist, according to Vossler; what is important for him is only the artistic sense of any given linguistic phenomenon.

Such is the nature of Vossler's purely aesthetic conception of language. In his own words: "Linguistic thought is essentially poetic thought; linguistic truth is artistic truth, is meaningful beauty."[13]

It is completely understandable, then, that for Vossler the basic manifestation, the basic reality, of language should not be language as a ready-made system, in the sense of a body of inherited, immediately usable forms—phonetic, grammatical, and other—but the *individual creative act of speech (Sprache als Rede)*. What follows from this is that, from the standpoint of language generation, the vital feature of every speech act does not consist in the grammatical forms, which are shared, stable, and immediately usable in all other utterances of a given language, but in stylistic concretization and modification of these abstract forms, which individualize and uniquely characterize any given utterance.

Only this stylistic individualization of language in concrete utterance is historical and creatively productive. It is here precisely that language is generated, later to solidify into grammatical forms: *everything that becomes a fact of grammar had once been a fact of style.* This is what Vossler's idea of the *precedence of style over grammar* amounts to.[14] Most of the linguistic studies published by the Vossler school stand on the boundary between linguistics (in the narrow sense) and stylistics. The Vosslerites consistently direct their efforts toward discerning meaningful ideological roots in each form of language.

That, basically, is the philosophical-linguistic view held by Vossler and his school.[15]

12. (Russian translation) "Grammar and the History of Language," *Logos*, I, 1910, p. 170.
13. *Ibid.*, p.167.
14. We shall return later to criticism of this idea.
15. Vossler's basic philosophico-linguistic studies, published after *Positivismus und Idealismus*, are collected in *Philosophie der Sprache* (1926). This book provides a complete picture of Vossler's philosophical and general linguistic outlook. Among linguistic studies that display the characteristic Vossler method, we might cite his *Frankreich Kultur im Spiegel seiner Sprachentwicklung* (1913). A complete bibliography of Vossler's writings up to 1922 will be found in *Idealistische Neuphilologie. Festschrift für K. Vossler* (1922). Two articles of Vossler's are available in Russian translation: "Grammatika i istorija jazyka" [Grammar and the History of Language], *Logos*, I, (1910), and "Otnošenie istorii jazykov k istorii literatury" [The Relationship of the History of Languages to the History of Literature], *Logos*, I-II (1912-1913). Both articles contribute to an understanding of the fundamentals of Vossler's outlook. No discussion whatever of the views of Vossler and his followers has been

Among contemporary representatives of the first trend in the philosophy of language, the name of the Italian philosopher and literary scholar, Benedetto Croce, must also be mentioned in view of the great influence he has had on contemporary European thought in the philosophy of language and literary studies.

Benedetto Croce's ideas are close in many respects to Vossler's. For Croce, language is also an aesthetic phenomenon. The basic, key term in his conception is *expression*. Any sort of expression is, at the root, artistic. Hence the notion that linguistics, as the study of expression par excellence (which is what the verbal medium is), coincides with aesthetics. And this means that for Croce, too, the individual act of verbal expression is the fundamental manifestation of language.[16]

Let us now go on to a characterization of the second trend of thought in philosophy of language.

The organizing center of all linguistic phenomena, that which makes them the specific object of a special science of language, shifts in the case of the second trend to an entirely different factor—*to the linguistic system as a system of the phonetic, grammatical, and lexical forms of language.*

If, for the first trend, language is an ever-flowing stream of speech acts in which nothing remains fixed and identical to itself, then, for the second trend, language is the stationary rainbow arched over that stream.

Each individual creative act, each utterance, is idiosyncratic and unique, but each utterance contains elements identical with elements in other utterances of the given speech group. And it is precisely these factors—the phonetic, grammatical, and lexical factors that are *identical* and therefore *normative* for all utterances—that insure the unity of a given language and its comprehension by all the members of a given community.

If we take any sound in a language, for instance the phoneme /b/ in "rainbow," then this sound as produced by the physiological articulatory apparatus of individual organisms is idiosyncratic and unique for each speaker. The /b/ in "rainbow" will have as many different pronunciations as there are people who pronounce the word (even though our ear may resist or be incapable of distinguishing these peculiarities). Physiological sound (i.e., sound produced by the individual physiological apparatus) is, after all, just as unique as are a person's fingerprints or as is the chemical composition of each individual person's blood (not-

16. The first part of B. Croce's *Aesthetics as a Science of Expression and General Linguistics* has been translated into Russian (Moscow, 1920). Croce's overall views on language and linguistics are already specified in the first section of his book.

undertaken in Russian linguistic literature. A few references to them are given only in an article by V. M. Žirmunskij about contemporary German literary scholarship (in Poètika, sb. III, "Academia," 1927). In the above-cited survey by R. Šor, the Vossler school is mentioned only in a footnote. In due time, we shall have something to say about works by Vossler's followers that have a philosophical and methodological significance.

withstanding the fact that science has not yet been able to provide the formula for individual blood).

However, the question is: How important, from the standpoint of language, are all these idiosyncratic peculiarities in the pronunciation of /b/—peculiarities for which, we may hypothesize, the shape of the individual person's lips and oral cavity are responsible (assuming that we were in a position to distinguish and pinpoint all these peculiarities)? The answer is, of course, that they are totally unimportant. What is important is precisely the *normative identity* of the sound in all instances in which the word "rainbow" is pronounced. It is this normative identity (factual identity being, after all, nonexistent) that constitutes the unity of the sound system of a language (at some particular moment in its life) and that guarantees that the word in question will be understood by all members of the language community. This normatively identical phoneme /b/ may be said to be a linguistic fact, a specific object for study by the science of language.

The same is also true with respect to all other elements of language. Here, too, we find the same normative identity of linguistic form throughout (e.g., a syntactic pattern) and the individual-specific implementation and impletion of the particular form in the singular act of speech. The former belongs to the system of language, the latter is a fact belonging to individual processes of speaking conditioned by fortuitous (from the standpoint of language as system) physiological, subjective-psychological, and all other such factors as are not amenable to exact accountability.

It is clear that the system of language in the sense characterized above is completely independent of individual creative acts, intentions, or motives. From the point of view of the second trend, meaningful language creativity on the speaker's part is simply out of the question.[17] Language stands before the individual as an inviolable, incontestable norm which the individual, for his part, can only accept. If the individual fails to perceive a linguistic form as an incontestable norm, then it does not exist for him as a form of language but simply as a natural possibility for his own individual, psychophysical apparatus. The individual acquires the system of language from his speech community completely ready-made. Any change within that system lies beyond the range of his individual consciousness. The individual act of articulating sounds becomes a linguistic act only by measure of its compliance with the fixed (at any given moment in time) and incontestable (for the individual) system of language.

What, then, is the nature of the set of laws in force within the language system?

---

17. Though, as we shall see, the bases just described of the second trend of thought in philosophy of language did, on the grounds of rationalism, incorporate the idea of an artificially constructed, logical, universal language.

This set of laws has a purely *immanent and specific* nature that is not reducible to any other set of laws—ideological, artistic, or otherwise. All forms of language at any given point in time, i.e., *synchronically*, are in a position of mutual indispensability and complementariness, whereby they transform language into an orderly system pervaded by laws of a specifically linguistic nature. *This specifically linguistic systematicity, in distinction from the systematicity of ideology*—of cognition, creative art, and ethics—*cannot become a motive for the individual consciousness.* The individual must accept and assimilate this system entirely as is; there is no place in it for evaluative, ideological discriminations—such as whether something is better, worse, beautiful, ugly, or the like. In fact, there is only one linguistic criterion: correct versus incorrect, wherein *linguistically correct* is understood to mean only the *correspondence of a given form to the normative system of language.* Consequently, no such thing as linguistic taste or linguistic truth comes up for discussion. From the individual's point of view, linguistic systematicity is arbitrary, i.e., utterly lacking any natural or ideological (for instance, artistic) comprehensibility or motivation. Thus between the phonetic design of a word and its meaning, there is neither a natural connection nor an artistic correspondence.

If language, as a system of forms, is completely independent of creative impulses or activities on the part of the individual, then it follows that language is the product of collective creativity—that it is a social entity and therefore, like all social institutions, is normative for each separate individual.

However, this system of language, which is an immutable unity at any given point in time, i.e., synchronically, does change, does evolve in the process of the historical evolution of the speech community. After all, the normative identity of the phoneme we established above will be different at different periods in the development of the language in question. In short, language does have its history. Now, how can this history be understood in the outlook of the second trend?

An overriding characteristic of the second trend of thought in the philosophy of language is its assuming a special kind of *discontinuity between the history of language and the system of language* (i.e., language in its a-historical, synchronic dimension). From the standpoint of the basic principles of the second trend, this dualistic discontinuity is absolutely insurmountable. There can be nothing in common between the logic governing the system of linguistic forms at any given moment in time and the logic (or rather "a-logic") of the historical change of these forms. The logic is of two different kinds; or rather, if we recognize only one of them as logic, the other will be a-logic, i.e., sheer violation of the logic accepted.

Indeed, the linguistic forms that comprise the system of language are mutually indispensable and complementary to one another in just the way that terms in a mathematical formula are. A change of one member of the system creates a new system, just as a change of one term in a formula creates a new formula. The interconnection and regularity governing the relationship between terms in one formula do not, of course, extend, nor can they extend, to the relationships between that particular formula or system and another, subsequent formula or system.

A rough analogy can be used here that will adequately portray the attitude of the second trend of thought in the philosophy of language toward the history of language. Let us liken the system of language to Newton's formula for the solution of binomials. Within this formula reigns a strict set of regulations under which each term of the formula is subsumed and given its fixed function. Now let us suppose that a student using this formula has misconstrued it (for instance, has mixed up the exponents or the plus and minus signs). In this way, a new formula with its own inner regulatory principles is obtained (of course, the new formula does not work for the solution of binomials, but that is beside the point of the analogy). Between the first and the second formulas there is no mathematical connection analogous to that which holds for the terms within each formula.

The situation is exactly the same in language. Systematic relationships connecting two linguistic forms together in the system of a language (at some particular point in time) have nothing in common with relationships that connect one of these forms with its altered aspect in a subsequent period of the historical evolution of that language. Up until the 16th century, a German formed the past tense of the verb "to be" as: *ich was; wir waren.* The German of today uses: *ich war; wir waren.* "Ich was," therefore, changed into "ich war." Between the forms "ich was" and "wir waren" and between the forms "ich war" and "wir waren," systematic linguistic connection and complementariness exist. They connect with and complement each other, to be precise, as the first person singular and plural of the same verb. Between "ich was" and "ich war" and between "ich war" (modern times) and "wir waren" (15th and 16th centuries), there exists a different, entirely separate relationship having nothing in common with the first, systematic, one. The form "ich war" came about by analogy with "wir waren"; under the influence of "wir waren" people (separate individuals) began creating "ich war" in place of "ich was."[18] This phenomenon became widespread and, as a result, an individual error turned into a linguistic norm. Thus, between the following two series:

I. *ich was—wir waren* (in the synchronic cross section of the 15th century, let us say) or *ich war—wir waren* (in the synchronic cross section of, say, the 19th century) and

II. *ich was—ich war*

      wir waren (as a factor promoting analogy)

18. Compare, English "I was."

there exist profound and fundamental differences. The first—the synchronic—series is governed by the systematic linguistic connectedness of mutually indispensable and complementary elements. This series stands apart from the individual in its capacity as an incontestable linguistic norm. The second—the historical or diachronic—series is governed by its own special set of principles—strictly speaking, that of error by analogy.

The logic of the history of language—the logic of individual errors or deviations (the shift from "ich was" to "ich war")—operates beyond the range of the individual consciousness. The shift is unintentional and unnoticed and only as such can it come about. At any one period of time only one linguistic norm can exist: either "ich was" or "ich war." A norm can coexist only with its violation and not with another, contradictory norm (for which reason there can be no "tragedies" in language). If the violation does not make itself felt and consequently is not corrected, and if there is favorable ground for this particular violation to become a widespread fact—and analogy in our instance qualifies as favorable ground—then such a violation will become the next linguistic norm.

It turns out, then, that there is nothing in common—no connection—between the logic of language as a system of forms and the logic of its historical evolution. Completely different sets of principles and sets of factors hold sway in each of the two domains. What endows language with meaning and unity in its synchronic dimension is overridden and ignored in its diachronic dimension. *The present state of a language and the history of a language do not enter into and are incapable of entering into mutual comprehensibility.*

At this point we come upon a cardinal difference between the first and second trends in the philosophy of language. Indeed, for the first trend the very essence of language is revealed precisely in its history; the logic of language is not at all a matter of reproducing a normatively identical form but of continuous renovation and individualization of that form via the stylistically unreproducible utterance. *The reality of language is, in fact, its generation.* Complete mutual comprehensibility obtains in language between any given moment in its life and its history. The same ideological motives prevail in the one and the other. In Vosslerian terms, *linguistic taste creates the unity of a language at any given moment in time; and it is the same linguistic taste that creates and secures the unity of a language's historical evolution.* The transition from one historical form to another occurs basically within the individual consciousness, since, for Vossler, as we know, each grammatical form was originally a free stylistic form.

The difference between the first and second trends is very graphically brought out in the following contrast. The self-identical forms comprising the immutable system of language (*ergon*) represented for the first trend only the inert crust of the actual generative process of language, i.e., of the true essence of language implemented in the unreproducible, individual act of creation. Meanwhile, for the second trend, it is exactly this system of self-identical forms that becomes the essence of language; individual creative refraction and variation of linguistic forms are, for this trend, only the dross of linguistic life or, rather, of linguistic monumentality, only the mercurial and extraneous overtones of the basic, fixed tone of linguistic forms.

The outlook of the second trend can, on the whole, be summarized in the following basic principles:

1. *Language is a stable, immutable system of normatively identical linguistic forms which the individual consciousness finds ready-made and which is incontestable for that consciousness.*

2. *The laws of language are the specifically linguistic laws of connection between linguistic signs within a given, closed linguistic system.* These laws are objective with respect to *any* subjective consciousness.

3. *Specifically linguistic connections have nothing in common with ideological values* (artistic, cognitive, or other). Language phenomena are not grounded in ideological motives. No connection of a kind natural and comprehensible to the consciousness or of an artistic kind obtains between the word and its meaning.

4. *Individual acts of speaking are, from the viewpoint of language, merely fortuitous refractions and variations or plain and simple distortions of normatively identical forms;* but precisely these acts of individual discourse explain the historical changeability of linguistic forms, a changeability that in itself, from the standpoint of the language system, is irrational and senseless. *There is no connection, no sharing of motives, between the system of language and its history. They are alien to one another.*

The reader will note that the four basic principles we have just formulated to characterize the second trend of thought in the philosophy of language represent antitheses to the corresponding four basic principles of the first trend.

The historical development of the second trend is a great deal more difficult to trace back. In this case, no representative, no founder equal to Wilhelm von Humboldt appears at the dawn of our era. The roots of this trend must be sought in the rationalism of the 17th and 18th centuries. These roots go back to Cartesian grounds.[19]

The ideas behind the second trend received their first and very sharply delineated expression in Leibniz's conception of universal grammar.

The idea of the *conventionality, the arbitrariness of language,* is a typical one for rationalism as a whole, and no less typical is the *comparison of language to the system of mathematical signs.* What interests the mathematically

19. There can be no doubt that the second trend has profound inner connection with Cartesian thought and with the overall world view of neoclassicism and its cult of autonomous, rational, fixed form. Descartes himself produced no studies in the philosophy of language, but characteristic pronouncements of his can be found in his letters. See Cassirer, *Philosophie der symbolischen Formen*, pp. 67-68.

minded rationalists is not the relationship of the sign to the actual reality it reflects nor to the individual who is its originator, but the *relationship of sign to sign within a closed system* already accepted and authorized. In other words, they are interested only in the *inner logic of the system of signs itself*, taken, as in algebra, completely independently of the ideological meanings that give the signs their content. Rationalists are not averse to taking the understander's viewpoint into account, but are least of all inclined to consider that of the speaker, as the subject expressing his own inner life. For the fact is that the mathematical sign is least amenable to interpretation as an expression of the individual psyche —and it is the mathematical sign, after all, that rationalists hold to be the ideal of any sign, including the verbal sign. This is exactly what found graphic expression in Leibniz's idea of universal grammar.[20]

It should be noted at this point that the precedence of the understander's viewpoint over the speaker's has remained a constant feature of the second trend. This means that on the basis of this trend, there is no access to the problem of expression nor, consequently, to the problem of the verbal generation of thought and the subjective psyche (one of the fundamental problems for the first trend).

In somewhat simplified form, the idea of language as a system of conventional, arbitrary signs of a fundamentally rational nature was propounded by representatives of the Age of the Enlightenment in the 18th century.

Engendered on French soil, the ideas of abstract objectivism still hold sway predominantly in France.[21] Let us pass over its intermediary stages of development and turn directly to a characterization of the modern state of the second trend.

Abstract objectivism finds its most striking expression at the present time in the so-called Geneva school of Ferdinand de Saussure. Its representatives, particularly Charles Bally, are among the most prominent linguists of modern times. The ideas of this second trend all have been endowed with amazing clarity and precision by Ferdinand de Saussure. His formulations of the basic concepts of linguistics can well be accounted classics of their kind. Moreover, Saussure undauntedly carried his ideas out to their conclusions, providing all the basic lines of abstract objectivism with exceptionally clear-cut and rigorous definition.

In Russia, the Saussure school is as popular and influential as the Vossler school is not. It can be claimed that the majority of Russian thinkers in linguis-

20. The reader can acquaint himself with the views of Leibniz pertinent here by referring to Cassirer's book, *Leibniz' System in seinen wissenschaftlichen Grundlagen* (Marburg, 1902).

21. Curiously, the first trend, in contradistinction to the second, has developed and continues to develop primarily on German soil.

tics are under the determinative influence of Saussure and his disciples, Bally and Sèchehaye.[22]

In view of the fundamental importance of Saussure's views for the whole second trend and for Russian linguistic thought in particular, we shall consider those views in some detail. Here as elsewhere, to be sure, we shall confine ourselves to basic philosophical-linguistic positions only.[23]

Saussure's point of departure is a distinction among three aspects of language: *language-speech* (langage), *language as a system of forms* (langue) and *the individual speech act—the utterance* (parole). Language (in the sense of *langue:* a system of forms) and utterance *(parole)* are constituents of language-speech *(langage)*, and the latter is understood to mean the sum total of all the phenomena—physical, physiological, and psychological—involved in the realization of verbal activity.

Language-speech *(langage)*, according to Saussure, cannot be the object of study for linguistics. In and of itself, it lacks inner unity and validity as an autonomous entity; it is a heterogeneous composite. Its contradictory composition makes it difficult to handle. Precise definition of linguistic fact would be an impossibility on its grounds. Language-speech cannot be the point of departure for linguistic analysis.

What, then, does Saussure propose should be chosen as the correct methodological procedure for the identification of the specific object of linguistics? We shall let him speak for himself:

> In our opinion, there can be but one solution to all these difficulties [i.e., difficulties entailed in taking *langage* as the point of departure for analysis—*V.V.*]: *we must first and foremost take our stand on the grounds of language* (langue) *and accept it as the norm for all other manifestations of speech* (langage). Indeed, amidst so many dualities, language alone appears susceptible to autonomous definition, and it alone can provide the mind a satisfactory base of operations.[24]

22. R. Šor's *Jazyk i obščestvo* [Language and Society] (Moscow, 1926), is entrenched in the spirit of the Geneva School. She also functions as an ardent apologist of Saussure's basic ideas in her article, "Krizis sovremennoj lingvistiki," already cited. The linguist V. V. Vinogradov may be regarded a follower of the Geneva School. Two schools of Russian linguistics, the Fortunatov school and the so-called Kazan' school (Kruševskij and Baudouin de Courtenay), both of them vivid expressions of linguistic formalism, fit entirely within the framework we have mapped out as that of the second trend of thought in philosophy of language.

23. Saussure's basic theoretical work, published after his death by his students, is *Cours de linguistique générale* (1916). We shall be quoting from the second edition of 1922. Puzzlingly enough, Saussure's book, for all its influence, has not as yet been translated into Russian. A brief summary of Saussure's views can be found in the above-cited article by R. Šor and in an article by Peterson, "Obščaja lingvistika" [General Linguistics], *Pečat' i Revoljucija*, 6, 1923.

24. Saussure, *Cours de linguistique*, p. 24.

And in what does Saussure see the fundamental difference between speech *(langage)* and language *(langue)*?

> Taken in its totality, speech is manifold and anomalous. Astride several domains at once—the physical, the physiological, the psychological, it pertains, also, both to the domain of the individual and to the domain of society. It resists classification under any of the categories of human facts because there is no knowing how to elicit its unity.
> Language, on the contrary, is a self-contained whole and a principle of classification. Once we give it first place among the facts of speech, we introduce a natural order into an assemblage that is amenable to no other classification.[25]

Thus, Saussure's contention is that language as a system of normatively identical forms must be taken as the point of departure and that all manifestations of speech must be illuminated from the angle of these stable and autonomous forms.

After having distinguished language from speech (speech meaning the sum total of all manifestations of the verbal faculty, i.e., *langage*), Saussure proceeds to distinguish language from acts of individual speaking, i.e., from utterance *(parole)*:

> In distinguishing language *(langue)* from utterance *(parole)*, we by the same token distinguish (1) what is social from what is individual, and (2) what is essential from what is accessory and more or less random.
> Language is not a function of the speaker; it is a product that the individual registers passively: it never relies upon premeditation and reflection plays no part in it, except in the matter of classification—which is a topic for later consideration.
> Utterance, on the contrary, is an individual act of will and intelligence in which we must distinguish between (1) the combinations through which a speaker utilizes a particular language code for expressing his own personal thoughts, and (2) the psychophysical mechanism that enables him to exteriorize those combinations.[26]

Linguistics, as Saussure conceives it, cannot have the utterance as its object of study.[27] What constitutes the linguistic element in the utterance are the normatively identical forms of language present in it. Everything else is "accessory and random."

Let us underscore Saussure's main thesis: *language stands in opposition to utterance in the same way as does that which is social to that which is individual.*

25. *Ibid.*, p. 25.
26. *Ibid.*, p. 30.
27. Saussure does, it is true, allow the possibility of a special linguistics of utterance ("linguistique de la parole"), but he remains silent on just what sort of linguistics that would be. Here is what he says on this point:

> Il faut choisir entre deux routes qu'il est impossible de prendre en même temps; elles doivent être suivies séparément. On peut à la rigueur conserver le nom de linguistique de la parole. Mais il ne faudra pas la confondre avec la linguistique proprement dite, celle dont la langue est l'unique objet [*Ibid.*, p. 39].

The utterance, therefore, is considered a thoroughly individual entity. This point, as we shall see later, contains the *pseudos proton* of Saussure's views and of the whole abstract objectivist trend.

The individual act of speaking, the utterance *(parole)*, so decisively cast aside from linguistics, does return, however, as an essential factor in the history of language.[28] Saussure, in the spirit of the second trend, sharply opposes the history of language to language as a synchronic system. History is dominated by "utterance" with its individuality and randomness, and therefore a completely different set of principles holds for the history of language than for the system of language. Saussure declares:

> Such being the case, the synchronic "phenomenon" can have nothing in common with the diachronic . . . . *Synchronic linguistics* will be concerned with the logical and psychological relations that bind together coexistant terms and form a system, such as these relations are perceived by one and the same collective mind.
> *Diachronic linguistics,* on the contrary, must study relations binding successive terms together, which relations are not perceived by the collective mind and replace one another without forming a system.[29]

Saussure's views on history are extremely characteristic for the spirit of rationalism that continues to hold sway in this second trend of thought in the philosophy of language and that regards history as an irrational force distorting the logical purity of the language system.

Saussure and the Saussure school are not the only high point of abstract objectivism in our time. Looming alongside the Saussure school is another—the sociological school of Durkheim, represented in linguistics by a figure such as Meillet. We shall not dwell on a characterization of Meillet's views.[30] They fit entirely within the framework of the basic principles of the second trend. For Meillet, too, language is a social phenomenon, not in its aspect as a process, but as a stable system of linguistic norms. The compulsory nature of language and the fact that language is exterior to the individual consciousness are for Meillet its fundamental social characteristics.

So much, then, for the views of the second trend of thought in philosophy of language—the trend of abstract objectivism.

Needless to say, there are numerous schools and movements in linguistics, sometimes highly significant ones, that do not fit into the framework of the two trends we have described. It was our purpose to trace the major arteries only. All other manifestations of philosophical-linguistic thought are in the nature of

28. Saussure says: *"Tout ce qui est diachronique dans la langue ne l'est que par la parole. C'est dans la parole que se trouve le germe de tout les changements [Ibid., p. 138].*

29. *Ibid.,* pp. 129 and 140.

30. An exposition of Meillet's views in connection with the principles of Durkheim's sociological method is given in the above-cited article by M. N. Peterson, "Jazyk kak social'noe javlenie." The article includes a bibliography.

combinations or compromises with respect to the trends discussed or are entirely devoid of any appreciable theoretical orientation.

Let us take the example of the neogrammarian movement, a phenomenon of no small importance in the linguistics of the latter half of the 19th century. The neogrammarians, with respect to part of their basic principles, are associated with the first trend, tending toward its physiological extreme. For them, the individual who creates language is essentially a physiological being. On the other hand, the neogrammarians did attempt to construct, on psychophysiological grounds, invariable natural scientific laws of language completely removed from anything describable as the individual will of speakers. From this issued the neogrammarians' notion of sound laws *(Lautgesetze).*[31]

In linguistics, as in any other discipline, there are two basic devices for avoiding the obligation and trouble of thinking in responsible, theoretical, and, consequently, philosophical terms. The first way is to accept all theoretical views wholesale (academic eclecticism), and the second is not to accept a single point of view of a theoretical nature and to proclaim "fact" as the ultimate basis and criterion for any kind of knowledge (academic positivism).

The philosophical effect of both these devices for avoiding philosophy amounts to one and the same thing, since in the second case, too, all possible theoretical points of view can and do creep into investigation under the cover of "fact." Which of these devices an investigator will choose depends entirely upon his temperament: the eclectic tends more to the blithe side; the positivist, to the surreptitious.

There have been in linguistics a great many developments, and entire schools (here, school has the sense of scientific and technical training) that have avoided the trouble of a philosophical linguistic orientation. They, of course, did not find a place in the present survey.

We shall have occasion to mention later, in connection with our analysis of the problem of verbal interaction and the problem of meaning, certain linguists and philosophers of language not mentioned here—for instance, Otto Deitrich and Anton Marty.

At the beginning of this chapter, we posed the *problem of the identification and delimitation of language as a specific object for investigation.* We endeavored to bring into view those guideposts already placed along the road of the solution to the problem by the preceding trends of thought in the philosophy of language. As a result, we find ourselves confronted by two series of guideposts pointing in

31. The basic works of the neogrammarian movement are: Osthoff, *Das physiologische und psychologische Moment in der Sprachlichen Formenbildung* (Berlin, 1879); Brugmann and Delbrück, *Grundriss der vergleichenden Grammatik der indogermanischen Sprachen,* 5 Volumes (Vol. I, 1st edition, 1886). The neogrammarian program is spelled out in the preface to the book by Osthoff and Brugmann, *Morphologische Untersuchungen,* Vol. I (Leipzig, 1878).

diametrically opposite directions: *the theses of individualistic subjectivism and the antitheses of abstract objectivism.*

What, then, is the true center of linguistic reality: the individual speech act—the utterance—or the system of language? And what is the real mode of existence of language: unceasing creative generation or inert immutability of self-identical norms?

CHAPTER 2

Language, Speech, and Utterance

Can language as a system of normative, self-identical forms be considered an objective fact? Language as a system of norms and the actual viewpoint on language in a speaker's consciousness. What kind of linguistic reality underlies a linguistic system? The problem of the alien, foreign word. The errors of abstract objectivism. Summary and conclusions.

In the preceding chapter, we tried to give an entirely objective picture of the two main trends of thought in the philosophy of language. Now we must submit those trends to a thorough critical analysis. Only after having done so will we be able to answer the question posed at the end of the preceding chapter.

Let us begin with critical analysis of the second trend, that of abstract objectivism.

First of all, let us pose a question: to what degree may the system of self-identical linguistic norms (i.e., the system of language, as the representatives of the second trend understand it) be considered a real entity?

None of the representatives of abstract objectivism would, of course, ascribe concrete material reality to the system of language. True, that system is expressed in material things—in signs—but as a system of normatively identical forms, it has reality only in the capacity of the social norm.

Representatives of abstract objectivism constantly stress—and it is one of their basic principles—that the system of language is an objective fact external to and independent of *any* individual consciousness. Actually, represented as a system of self-identical, immutable norms, it can be perceived in this way only by the individual consciousness and from the point of view of that consciousness.

Indeed, if we were to disregard the subjective, individual consciousness vis-à-vis the language system, the system of norms incontestable for that consciousness,

65

if we were to look at language in a truly objective way — from the side, so to speak, or more accurately, from above it, we would discover no inert system of self-identical norms. Instead, we would find ourselves witnessing the ceaseless generation of language norms.

From a truly objective viewpoint, one that attempts to see language in a way completely apart from how it appears to any given individual at any given moment in time, language presents the picture of a ceaseless flow of becoming. From the standpoint of observing a language objectively, from above, there is no real moment in time when a synchronic system of language could be constructed.

Thus *a synchronic system, from the objective point of view, does not correspond to any real moment in the historical process of becoming.* And indeed, to the historian of language, with his diachronic point of view, a synchronic system is not a real entity; it merely serves as a conventional scale on which to register the deviations occuring at every real instant in time.

So, then, a synchronic system may be said to exist only from the point of view of the subjective consciousness of an individual speaker belonging to some particular language group at some particular moment of historical time. From an objective point of view, no such system exists at any real instant of historical time. We may suppose, for instance, that while Caesar was engaged in writing his works, the Latin language was for him a fixed, incontestable system of self-identical norms; but, for the historian of Latin, a continuous process of linguistic change was going on at the very moment that Caesar was working (whether or not the historian of Latin would be able to pinpoint those changes).

Any system of social norms occupies an analogous position. It exists only with respect to the subjective consciousness of individuals belonging to some particular community governed by norms. Such is the nature of a system of moral norms, of judicial norms, of norms for aesthetic taste (there are, indeed, such norms), and so on. Of course, these norms vary: their obligatory nature varies, as does the breadth of their social compass, as does also the degree of their social significance, determined by their proximity to the basis, etc. But the nature of their existence as norms remains the same—they exist only with respect to the subjective consciousness of members of some particular community.

Does it follow, then, that this relationship between the subjective consciousness and language as a system of objective, incontestable norms is itself bereft of any objectivity? Of course not. Properly understood, this relationship can be considered an objective fact.

If we claim that language as a system of incontestable and immutable norms exists objectively, we commit a gross error. But if we claim that language, with respect to the individual consciousness, is a system of immutable norms, that such is the mode of existence of language for each member of any given language community, then what we are expressing in these terms is a completely objective relationship. Whether the fact itself is correctly constituted, whether language actually does appear only as a fixed and inert system of norms to the speaker's consciousness—that is another question. For the time being we shall leave that question open. But the point, in any case, is that a certain kind of objective relationship can be established.

Now, how do representatives of abstract objectivism themselves regard this matter? Do they assert that language is a system of objective and incontestable self-identical norms, or are they aware of the fact that this is only the mode of existence of the language for the subjective consciousness of a speaker of any given language?

No better answer can be given than the following: Most representatives of abstract objectivism are inclined to assert *the unmediated reality, the unmediated objectivity of language as a system of normatively identical forms.* In the case of these representatives of the second trend, abstract objectivism converts directly into *hypostasizing abstract objectivism.* Other representatives of the trend (Meillet, for instance) have a more critical attitude and do take account of the abstract and conventional nature of the linguistic system. However, not a single representative of abstract objectivism has arrived at a clear and distinct conception of the kind of reality that language as an objective system does possess. In the majority of cases, these representatives walk the tightrope between two conceptions of the word "objective" as applied to the system of language: one in quotation marks, so to speak (from the standpoint of the speaker's subjective consciousness), and one without quotation marks (from the objective standpoint). This, incidentally, is the way that Saussure, too, handles the question—he provides no clear-cut solution.

Now we must ask: Does language really exist for the speaker's subjective consciousness as an objective system of incontestable, normatively identical forms? Has abstract objectivism correctly understood the point of view of the speaker's subjective consciousness? Or, to put it another way: Is the mode of being of language in the subjective speech consciousness really what abstract objectivism says it is?

We must answer this question in the negative. The speaker's subjective consciousness does not in the least operate with language as a system of normatively identical forms. That system is merely an abstraction arrived with a good deal of trouble and with a definite cognitive and practical focus of attention. The system of language is the product of deliberation on language, and deliberation of a kind by no means carried out by the consciousness of the native speaker himself and by no means carried out for the immediate purposes of speaking.

In point of fact, the speaker's focus of attention is brought about in line with the particular, concrete utterance he is making. What matters to him is applying a normatively identical form (let us grant there is such a thing for the time being) in some particular, concrete context. For him, the center of gravity lies not in the identity of the form but in that new and concrete meaning it acquires in the particular context. What the speaker values is not that aspect of the form which is invariably identical in all instances of its usage, despite the nature of those instances, but that aspect of the linguistic form because of which it can figure in the given, concrete context, because of which it becomes a sign adequate to the conditions of the given, concrete situation.

We can express it this way: *what is important for the speaker about a linguistic form is not that it is a stable and always self-equivalent signal, but that it is an always changeable and adaptable sign.* That is the speaker's point of view.

But doesn't the speaker also have to take into account the point of view of the listener and understander? Isn't it possible that here, exactly, is where the normative identity of a linguistic form comes into force?

This, too, is not quite so. The basic task of understanding does not at all amount to recognizing the linguistic form used by the speaker as the familiar, "that very same," form, the way we distinctly recognize, for instance, a signal that we have not quite become used to or a form in a language that we do not know very well. No, the task of understanding does not basically amount to recognizing the form used, but rather to understanding it in a particular, concrete context, to understanding its meaning in a particular utterance, i.e., it amounts to understanding its novelty and not to recognizing its identity.

In other words, the understander, belonging to the same language community, also is attuned to the linguistic form not as a fixed, self-identical signal, but as a changeable and adaptable sign.

The process of understanding is on no account to be confused with the process of recognition. These are thoroughly different processes. Only a sign can be understood; what is recognized is a signal. A signal is an internally fixed, singular thing that does not in fact stand for anything else, or reflect or refract anything, but is simply a technical means for indicating this or that object (some definite, fixed object) or this or that action (likewise definite and fixed).[1] Under no circumstances does the signal relate to the domain of the ideological; it relates to the world of technical devices, to instruments of production in the broad sense of the term. Even further removed from ideology are the signals with which reflexology is concerned. These signals, taken in relation to the organism of the animal subject, i.e., as signals for that subject, have no relation to techniques of production. In this capacity they are not signals but stimuli of a special kind. They become instruments of production only in the hands of the experimenter. The grievous misconceptions and ingrained habits of mechanistic

---

1. For interesting and ingenious distinctions between a signal or combinations of signals (in maritime usage, for instance) and a linguistic form or combinations of linguistic forms in connection with the problem of syntax, see K. Bühler, "Vom Wesen der Syntax," *Festschrift für Karl Vossler*, pp. 61-69.

thought are alone responsible for the attempt to take these "signals" and very nearly make of them the key to the understanding of language and of the human psyche (inner word).

Should a linguistic form remain only a signal, recognized as such by the understander, it, then, does not exist for him as a linguistic form. Pure signality is not evinced even in the early stages of language learning. In this case, too, the linguistic form is oriented in context; here, too, it is a sign, although the factor of signality and its correlative, the factor of recognition, are operative.

Thus the constituent factor for the linguistic form, as for the sign, is not at all its self-identity as signal but its specific variability; and the constituent factor for understanding the linguistic form is not recognition of "the same thing," but understanding in the proper sense of the word, i.e., orientation in the particular, given context and in the particular, given situation—orientation in the dynamic process of becoming and not "orientation" in some inert state.[2]

It does not, of course, follow from all that has been said that the factors of signalization and its correlative, recognition, are absent from language. They are present, but they are not constituents of language as such. They are dialectically effaced by the new quality of the sign (i.e., of language as such). In the speaker's native language, i.e., for the linguistic consciousness of a member of a particular language community, signal-recognition is certainly dialectically effaced. In the process of mastering a foreign language, signality and recognition still make themselves felt, so to speak, and still remain to be surmounted, the language not yet fully having become language. The ideal of mastering a language is absorption of signality by pure semioticity and of recognition by pure understanding.[3]

2. We shall see later that precisely this kind of understanding in the proper sense, an understanding of process, lies at the basis of response, i.e., at the basis of verbal interaction. No sharp dividing line can be drawn between understanding and response. Any act of understanding is a response, i.e., it translates what is being understood into a new context from which a response can be made.

3. The principle advanced here underlies the practice (though proper theoretical awareness may be lacking) of all sensible methods of teaching living foreign languages. What is central to all these methods is that students become acquainted with each linguistic form only in concrete contexts and situations. So, for instance, students are acquainted with some word only through the presentation of a variety of contexts in which that word figures. Thanks to this procedure, the factor of recognition of identical word is dialectically combined with and submerged under the factor of the word's contextual changeability, diversity, and capacity for new meanings. A word extracted from context, written down in an exercise book, and then memorized together with its Russian translation undergoes signalization, so to speak. It becomes a particular hard-and-fast thing, and the factor of recognition intensifies in the process of understanding it. To put it briefly, under a sound and sensible method of practical instruction, a form should be assimilated not in its relation to the abstract system of the language, i.e., as a self-identical form, but in the concrete structure of utterance, i.e., as a mutable and pliable sign.

The linguistic consciousness of the speaker and of the listener-understander, in the practical business of living speech, is not at all concerned with the abstract system of normatively identical forms of language, but with language-speech in the sense of the aggregate of possible contexts of usage for a particular linguistic form. For a person speaking his native tongue, a word presents itself not as an item of vocabulary but as a word that has been used in a wide variety of utterances by co-speaker A, co-speaker B, co-speaker C and so on, and has been variously used in the speaker's own utterances. A very special and specific kind of orientation is necessary, if one is to go from there to the self-identical word belonging to the lexicological system of the language in question—the dictionary word. For that reason, a member of a language community does not normally feel himself under the pressure of incontestable linguistic norms. A linguistic form will bring its normative significance to the fore only in exceptionally rare instances of conflict, instances that are not typical for speech activity (and which for modern man are almost exclusively associated with writing).

One other extremely pertinent consideration needs to be added here. The verbal consciousness of speakers has, by and large, nothing whatever to do with linguistic form as such or with language as such.

In point of fact, the linguistic form, which, as we have just shown, exists for the speaker only in the context of specific utterances, exists, consequently, only in a specific ideological context. In actuality, we never say or hear *words,* we say and hear what is true or false, good or bad, important or unimportant, pleasant or unpleasant, and so on. *Words are always filled with content and meaning drawn from behavior or ideology.* That is the way we understand words, and we can respond only to words that engage us behaviorally or ideologically.

Only in abnormal and special cases do we apply the criterion of correctness to an utterance (for instance, in language instruction). Normally, the criterion of linguistic correctness is submerged by a purely ideological criterion: an utterance's correctness is eclipsed by its truthfulness or falsity, its poeticalness or banality, etc.[4]

Language, in the process of its practical implementation, is inseparable from its ideological or behavioral impletion. Here, too, an orientation of an entirely special kind—one unaffected by the aims of the speaker's consciousness—is required if language is to be abstractly segregated from its ideological or behavioral impletion.

---

4. On this basis, as we shall see later, one would have to disagree with Vossler in his postulating the existence of a separate and distinct kind of linguistic taste that in each instance would remain apart from some specific kind of ideological "taste"—aesthetic, cognitive, ethical, or other.

If we advance this abstract segregation to the status of a principle, if we reify linguistic form divorced from ideological impletion, as do certain representatives of the second trend, then we end up dealing with a signal and not with a sign of language-speech.

The divorce of language from its ideological impletion is one of abstract objectivism's most serious errors.

In sum, then, for the conciousness of a speaker of a language, the real mode of existence for that language is not as a system of normatively identical forms. From the viewpoint of the speaker's consciousness and his real-life practice in social intercourse, there is no direct access to the system of language envisioned by abstract objectivism.

What, then, in such a case, is this system?

It is clear from the start that that system is obtained by way of abstraction, that it is composed of elements extracted in an abstract way from the real units that make up the stream of speech—from utterances. Any abstraction, if it is to be legitimate, must be justified by some specific theoretical and practical goal. An abstraction may be productive or not productive, or may be productive for some goals and tasks and not productive for others.

What are the goals that underlie the kind of linguistic abstraction that leads to the synchronic system of language? And from what point of view may this system be regarded productive and necessary?

At the basis of the modes of linguistic thought that lead to the postulation of language as a system of normatively identical forms lies a *practical and theoretical focus of attention on the study of defunct, alien languages preserved in written monuments.*

This philological orientation has determined the whole course of linguistic thinking in the European world to a very considerable degree, and we must stress this point with all possible insistence. European linguistic thought formed and matured over concern with the cadavers of written languages; almost all its basic categories, its basic approaches and techniques were worked out in the process of reviving these cadavers.

Philologism is the inevitable distinguishing mark of the whole of European linguistics as determined by the historical vicissitudes of its birth and development. However far back we may go in tracing the history of linguistic categories and methods, we find philologists everywhere. Not just the Alexandrians, but the ancient Romans were philologists, as were the Greeks (Aristotle is a typical philologist). Also, the ancient Hindus were philologists.

We can state outright: *linguistics makes its appearance wherever and whenever philological need has appeared.* Philological need gave birth to linguistics, rocked its cradle, and left its philological flute wrapped in its swaddling clothes. That flute was supposed to be able to awaken the dead. But it lacked the range necessary for mastering living speech as actually and continuously generated.

N. Ja. Marr is perfectly correct in pointing out this philological essence in Indo-European linguistic thought:

> Indo-European linguistics, commanding an already established and a long since fully formed object of investigation—the Indo-European languages of the historical epochs— and taking its departure, moreover, almost exclusively from the petrified forms of written languages—dead languages foremost among them—is naturally itself incapable of bringing to light the process of the emergence of speech in general and the origination of its species.[5]

Or in another passage:

> The greatest obstacle [to the study of aboriginal speech—*V. V.*] is caused not by the difficulty of the research itself, nor the lack of solid data, but by our scientific thinking, which is locked into the traditional outlook of philology or the history of culture and has not been nurtured by ethnological and linguistic perception of living speech in its limitlessly free, creative ebb and flow.[6]

Marr's words hold true not only, of course, for Indo-European studies, which have set the tone for all contemporary linguistics, but also for the whole of linguistics as we know it from history. Everywhere, as we have said, linguistics is the child of philology.

Guided by philological need, linguistics has always taken as its point of departure the finished monologic utterance—the ancient written monument, considering it the ultimate realium. All its methods and categories were elaborated in its work on this kind of defunct, monologic utterance or, rather, on a series of such utterances constituting a corpus for linguistics by virtue of common language alone.

But the monologic utterance is, after all, already an abstraction, though, to be sure, an abstraction of a "natural" kind. Any monologic utterance, the written monument included, is an inseverable element of verbal communication. Any utterance—the finished, written utterance not excepted—makes response to something and is calculated to be responded to in turn. It is but one link in a continuous chain of speech performances. Each monument carries on the work of its predecessors, polemicizing with them, expecting active, responsive understanding, and anticipating such understanding in return. Each monument in actuality is an integral part of science, literature, or political life. The monument, as any other monologic utterance, is set toward being perceived in the context of current scientific life or current literary affairs, i.e., it is perceived in the generative process of that particular ideological domain of which it is an integral part.

---

5. N. Ja. Marr, *Po ètapam jafetskoj teorii* [Through the Stages of the Japhetic Theory] (1926), p. 269.
6. *Ibid.*, pp. 94-95.

The philologist-linguist tears the monument out of that real domain and views it as if it were a self-sufficient, isolated entity. He brings to bear on it not an active ideological understanding but a completely passive kind of understanding, in which there is not a flicker of response, as there would be in any authentic kind of understanding. The philologist takes the isolated monument as a document of language and places it in relation with other monuments on the general plane of the language in question. All the methods and categories of linguistic thought were formed in this process of comparing and correlating isolated monologic utterances on the plane of language.

The dead language the linguist studies is, of course, an alien language. Therefore, the system of linguistic categories is least of all a product of cognitive reflection on the part of the linguistic consciousness of a speaker of that language. Here reflection does not involve a native speaker's feeling for his own language. No, this kind of reflection is that of a mind striking out into, breaking trails through, the unfamiliar world of an alien language.

Inevitably, the philologist-linguist's passive understanding is projected onto the very monument he is studying from the language point of view, as if that monument were in fact calculated for just that kind of understanding, as if it had, in fact, been written for the philologist.

The result of all this is a fundamentally erroneous theory of understanding that underlies not only the methods of linguistic interpretation of texts but also the whole of European semasiology. Its entire position on word meaning and theme is permeated through and through with the false notion of *passive understanding,* the kind of understanding of a word that excludes active response in advance and on principle.

We shall see later that this kind of understanding, with built-in exclusion of response, is not at all in fact the kind of understanding that applies in language-speech. The latter kind of understanding inextricably merges with an active position taken apropos of what has been said and is being understood. The characteristic feature of passive understanding is exactly a distinct sense of the identity factor in a linguistic sign, i.e., perception of it as an artifact-signal and, in correlation with this, the predominance of the recognition factor.

Thus *dead, written, alien language* is the true description of the language with which linguistic thought has been concerned.

The *isolated, finished, monologic utterance,* divorced from its verbal and actual context and standing open not to any possible sort of active response but to passive understanding on the part of a philologist—that is the ultimate "donnée" and the starting point of linguistic thought.

Engendered in the process of mastering a dead, alien language for purposes of scientific investigation, linguistic thought has also served another, not investigatory, but instructional purpose: the purpose not of deciphering a language but of teaching an already deciphered language. Monuments were made over from heuristic documents into a classical model of language for the lecture hall.

This second basic task of linguistics—its creating the apparatus essential for instruction in a deciphered language, for codifying it, so to speak, in line with the aims of lecture-hall transmission, made a substantial imprint on linguistic thinking. *Phonetics, grammar, lexicon*—the three branches of the system of language, the three organizing centers for linguistic categories—took shape within the channel of these two major tasks of linguistics: *the heuristic and the pedogogical.*

What is a philologist?

Despite the vast differences in cultural and historical lineaments from the ancient Hindu priests to the modern European scholar of language, the philologist has always and everywhere been a decipherer of alien, "secret" scripts and words, and a teacher, a disseminator, of that which has been deciphered and handed down by tradition.

The first philologists and the first linguists were always and everywhere *priests.* History knows no nation whose sacred writings or oral tradition were not to some degree in a language foreign and incomprehensible to the profane. To decipher the mystery of sacred words was the task meant to be carried out by the priest-philologists.

It was on these grounds that ancient philosophy of language was engendered: the Vedic teaching about the word, the Logos of the ancient Greek thinkers, and the biblical philosophy of the word.

To understand these philosophemes properly, one must not forget for one instant that they were *philosophemes of the alien word.* If some nation had known only its own native tongue; if, for that nation, word had always coincided with native word of that nation's life; if no mysterious, alien word, no word from a foreign tongue, had ever entered its purview, then such a nation would never have created anything resembling these philosophemes.[7] It is an astonishing feature: from remotest antiquity to the present day, the philosophy of word and linguistic thought have been built upon specific sensibility to the alien, foreign-language word and upon those tasks which precisely that kind of word presents to the mind—deciphering and teaching what has been deciphered.

The Vedic priest and the contemporary philologist-linguist are spellbound and held captive in their thinking about language by one and the same phenomenon—the phenomenon of alien, foreign-language word.

_____

7. According to Vedic religion, the sacred word—in that usage to which it is put by the "gnostic" consecrated priest —becomes the sovereign of all Being, including both gods and men. The priest-gnostic is defined here as the one who commands the word—therein lies all his power. The doctrine to this effect is contained already in the Rig Veda. The ancient Greek philosopheme of Logos and the Alexandrian doctrine of Logos are well known.

One is sensible of one's native word in a completely different way or, to be more precise, one is ordinarily not sensible of one's native word as a word crammed with all those categories that it has generated in linguistic thought and that it generated in the philosophical-religious thought of the ancients. Native word is one's "kith and kin"; we feel about it as we feel about our habitual attire or, even better, about the atmosphere in which we habitually live and breathe. It contains no mystery; it can become a mystery only in the mouth of others, provided they are hierarchically alien to us—in the mouth of the chief, in the mouth of the priests. But in that case, it has already become a word of a different kind, externally changed and removed from the routine of life (taboo for usage in ordinary life, or an archaism of speech); that is, if it had not already been from the start a foreign word in the mouth of a conqueror-chief. Only at this point is the "Word" born, and only at this point—*incipit philosophia, incipit philologia.*

Orientation in linguistics and the philosophy of language toward the alien, foreign word is by no means an accidental occurrence or a whim on the part of linguistics and philosophy. No, that orientation is the expression of the enormous historical role that the alien word has played in the formation of all the historical cultures. It has played that role with respect to all domains of ideo-logical creativity without exception, from the sociopolitical order to the behavioral code of daily life. Indeed, it was the alien, foreign-language word that brought civilization, culture, religion, and political organization (e.g., the role of the Sumerians with respect to the Babylonian Semites, of the Japhites to the Hellenes, of Rome and of Christianity to the barbarian peoples, of Byzantium, the "Varangians," the South Slavic tribes to the Eastern Slavs, etc.). This grandiose organizing role of the alien word, which always either entered upon the scene with alien force of arms and organization or was found on the scene by the young conqueror-nation of an old and once mighty culture and captivated, from its grave, so to speak, the ideological consciousness of the newcomer-nation—this role of the alien word led to its coalescence in the depths of the historical consciousness of nations with the idea of authority, the idea of power, the idea of holiness, the idea of truth, and dictated that notions about the word be preeminently oriented toward the alien word.

However, the philosophy of language and linguistics never were, and are still not today, objectively aware of the enormous historical role played by the foreign word. No, linguistics is still enslaved by it; linguistics represents, as it were, the last wave to reach us of the once-upon-a-time fructifying inundation of alien speech, the last residue of its dictatorial and culture-creating role.

For this very reason, linguistics, itself the product of foreign word, is far from any proper understanding of the role played by the foreign word in the history of language and linguistic consciousness. On the contrary, Indo-European studies have fashioned categories of understanding for the history of language of a kind that preclude proper evaluation of the role of alien word. Meanwhile, that role, to all appearances, is enormous.

The idea of *linguistic "crossing" as the basic factor in the evolution of languages* has been definitively advanced by Marr. He also recognized linguistic crossing to be the main factor in the solution of the problem of how language originated:

> Crossing in general, as a factor in the emergence of different language species and even types of language, being *the* source for the formation of new species, has been observed and traced throughout all the Japhetic languages, and this must be considered one of the most momentous achievements of Japhetic linguistics. . . . The point is that no primigene of sound language, no single-tribal language exists or, as we shall see, existed or could have existed. Language, the creation of sociality which had arisen on the basis of intertribal communication brought about by economic needs, is the accumulation of precisely this kind of sociality, which is always multitribal.[8]

In his article, "On the Origin of Language," Marr has the following to say on our topic:

> In short, the approach to this or that language in terms of so-called national culture, as the mass, native language of an entire population, is unscientific and unrealistic; the ecumenical, classless national language remains a fiction. But that is not the half of it. Just as castes in the early stages of development issue from tribes—or really from tribal formations, that are also by no means simple in themselves—so by way of crossing, did concrete tribal languages and, even more so, national languages, come to represent crossbred types of languages, crossbred from the combination of simple elements through which, in one way or another, every language is formed. Paleontological analysis of human speech goes no further than definition of these tribal elements, but the Japhetic theory accomodates these elements in such a decisive and definitive way that the question of the origin of language is boiled down to the question of the emergence of these elements, which are in fact nothing more than tribal names.[9]

Here we can only take note of the significance of the alien word for the problem of the origin of language and its evolution. These problems exceed the scope of our present study. For us the importance of the alien word consists in its role as a factor determining philosophical linguistic thought and the categories and approaches stemming from that thought.

We shall now disregard the particularities of aboriginal thought about the alien word[10] and also the categories of the ancient philosophemes of word mentioned above. We shall attempt to note down here only those particular features

---

8. N. Ja. Marr, *Japhetic theory*, p. 268.

9. *Ibid.*, pp. 315-316.

10. Thus to a significant degree it was the alien word that determined prehistoric man's magical perception of the word. We have in mind in this connection all the relevant phenomena in toto.

in thought about the word that have persisted through the centuries and have had determinative effect on contemporary linguistic thought. We may safely assume that these are precisely the categories that have found their most marked and most clear-cut expression in the doctrine of abstract objectivism.

We shall now attempt to reformulate, in the following series of concise premises, those features of cognizance of the alien word that underlie abstract objectivism. In doing so, we shall also be summarizing our preceding exposition and supplementing it at certain crucial points.[11]

1. *The factor of stable self-identity in linguistic forms takes precedence over their mutability.*
2. *The abstract takes precedence over the concrete.*
3. *Abstract systematization takes precedence over historical actuality.*
4. *The forms of elements take precedence over the form of the whole.*
5. *Reification of the isolated linguistic element to the neglect of the dynamics of speech.*
6. *Singularization of word meaning and accent to the neglect of its living multiplicity of meaning and accent.*
7. *The notion of language as a ready-made artifact handed down from one generation to another.*
8. *Inability to conceptualize the inner generative process of a language.*

Let us consider briefly each of these features of the system of thought dominated by the alien word.

1.   The first feature needs no further commentary. We have already pointed out that understanding one's own language is focused not on recognizing identical elements of speech but on understanding their new, contextual meaning. The construction of a system of self-identical forms may then be said to be an indispensable and vital stage in the processes of deciphering an alien language and handing it on.

2.   The second point, too, is clear enough on the basis of what has already been said. The finished monologic utterance is an abstraction, in point of fact. Concretization of a word is possible only by way of including that word into the actual historical context of its original implementation. By propounding the

11. One should not forget in this connection that abstract objectivism in its new formation is an expression of the condition that the alien word had reached when it had already lost its authoritativeness and productivity to a significant degree. Moreover, specificity of perception of the alien word has declined in abstract objectivism, owing to that fact that the latter's basic categories of thought have been extended to perception of living and native languages. Linguistics studies a living language as if it were a dead language, and native language as if it were an alien tongue. That is why the postulations of abstract objectivism are so different from the ancient philosophemes of alien word.

isolated monologic utterance, all those ties that bind an utterance to the full concreteness of historical generation are torn away.

3.   Formalism and systematicity are the typical distinguishing marks of any kind of thinking focused on a ready-made and, so to speak, arrested object.

This particular feature of thought has many different manifestations. Characteristically, what undergoes systematization is usually (if not exclusively) someone else's thought. True creators—the initiators of new ideological trends—are never formalistic systematizers. Systematization comes upon the scene during an age which feels itself in command of a ready-made and handed-down body of authoritative thought. A creative age must first have passed; then and only then does the business of formalistic systematizing begin—an undertaking typical of heirs and epigones who feel themselves in possession of someone else's, now voiceless word. Orientation in the dynamic flow of generative process can never be of the formal, systematizing kind. Therefore, formal, systematizing grammatical thought could have developed to its full scope and power only on the material of an alien, dead language, and only could have done so provided that that language had already, to a significant degree, lost its affective potency— its sacrosanct and authoritative character. With respect to living language, systematic, grammatical thought must inevitably adopt a conservative position, i.e., it must interpret living language as if it were already perfected and ready-made and thus must look upon any sort of innovation in language with hostility. Formal, systematic thought about language is incompatible with living, historical understanding of language. From the system's point of view, history always seems merely a series of accidental transgressions.

4.   Linguistics, as we have seen, is oriented toward the isolated, monologic utterance. Linguistic monuments comprise the material for study, and the passively understanding mind of the philologist is brought to bear on that material. Thus all the work goes on within the bounds of some given utterance. As for the boundaries that demarcate the utterance as a whole entity, they are perceived faintly or sometimes not at all. Research is wholly taken up in study of immanent connections on the inside territory of the utterance. Considerations of the utterance's external affairs, so to speak, remain beyond the field of study. Thus, all connections that exceed the bounds of the utterance as a monologic whole are ignored. One might well expect, then, that the very nature of an utterance's wholeness and the forms that that wholeness may take are left outside of linguistic thought. And indeed, linguistic thought goes no further than the elements that make up the monologic utterance. The structure of a complex sentence (a period)—that is the furthest limit of linguistic reach. The structure of a whole utterance is something linguistics leaves to the competence of other disciplines—to rhetoric and poetics. Linguistics lacks any approach to the compositional forms of the whole. Therefore, there is no direct transition between

the linguistic forms of the elements of an utterance and the forms of its whole, indeed, no connection at all! Only by making a jump from syntax can we arrive at problems of composition. This is absolutely inevitable, seeing that the forms making up the whole of an utterance can only be perceived and understood against the background of other whole utterances belonging to a unity of some particular domain of ideology. Thus, for instance, the forms of a literary utterance—a literary work of art—can only be understood in the unity of literary life, indissolubly connected with other kinds of *literary* forms. When we relegate a literary work to the history of language as a system, when we regard it only as a document of language, we lose access to its forms as the forms of a literary whole. There is a world of difference between referring a work to the system of language and referring a work to the concrete unity of literary life, and that difference is insurmountable on the grounds of abstract objectivism.

5.   Linguistic form is merely an abstractly extractable factor of the dynamic whole of speech performance—of the utterance. Abstraction of that sort is, of course, perfectly legitimate within the range of the specific tasks linguistics sets for itself. However, abstract objectivism supplies the grounds for the reification of the linguistic form, for its becoming an element supposedly extractable in actuality and supposedly capable of an isolated, historical existence of its own. This is completely understandable: after all, the system as a whole cannot undergo historical development. The utterance as a whole entity does not exist for linguistics. Consequently, the elements of the system, i.e., the separate linguistic forms, are all that is left. And so *they* must be what can undergo historical change.

History of language, then, amounts to the history of separate linguistic forms (phonetic, morphological, or other) that undergo development despite the system as a whole and apart from concrete utterances.[12]

Vossler is perfectly right in what he says about the history of language as conceived by abstract objectivism:

> Roughly speaking, the history of language, as it is given to us by historical grammar, is the same sort of thing as a history of clothing would be, which does not take the concept of fashion or the taste of the time as its point of departure, but provides a chronologically and geographically arranged list of buttons, clasps, stockings, hats, and ribbons. In historical grammar, such buttons and ribbons would have names like weak or strong *e*, voiceless *t*, voiced *d*, and so on.[13]

6.   The meaning of a word is determined entirely by its context. In fact, there are as many meanings of a word as there are contexts of its usage.[14] At the

---

12. Utterance is merely a neutral medium for change of linguistic form.

13. See Vossler, "Grammatika i istorija jazyka, *Logos,* I (1910), p. 170.

14. For the time being, we disregard the distinction between meaning and theme about which we shall speak below (Chapter 4).

same time, however, the word does not cease to be a single entity; it does not, so to speak, break apart into as many separate words as there are contexts of its usage. The word's unity is assured, of course, not only by the unity of its phonetic composition but also by that factor of unity which is common to all its meanings. How can the fundamental polysemanticity of the word be reconciled with its unity? To pose this question is to formulate, in a rough and elementary way, the cardinal problem of semantics. It is a problem that can only be solved dialectically. But how does abstract objectivism go about it? For abstract objectivism, the unity factor of a word solidifies, as it were, and breaks away from the fundamental multiplicity of its meanings. This multiplicity is perceived as the occasional overtones of a single hard-and-fast meaning. The focus of linguistic attention is exactly opposite that of real-life understanding on the part of the speakers engaged in a particular flow of speech. The philologist-linguist, when comparing different contexts in which a given word appears, focuses his attention on the identity factor in its usage, since to him what is important is to be able to remove the word from the contexts compared and to give it definition outside context, i.e., to create a dictionary word out of it. This process of isolating a word and fixing its meaning outside any context takes on added force when comparing different languages, i.e., when trying to match a word with an equivalent word in another language. In the process of linguistic treatment, meaning is constructed, as it were, on the border of at least two languages. These endeavors on the linguist's part are further complicated by the fact that he creates the fiction of a single and actual object corresponding to the given word. This object, being single and self-identical, is just what ensures the unity of meaning. The fiction of a word's literal realia promotes to an even greater degree the reification of its meaning. On these grounds, the dialectical combination of the unity of meaning with its multiplicity becomes impossible.

Another grave error on the part of abstract objectivism is to be seen in the following. The various contexts of usage for any one particular word are conceived of as all lying on the same plane. These contexts are thought of as forming a series of circumscribed, self-contained utterances all pointed in the same direction. In actual fact, this is far from true: contexts of usage for one and the same word often contrast with one another. The classical instance of such contrasting contexts of usage for one and the same word is found in dialogue. In the alternating lines of a dialogue, the same word may figure in two mutually clashing contexts. Of course, dialogue is only the most graphic and obvious instance of varidirectional contexts. Actually, any real utterance, in one way or another or to one degree or another, makes a statement of agreement with or a negation of something. Contexts do not stand side by side in a row, as if unaware of one another, but are in a state of constant tension, or incessant interaction and conflict. The change of a word's evaluative accent in different contexts is totally ignored by linguistics and has no reflection in its doctrine on

the unity of meaning. This accent is least amenable to reification, yet it is precisely a word's multiaccentuality that makes it a living thing. The problem of
multiaccentuality ought to be closely associated with the problem of multiplicity of meanings. Only provided that they are associated together can the two
problems be solved. But it is exactly this association that the basic principles of
abstract objectivism utterly preclude. Linguistics has thrown evaluative accent
overboard along with the unique utterance *(parole).*[15]

7.   According to the teaching of abstract objectivism, language is handed
down as a ready-made product from generation to generation. Of course, the
representatives of the second trend understand the transmission of the language
legacy, transmission of language as an artifact, in metaphorical terms, but still,
in their hands, such a comparison is not merely a metaphor. In reifying the
system of language and in viewing living language as if it were dead and alien,
abstract objectivism makes language something external to the stream of verbal
communication. This stream flows on, but language, like a ball, is tossed from
generation to generation. In actual fact, however, language moves together with
that stream and is inseparable from it. Language cannot properly be said to be
handed down—it endures, but it endures as a continuous process of becoming.
Individuals do not receive a ready-made language at all, rather, they enter upon
the stream of verbal communication; indeed, only in this stream does their
consciousness first begin to operate. Only in learning a foreign language does
a fully prepared consciousness—fully prepared thanks to one's native language—
confront a fully prepared language which it need only accept. People do not
"accept" their native language—it is in their native language that they first reach
awareness.[16]

8.   Abstract objectivism, as we have seen, is incapable of tying together the
existence of language in its abstract, synchronic dimension with the evolution
of language. Language exists for the consciousness of the speaker as a system of
normatively identical forms, but only for the historian as a process of generation.
This excludes any possibility for the speaker's consciousness to be actively in
touch with the process of historical evolution. The dialectical coupling of necessity with freedom and with, so to speak, linguistic responsibility is, of course,
utterly impossible on these grounds. A purely mechanistic conception of linguistic necessity holds sway here. No doubt this feature of abstract objectivism, too,
is connected with its subconscious fixation on dead and alien language.

15. We shall further amplify the points made here in the fourth chapter of this section of
our study.
16. The process of a child's assimilation of his native language is the process of his gradual
immersion into verbal communication. As that process of immersion proceeds, the child's
consciousness is formed and filled with content.

All that remains is for us to summarize our critical analysis of abstract objectivism. The problem we posed at the beginning of the first chapter—the problem of the actual mode of being of linguistic phenomena as a specific and unified object of study—was incorrectly solved by abstract objectivism. Language as a system of normatively identical forms is an abstraction justifiable in theory and practice only from the standpoint of deciphering and teaching a dead, alien language. This system cannot serve as a basis for understanding and explaining linguistic facts as they really exist and come into being. On the contrary, this system leads us away from the living, dynamic reality of language and its social functions, notwithstanding the fact that adherents of abstract objectivism claim sociological significance for their point of view. Underlying the theory of abstract objectivism are presuppositions of a rationalistic and mechanistic world outlook. These presuppositions are least capable of furnishing the grounds for a proper understanding of history—and language, after all, is a purely historical phenomenon.

Does it follow from this that the basic positions of the first trend, the trend of individualistic subjectivism, are the correct ones? Perhaps individualistic subjectivism has succeeded in grasping the true reality of language-speech? Or perhaps the truth lies somewhere in the middle, representing a compromise between the first and second trends, between the theses of individualistic subjectivism and the antitheses of abstract objectivism?

We believe that in this instance, as everywhere else, the truth is not to be found in the golden mean and is not a matter of compromise between thesis and antithesis, but lies over and beyond them, constituting a negation of both thesis and antithesis alike, i.e., constituting a *dialectical synthesis.* The theses of the first trend also do not hold up under critical examination, as we shall see in the next chapter.

Let us at this point direct attention to the following: Abstract objectivism, by taking the system of language and regarding it as the entire crux of linguistic phenomena, rejected the speech act—the utterance—as something individual. As we said once before, herein lies the *proton pseudos* of abstract objectivism. For individualistic subjectivism, the entire crux of the matter is just exactly the speech act—the utterance. However, individualistic subjectivism likewise defines this act as something individual and therefore endeavors to explain it in terms of the individual psychic life of the speaker. Herein lies its *proton pseudos.*

In point of fact, the speech act or, more accurately, its product—the utterance, cannot under any circumstances be considered an individual phenomenon in the precise meaning of the word and cannot be explained in terms of the individual psychological or psychophysiological conditions of the speaker. *The utterance is a social phenomenon.*

It shall be our concern to substantiate this thesis in the next chapter.

CHAPTER 3

Verbal Interaction

Individualistic subjectivism and its theory of expression. Criticism of the theory of expression. The sociological structure of experience and expression. The problem of behavioral ideology. The utterance as the basic unit in the generative process of speech. Approaches to the solution of the problem of the actual mode of existence of language. The utterance as a whole entity and its forms.

The second trend of thought in the philosophy of language was associated, as we saw, with rationalism and neoclassicism. The first trend—individualistic subjectivism—is associated with *romanticism.* Romanticism, to a considerable degree, was a reaction against the alien word and the categories of thought promoted by the alien word. More particularly and more immediately, romanticism was a reaction against the last resurgences of the cultural power of the alien word—the epochs of the Renaissance and neoclassicism. The romanticists were the first philologists of native language, the first to attempt a radical restructuring of linguistic thought. Their restructuring was based on experience with native language as the medium through which consciousness and ideas are generated. True, the romanticists remained philologists in the strict sense of the word. It was, of course, beyond their power to restructure a mode of thinking about language that had taken shape and had been sustained over the course of centuries. Nevertheless, new categories were introduced into that thinking, and these new categories were precisely what gave the first trend its specific characteristics. Symptomatically, even recent representatives of individualistic subjectivism have been specialists in modern languages, chiefly the Romance languages (Vossler, Leo Spitzer, Lorch, *et al.*).

However, individualistic subjectivism also took the monologic utterance as the ultimate reality and the point of departure for its thinking about language. To be sure, it did not approach the monologic utterance from the viewpoint of the passively understanding philologist but, rather, approached it from within, from the viewpoint of the person speaking and expressing himself.

What does the monologic utterance amount to, then, in the view of individualistic subjectivism? We have seen that it is a purely individual act, the expression of an individual consciousness, its ambitions, intentions, creative impulses, tastes, and so on. The category of expression for individualistic subjectivism is the highest and broadest category under which the speech act—the utterance—may be subsumed.

But what is expression?

Its simplest, rough definition is: something which, having in some way taken shape and definition in the psyche of an individual, is outwardly objectified for others with the help of external signs of some kind.

Thus there are two elements in expression: that inner something which is *expressible,* and its *outward objectification* for others (or possibly for oneself). Any theory of expression, however complex or subtle a form it may take, inevitably presupposes these two elements—the whole event of expression is played out between them. Consequently, any theory of expression inevitably presupposes that the expressible is something that can somehow take shape and exist apart from expression; that it exists first in one form and then switches to another form. This would have to be the case; otherwise, if the expressible were to exist from the very start in the form of expression, with quantitative transition between the two elements (in the sense of clarification, differentiation, and the like), the whole theory of expression would collapse. The theory of expression inevitably presupposes a certain dualism between the inner and outer elements and the explicit primacy of the former, since each act of objectification (expression) goes from inside out. Its sources are within. Not for nothing were idealistic and spiritualistic grounds the only grounds on which the theory of individualistic subjectivism and all theories of expression in general arose. Everything of real importance lies within; the outer element can take on real importance only by becoming a vessel for the inner, by becoming expression of spirit.

To be sure, by becoming external, by expressing itself outwardly, the inner element does undergo alteration. After all, it must gain control of outer material that possesses a validity of its own apart from the inner element. In this process of gaining control, of mastering outer material and making it over into a compliant medium of expression, the experiential, expressible element itself undergoes alteration and is forced to make a certain compromise. Therefore, idealistic grounds, the grounds on which all theories of expression have been established, also contain provision for the radical negation of expression as something that deforms the purity of the inner element.[1] In any case, all the creative and organizing forces of expression are within. Everything outer is merely passive material for manipulation by the inner element. Expression is formed basically within and then merely shifts to the outside. The understanding, interpretation, and explanation of an ideological phenomenon, it would follow from this argument, must also be directed inward; it must traverse a route the reverse of that for expression. Starting from outward objectification, the explanation must work down into its inner, organizing bases. That is how individualistic subjectivism understands expression.

The theory of expression underlying the first trend of thought in philosophy of language is fundamentally untenable.

The experiential, expressible element and its outward objectification are created, as we know, out of one and the same material. After all, there is no such thing as experience outside of embodiment in signs. Consequently, the very notion of a fundamental, qualitative difference between the inner and the outer element is invalid to begin with. Furthermore, the location of the organizing and formative center is not within (i.e., not in the material of inner signs) but outside. It is not experience that organizes expression, but the other way around—*expression organizes experience.* Expression is what first gives experience its form and specificity of direction.

Indeed, from whichever aspect we consider it, expression-utterance is determined by the actual conditions of the given utterance—above all, by its *immediate social situation.*

Utterance, as we know, is constructed between two socially organized persons, and in the absence of a real addressee, an addressee is presupposed in the person, so to speak, of a normal representative of the social group to which the speaker belongs. The *word is oriented toward an addressee,* toward *who* that addressee might be: a fellow-member or not of the same social group, of higher or lower standing (the addressee's hierarchical status), someone connected with the speaker by close social ties (father, brother, husband, and so on) or not. There can be no such thing as an abstract addressee, a man unto himself, so to speak. With such a person, we would indeed have no language in common, literally and figuratively. Even though we sometimes have pretensions to experiencing and saying things *urbi et orbi,* actually, of course, we envision this "world at large" through the prism of the concrete social milieu surrounding us. In the majority of cases, we presuppose a certain typical and stabilized *social purview* toward which the ideological creativity of our own social group and time is oriented,

---

1. "Spoken thought is a lie" (Tjutčev); "Oh, if one could speak from the soul without words" (Fet). These statements are extremely typical of idealistic romanticism.

i.e., we assume as our addressee a contemporary of our literature, our science, our moral and legal codes.

Each person's inner world and thought has its stabilized *social audience* that comprises the environment in which reasons, motives, values, and so on are fashioned. The more cultured a person, the more closely his inner audience will approximate the normal audience of ideological creativity; but, in any case, specific class and specific era are limits that the ideal of addressee cannot go beyond.

Orientation of the word toward the addressee has an extremely high significance. In point of fact, *word is a two-sided act.* It is determined equally by *whose* word it is and *for whom* it is meant. As word, it is precisely *the product of the reciprocal relationship between speaker and listener, addresser and addressee.* Each and every word expresses the "one" in relation to the "other." I give myself verbal shape from another's point of view, ultimately, from the point of view of the community to which I belong. A word is a bridge thrown between myself and another. If one end of the bridge depends on me, then the other depends on my addressee. A word is territory shared by both addresser and addressee, by the speaker and his interlocutor.

But what does being the speaker mean? Even if a word is not entirely his, constituting, as it were, the border zone between himself and his addressee— still, it does in part belong to him.

There is one instance of the situation wherein the speaker is the undoubted possessor of the word and to which, in this instance, he has full rights. This instance is the physiological act of implementing the word. But insofar as the act is taken in purely physiological terms, the category of possession does not apply.

If, instead of the physiological act of implementing sound, we take the implementation of word as sign, then the question of proprietorship becomes extremely complicated. Aside from the fact that word as sign is a borrowing on the speaker's part from the social stock of available signs, the very individual manipulation of this social sign in a concrete utterance is wholly determined by social relations. The stylistic individualization of an utterance that the Vosslerites speak about represents a reflection of social interrelationships that constitute the atmosphere in which an utterance is formed. *The immediate social situation and the broader social milieu wholly determine—and determine from within, so to speak—the structure of an utterance.*

Indeed, take whatever kind of utterance we will, even the kind of utterance that is not a referential message (communication in the narrow sense) but the verbal expression of some need—for instance, hunger—we may be certain that it is socially oriented in its entirety. Above all, it is determined immediately and directly by the participants of the speech event, both explicit and implicit participants, in connection with a specific situation. That situation shapes the utterance, dictating that it sound one way and not another—like a demand or request, insistence on one's rights or a plea for mercy, in a style flowery or plain, in a confident or hesitant manner, and so on.

The immediate social situation and its immediate social participants determine the "occasional" form and style of an utterance. The deeper layers of its structure are determined by more sustained and more basic social connections with which the speaker is in contact.

Even if we were to take an utterance still in process of generation "in the soul," it would not change the essence of the matter, since the structure of experience is just as social as is the structure of its outward objectification. The degree to which an experience is perceptible, distinct, and formulated is directly proportional to the degree to which it is socially oriented.

In fact, not even the simplest, dimmest apprehension of a feeling—say, the feeling of hunger not outwardly expressed—can dispense with some kind of ideological form. Any apprehension, after all, must have inner speech, inner intonation and the rudiments of inner style: one can apprehend one's hunger apologetically, irritably, angrily, indignantly, etc. We have indicated, of course, only the grosser, more egregious directions that inner intonation may take; actually, there is an extremely subtle and complex set of possibilities for intoning an experience. Outward expression in most cases only continues and makes more distinct the direction already taken by inner speech and the intonation already embedded in it.

Which way the intoning of the inner sensation of hunger will go depends upon the hungry person's general social standing as well as upon the immediate circumstances of the experience. These are, after all, the circumstances that determine in what evaluative context, within what social purview, the experience of hunger will be apprehended. The immediate social context will determine possible addressees, friends or foes, toward whom the consciousness and the experience of hunger will be oriented: whether it will involve dissatisfaction with cruel Nature, with oneself, with society, with a specific group within society, with a specific person, and so on. Of course, various degrees of perceptibility, distinctiveness, and differentiation in the social orientation of an experience are possible; but without some kind of evaluative social orientation there is no experience. Even the cry of a nursing infant is "oriented" toward its mother. There is the possibility that the experience of hunger may take on political coloring, in which case its structure will be determined along the lines of a potential political appeal or a reason for political agitation. It may be apprehended as a form of protest, and so on.

With regard to the potential (and sometimes even distinctly sensed) addressee, a distinction can be made between two poles, two extremes between which an experience can be apprehended and ideologically structured, tending now toward the one, now toward the other. Let us label these two extremes the *"I-experience"* and the *"we-experience."*

The "I-experience" actually tends toward extermination: the nearer it approaches its extreme limit, the more it loses its ideological structuredness and, hence, its apprehensible quality, reverting to the physiological reaction of the animal. In its course toward this extreme, the experience relinquishes all its potentialities, all outcroppings of social orientation, and, therefore, also loses its verbal delineation. Single experiences or whole groups of experiences can approach this extreme, relinquishing, in doing so, their ideological clarity and structuredness and testifying to the inability of the consciousness to strike social roots.[2]

The "we-experience" is not by any means a nebulous herd experience; it is differentiated. Moreover, ideological differentiation, the growth of consciousness, is in direct proportion to the firmness and reliability of the social orientation. The stronger, the more organized, the more differentiated the collective in which an individual orients himself, the more vivid and complex his inner world will be.

The "we-experience" allows of different degrees and different types of ideological structuring.

Let us suppose a case where hunger is apprehended by one of a disparate set of hungry persons whose hunger is a matter of chance (the man down on his luck, the beggar, or the like). The experience of such a declassé loner will be colored in some specific way and will gravitate toward certain particular ideological forms with a range potentially quite broad: humility, shame, enviousness, and other evaluative tones will color his experience. The ideological forms along the lines of which the experience would develop would be either the individualistic protest of a vagabond or repentant, mystical resignation.

Let us now suppose a case in which the hungry person belongs to a collective where hunger is not haphazard and does bear a collective character—but the collective of these hungry people is not itself tightly bound together by material ties, each of its members experiencing hunger on his own. This is the situation most peasants are in. Hunger is experienced "at large," but under conditions of material disparateness, in the absence of a unifying economic coalition, each person suffers hunger in the small, enclosed world of his own individual economy. Such a collective lacks the unitary material frame necessary for united action. A resigned but unashamed and undemeaning apprehension of one's hunger will be the rule under such conditions—"everyone bears it, you must bear it, too." Here grounds are furnished for the development of the philosophical and religious systems of the nonresistor or fatalist type (early Christianity, Tolstoyanism).

---

2. On the possibility of a set of human sexual experiences falling out of social context with concomitant loss of verbal cognizance, see our book, *Frejdizm* [Freudianism] (1927), pp. 135-136.

A completely different experience of hunger applies to a member of an objectively and materially aligned and united collective (a regiment of solders; workers in their association within the walls of a factory; hired hands on a large-scale, capitalist farm; finally, a whole class once it has matured to the point of "class unto itself"). The experience of hunger this time will be marked predominantly by overtones of active and self-confident protest with no basis for humble and submissive intonation. These are the most favorable grounds for an experience to achieve ideological clarity and structuredness.[3]

All these types of expression, each with its basic intonations, come rife with corresponding terms and corresponding forms of possible utterances. The social situation in all cases determines which term, which metaphor, and which form may develop in an utterance expressing hunger out of the particular intonational bearings of the experience.

A special kind of character marks the individualistic *self-experience*. It does not belong to the "I-experience" in the strict sense of the term as defined above. The individualistic experience is fully differentiated and structured. Individualism is a special ideological form of the "we-experience" of the bourgeois class (there is also an analogous type of individualistic self-experience for the feudal aristocratic class). The individualistic type of experience derives from a steadfast and confident social orientation. Individualistic confidence in oneself, one's sense of personal value, is drawn not from within, not from the depths of one's personality, but from the outside world. It is the ideological interpretation of one's social recognizance and tenability by rights, and of the objective security and tenability provided by the whole social order, of one's individual livelihood. The structure of the conscious, individual personality is just as social a structure as is the collective type of experience. It is a particular kind of interpretation, projected into the individual soul, of a complex and sustained socioeconomic situation. But there resides in this type of individualistic "we-experience," and also in the very order to which it corresponds, an inner contradiction that sooner or later will demolish its ideological structuredness.

An analogous structure is presented in solitary self-experience ("the ability and strength to stand alone in one's rectitude"), a type cultivated by Romain Rolland and, to some extent, by Tolstoj. The pride involved in this solitude also depends upon "we." It is a variant of the "we-experience" characteristic of the modern-day West European intelligentsia. Tolstoj's remarks about there being different kinds of thinking—"for oneself" and "for the public"—merely juxtapose two different conceptions of "public." Tolstoj's "for oneself" actually signifies

3. Interesting material about expressions of hunger can be found in Leo Spitzer's books, *Italienische Kriegsgefangenenbriefe* and *Die Umschreibungen des Begriffes Hunger*. The basic concern in these studies is the adaptability of word and image to the conditions of an exceptional situation. The author does not, however, operate with a genuine sociological approach.

only another social conception of addressee peculiar to himself. There is no such thing as thinking outside orientation toward possible expression and, hence, outside the social orientation of that expression and of the thinking involved.

Thus the personality of the speaker, taken from within, so to speak, turns out to be wholly a product of social interrelations. Not only its outward expression but also its inner experience are social territory. Consequently, the whole route between inner experience (the "expressible") and its outward objectification (the "utterance") lies entirely across social territory. When an experience reaches the stage of actualization in a full-fledged utterance, its social orientation acquires added complexity by focusing on the immediate social circumstances of discourse and, above all, upon actual addressees.

Our analysis casts a new light upon the problem of consciousness and ideology that we examined earlier.

Outside objectification, outside embodiment in some particular material (the material of gesture, inner word, outcry), *consciousness is a fiction.* It is an improper ideological construct created by way of abstraction from the concrete facts of social expression. But consciousness as organized, material expression (in the ideological material of word, a sign, drawing, colors, musical sound, etc.)—consciousness, so conceived, is an objective fact and a tremendous social force. To be sure, this kind of consciousness is not a supraexistential phenomenon and cannot determine the constitution of existence. It itself is part of existence and one of its forces, and for that reason it possesses efficacy and plays a role in the arena of existence. Consciousness, while still inside a conscious person's head as inner-word embryo of expression, is as yet too tiny a piece of existence, and the scope of its activity is also as yet too small. But once it passes through all the stages of social objectification and enters into the power system of science, art, ethics, or law, it becomes a real force, capable even of exerting in turn an influence on the economic bases of social life. To be sure, this force of consciousness is incarnated in specific social organizations, geared into steadfast ideological modes of expression (science, art, and so on), but even in the originial, vague form of glimmering thought and experience, it had already constituted a social event on a small scale and was not an inner act on the part of the individual.

From the very start experience is set toward fully actualized outward expression and, from the very start, tends in that direction. The expression of an experience may be realized or it may be held back, inhibited. In the latter case, the experience is inhibited expression (we shall not go into the extremely complex problem of the causes and conditions of inhibition). Realized expression, in its turn, exerts a powerful, reverse influence on experience: it begins to tie inner life together, giving it more definite and lasting expression.

This reverse influence by structured and stabilized expression on experience (i.e., inner expression) has tremendous importance and must always be taken into account. The claim can be made that it is a matter *not so much of expression accomodating itself to our inner world but rather of our inner world accomodating itself to the potentialities of our expression, its possible routes and directions.*

To distinguish it from the established systems of ideology—the systems of art, ethics, law, etc.—we shall use the term *behavioral ideology* for the whole aggregate of life experiences and the outward expressions directly connected with it. Behavioral ideology is that atmosphere of unsystematized and unfixed inner and outer speech which endows our every instance of behavior and action and our every "conscious" state with meaning. Considering the sociological nature of the structure of expression and experience, we may say that behavioral ideology in our conception corresponds basically to what is termed "social psychology" in Marxist literature. In the present context, we should prefer to avoid the word "psychology," since we are concerned exclusively with the content of the psyche and the consciousness. That content is ideological through and through, determined not by individual, organismic (biological or physiological) factors, but by factors of a purely sociological character. The individual, organismic factor is completely irrelevant to an understanding of the basic creative and living lineaments of the content of consciousness.

The established ideological systems of social ethics, science, art, and religion are crystallizations of behavioral ideology, and these crystallizations, in turn, exert a powerful influence back upon behavioral ideology, normally setting its tone. At the same time, however, these already formalized ideological products constantly maintain the most vital organic contact with behavioral ideology and draw sustenance from it; otherwise, without that contact, they would be dead, just as any literary work or cognitive idea is dead without living, evaluative perception of it. Now, this ideological perception, for which alone any ideological piece of work can and does exist, is carried out in the language of behavioral ideology. Behavioral ideology draws the work into some particular social situation. The work combines with the whole content of the consciousness of those who perceive it and derives its apperceptive values only in the context of that consciousness. It is interpreted in the spirit of the particular content of consciousness (the consciousness of the perceiver) and is illuminated by it anew. This is what constitutes the vitality of an ideological production. In each period of its historical existence, a work must enter into close association with the changing behavioral ideology, become permeated with it, and draw new sustenance from it. Only to the degree that a work can enter into that kind of integral, organic association with the behavioral ideology of a given period is it viable for that period (and of course, for a given social group). Outside its connection with behavioral ideology it ceases to exist, since it ceases to be experienced as something ideologically meaningful.

We must distinguish several different strata in behavioral ideology. These strata are defined by the social scale on which experience and expression are measured, or by the social forces with respect to which they must directly orient themselves.

The purview in which an experience or expression comes into being may, as we know, vary in scope. The world of an experience may be narrow and dim; its social orientation may be haphazard and ephemeral and characteristic only for some adventitious and loose coalition of a small number of persons. Of course, even these erratic experiences are ideological and sociological, but their position lies on the borders of the normal and the pathological. Such an experience will remain an isolated fact in the psychological life of the person exposed to it. It will not take firm root and will not receive differentiated and full-fledged expression; indeed, if it lacks a socially grounded and stable audience, where could it possibly find bases for its differentiation and finalization? Even less likely would such an adventitious experience be set down, in writing or even more so in print. Experiences of that kind, experiences born of a momentary and accidental state of affairs, have, of course, no chance of further social impact or efficacy.

The lowest, most fluid, and quickly changing stratum of behavioral ideology consists of experiences of that kind. To this stratum, consequently, belong all those vague and undeveloped experiences, thoughts, and idle, accidental words that flash across our minds. They are all of them cases of miscarriages of social orientations, novels without heroes, performances without audiences. They lack any sort of logic or unity. The sociological regulatedness in these ideological scraps is extremely difficult to detect. In this lowest stratum of behavioral ideology only statistical regularity is detectable; given a huge quantity of products of this sort, the outlines of socioeconomic regulatedness could be revealed. Needless to say, it would be a practical impossibility to descry in any one such accidental experience or expression its socioeconomic premises.

The upper strata of behavioral ideology, the ones directly linked with ideological systems, are more vital, more serious and bear a creative character. Compared to an established ideology, they are a great deal more mobile and sensitive: they convey changes in the socioeconomic basis more quickly and more vividly. Here, precisely, is where those creative energies build up through whose agency partial or radical restructuring of ideological systems comes about. Newly emerging social forces find ideological expression and take shape first in these upper strata of behavioral ideology before they can succeed in dominating the arena of some organized, official ideology. Of course, in the process of this struggle, in the process of their gradual infiltration into ideological organizations (the press, literature, and science), these new currents in behavioral ideology, no matter how revolutionary they may be, undergo the influence of the established ideological systems and, to some extent, incorporate forms, ideological practices, and approaches already in stock.

What usually is called "creative individuality" is nothing but the expression of a particular person's basic, firmly grounded, and consistent line of social orientation. This concerns primarily the uppermost, fully structured strata of inner speech (behavioral ideology), each of whose terms and intonations have gone through the stage of expression and have, so to speak, passed the test of expression. Thus what is involved here are words, intonations, and inner-word gestures that have undergone the experience of outward expression on a more or less ample social scale and have acquired, as it were, a high social polish and lustre by the effect of reactions and responses, resistance or support, on the part of the social audience.

In the lower strata of behavioral ideology, the biological-biographical factor does, of course, play a crucial role, but its importance constantly diminishes as the utterance penetrates more deeply into an ideological system. Consequently, while bio-biographical explanations are of some value in the lower strata of experience and expression (utterance), their role in the upper strata is extremely modest. Here the objective sociological method takes full command.

So, then, the theory of expression underlying individualistic subjectivism must be rejected. *The organizing center of any utterance, of any experience, is not within but outside—in the social milieu surrounding the individual being.* Only the inarticulate cry of an animal is really organized from inside the physiological apparatus of an individual creature. Such a cry lacks any positive ideological factor vis-à-vis the physiological reaction. Yet, even the most primitive human utterance produced by the individual organism is, from the point of view of its content, import, and meaning, organized outside the organism, in the extraorganismic conditions of the social milieu. Utterance as such is wholly a product of social interaction, both of the immediate sort as determined by the circumstances of the discourse, and of the more general kind, as determined by the whole aggregate of conditions under which any given community of speakers operates.

The individual utterance(*parole*), despite the contentions of abstract objectivism, is by no means an individual fact not susceptible to sociological analysis by virtue of its individuality. Indeed, if this were so, neither the sum total of these individual acts nor any abstract features common to all such individual acts (the "normatively identical forms") could possibly engender a social product.

Individualistic subjectivism is *correct* in that individual utterances *are* what constitute the actual, concrete reality of language, and in that they *do have* creative value in language.

But individualistic subjectivism is *wrong* in ignoring and failing to understand the social nature of the utterance and in attempting to derive the utterance from the speaker's inner world as an expression of that inner world. The structure of the utterance and of the very experience being expressed is a *social structure.* The stylistic shaping of an utterance is shaping of a social kind, and the very verbal stream of utterances, which is what the reality of language actually amounts to, is a social stream. Each drop of that stream is social and the entire dynamics of its generation is social.

Individualistic subjectivism is also completely *correct* in that linguistic form and its ideological impletion are *not* severable. Each and every word is ideological and each and every application of language involves ideological change. But individualistic subjectivism is *wrong* insofar as it also derives this ideological impletion of the word from the conditions of the individual psyche.

Individualistic subjectivism is *wrong* in taking the monologic utterance, just as abstract objectivism does, as its basic point of departure. Certain Vosslerites, it is true, have begun to consider the problem of dialogue and so to approach a more correct understanding of verbal interaction. Highly symptomatic in this regard is one of Leo Spitzer's books we have already cited— his *Italienische Umgangssprache*, a book that attempts to anlyze the forms of Italian conversational language in close connection with the conditions of discourse and above all with the issue of the addressee.[4] However, Leo Spitzer utilizes a *descriptive psychological* method. He does not draw from his analysis the fundamentally sociological conclusions it suggests. For the Vosslerites, therefore, the monologic utterance still remains the basic reality.

The problem of verbal interaction has been posed clearly and distinctly by Otto Dietrich.[5] He proceeds by way of subjecting to criticism the theory of utterance as expression. For him, the basic function of language is not expression but *communication* (in the strict sense), and this leads him to consider the role of the addressee. The minimal condition for a linguistic manifestation is, according to Dietrich, *twofold* (speaker and listener). However, Dietrich shares assumptions of a general psychological type with individualistic subjectivism. Dietrich's investigations likewise lack any determinate sociological basis.

Now we are in a position to answer the question we posed at the end of the first chapter of this section of our study. *The actual reality of language-speech is not the abstract system of linguistic forms, not the isolated monologic utterance, and not the psychophysiological act of its implementation, but the social event of verbal interaction implemented in an utterance or utterances.*

Thus, verbal interaction is the basic reality of language.

---

4. In this respect, the very organization of the book is symptomatic. The book divides into four main chapters. Their titles are as follows: I. *Eröffnungsformen des Gesprächs.* II. *Sprecher und Hörer;* A. *Höflichkeit (Rücksicht auf den Partner).* B. *Sparsamkeit und Verschwendung im Ausdruck;* C. *In einandergreifen von Rede und Gegenrede.* III. *Sprecher und Situation.* IV. *Der Abschluss des Gesprächs.* Spitzer's predecessor in the study of conversational language under conditions of real-life discourse was Hermann Wunderlich. See his book, *Unsere Umgangssprache* (1894).

5. See *Die Probleme der Sprachpsychologie* (1914).

Dialogue, in the narrow sense of the word, is, of course, only one of the forms—a very important form, to be sure—of verbal interaction. But dialogue can also be understood in a broader sense, meaning not only direct, face-to-face, vocalized verbal communication between persons, but also verbal communication of any type whatsoever. A book, i.e., a *verbal performance in print*, is also an element of verbal communication. It is something discussable in actual, real-life dialogue, but aside from that, it is calculated for active perception, involving attentive reading and inner responsiveness, and for organized, *printed* reaction in the various forms devised by the particular sphere of verbal communication in question (book reviews, critical surveys, defining influence on subsequent works, and so on). Moreover, a verbal performance of this kind also inevitably orients itself with respect to previous performances in the same sphere, both those by the same author and those by other authors. It inevitably takes its point of departure from some particular state of affairs involving a scientific problem or a literary style. Thus the printed verbal performance engages, as it were, in ideological colloquy of large scale: it responds to something, objects to something, affirms something, anticipates possible responses and objections, seeks support, and so on.

Any utterance, no matter how weighty and complete in and of itself, *is only a moment in the continuous process of verbal communication.* But that continuous verbal communication is, in turn, itself only a moment in the continuous, all-inclusive, generative process of a given social collective. An important problem arises in this regard: the study of the connection between concrete verbal interaction and the extraverbal situation—both the immediate situation and, through it, the broader situation. The forms this connection takes are different, and different factors in a situation may, in association with this or that form, take on different meanings (for instance, these connections differ with the different factors of situation in literary or in scientific communication). *Verbal communication can never be understood and explained outside of this connection with a concrete situation.* Verbal intercourse is inextricably interwoven with communication of other types, all stemming from the common ground of production communication. It goes without saying that word cannot be divorced from this eternally generative, unified process of communication. In its concrete connection with a situation, verbal communication is always accompanied by social acts of a nonverbal character (the performance of labor, the symbolic acts of a ritual, a ceremony, etc.), and is often only an accessory to these acts, merely carrying out an auxiliary role. *Language acquires life and historically evolves precisely here, in concrete verbal communication, and not in the abstract linguistic system of language forms, nor in the individual psyche of speakers.*

From what has been established, it follows that the methodologically based order of study of language ought to be: (1) the forms and types of verbal interaction in connection with their concrete conditions; (2) forms of particular utterances, of particular speech performances, as elements of a closely linked interaction—i.e., the genres of speech performance in human behavior and ideological creativity as determined by verbal interaction; (3) a reexamination, on this new basis, of language forms in their usual linguistic presentation.

This is the order that the actual generative process of language follows: *social intercourse is generated* (stemming from the basis); *in it verbal communication and interaction are generated; and in the latter, forms of speech performances are generated; finally, this generative process is reflected in the change of language forms.*

One thing that emerges from all that has been said is the extreme importance of the problem of the forms of an utterance *as a whole.* We have already pointed out that contemporary linguistics lacks any approach to the utterance itself. Its analysis goes no further than the elements that constitute an utterance. Meanwhile, utterances are the real units that make up the stream of language-speech. What is necessary in order to study the forms of this real unit is precisely that it not be isolated from the historical stream of utterances. As a whole entity, the utterance is implemented only in the stream of verbal intercourse. The whole is, after all, defined by its boundaries, and these boundaries run along the line of contact between a given utterance and the extraverbal and verbal (i.e., made up of other utterances) milieu.

The first and last words, the beginning and end points of real-life utterance— that is what already constitutes the problem of the whole. The process of speech, broadly understood as the process of inner and outer verbal life, goes on continuously. It knows neither beginning nor end. The outwardly actualized utterance is an island rising from the boundless sea of inner speech; the dimensions and forms of this island are determined by the particular *situation* of the utterance and its *audience.* Situation and audience make inner speech undergo actualization into some kind of specific outer expression that is directly included into an unverbalized behavioral context and in that context is amplified by actions, behavior, or verbal responses of other participants of the utterance. The full-fledged question, exclamation, command, request—these are the most typical forms of wholes in behavioral utterances. All of them (especially the command and request) require an extraverbal complement and, indeed, an extraverbal commencement. The very type of structure these little behavioral *genres* will achieve is determined by the effect of its coming up against the extraverbal milieu and against another word (i.e., the words of other people). Thus, the form a command will take is determined by the obstacles it may encounter, the degree of submissiveness expected, and so on. The structure of the genre in these instances will be in accord with the accidental and unique features of behavioral situations. Only when social custom and circumstances have fixed and stabilized certain forms in behavioral interchange to some appreciable degree, can one speak of specific types of structure in genres of behavioral speech. So, for instance, an entirely special type of structure has been worked out for the genre of the light and casual causerie of the drawing room where everyone "feels at home" and where the basic differentiation within the gathering (the audience) is that between men and women. Here we find devised special forms of insinuation, half-sayings, allusions to little tales of an intentionally nonserious character, and so on. A different type of structure is worked out in the case of conversation between husband and wife, brother and sister, etc. In the case where a random assortment of people gathers—while waiting in a line or conducting some business—statements and exchanges of words will start and finish and be constructed in another, completely different way. Village sewing circles, urban carouses, workers' lunchtime chats, etc., will all have their own types. Each situation, fixed and sustained by social custom, commands a particular kind of organization of audience and, hence, a particular repertoire of little behavioral genres. The behavioral genre fits everywhere into the channel of social intercourse assigned to it and functions as an ideological reflection of its type, structure, goal, and social composition. The behavioral genre is a fact of the social milieu: of holiday, leisure time, and of social contact in the parlor, the workshop, etc. It meshes with that milieu and is delimited and defined by it in all its internal aspects.

The production processes of labor and the processes of commerce know different forms for constructing utterances.

As for the forms of ideological intercourse in the strict sense of the term—forms for political speeches, political acts, laws, regulations, manifestos, and so forth; and forms for poetic utterances, scientific treatises, etc.—these have been the object of special investigation in rhetoric and poetics, but, as we have seen, these investigations have been completely divorced from the problem of language on the one hand, and from the problem of social intercourse on the other.[6] Productive analysis of the forms of the whole of utterances as the real units in the stream of speech is possible only on a basis that regards the individual utterance as a purely sociological phenomenon. Marxist philosophy of language should and must stand squarely on the utterance as the real phenomenon of language-speech and as a socioideological structure.

Now that we have outlined the sociological structure of the utterance, let us return to the two trends in philosophical linguistic thought and make a final summing up.

---

6. On the topic of disjuncture of a literary work of art with conditions of artistic communication and the resulting inertness of the work, see our study, "Slovo v Žizni i slovo v poèzii" [Word in Life and Word in Poetry], *Zvezda*, 6 (1926).

R. Šor, a Moscow linguist and an adherent of the second trend of thought in philosophy of language, ends a brief sketch of the contemporary state of linguistics with the following words:

> "Language is not an artifact (*ergon*) but a natural and congenital activity of mankind"— so claimed the romanticist linguistics of the 19th century. Theoretical linguistics of modern times claims otherwise: "Language is not individual activity (*energiea*) but a cultural-historical legacy of mankind (*ergon*). [7]

This conclusion is amazing in its bias and one-sidedness. On the factual side, it is completely untrue. Modern theoretical linguistics includes, after all, the Vossler school, one of Germany's most powerful movements in contemporary linguistic thought. It is impermissible to identify modern linguistics with only one of its trends.

From the theoretical point of view, both the thesis and the antithesis made up by Šor must equally be rejected, since they are equally inadequate to the real nature of language.

Let us conclude the argument with an attempt to formulate our own point of view in the following set of propositions:

1. *Language as a stable system of normatively identical forms is merely a scientific abstraction,* productive only in connection with certain particular practical and theoretical goals. This abstraction is not adequate to the concrete reality of language.

2. *Language is a continuous generative process implemented in the social-verbal interaction of speakers.*

3. *The laws of the generative process of language are not at all the laws of individual psychology, but neither can they be divorced from the activity of speakers.* The laws of language generation are *sociological* laws.

4. *Linguistic creativity does not coincide with artistic creativity nor with any other type of specialized ideological creativity. But, at the same time, linguistic creativity cannot be understood apart from the ideological meanings and values that fill it.* The generative process of language, as is true of any historical generative process, can be perceived as blind mechanical necessity, but it can also become "free necessity" once it has reached the position of a conscious and desired necessity.

5. *The structure of the utterance is a purely sociological structure.* The utterance, as such, obtains between speakers. The individual speech act (in the strict sense of the word "individual") is *contradictio in adjecto.*

7. R. Šor, "Krizis sovremennoj linvistiki" [The Crisis in Contemporary Linguistics], *Jafetičeskij sbornik,* **V** (1927), p. 71.

CHAPTER 4

Theme and Meaning in Language

Theme and meaning. The problem of active perception. Evaluation and meaning. The dialectics of meaning.

The problem of meaning is one of the most difficult problems of linguistics. Efforts toward solving this problem have revealed the one-sided monologism of linguistic science in particularly strong relief. The theory of passive understanding precludes any possibility of engaging the most fundamental and crucial features of meaning in language.

The scope of the present study compels us to limit ourselves to a very brief and perfunctory examination of this issue. We shall attempt only to map out the main lines of its productive treatment.

A definite and unitary meaning, a unitary significance, is a property belonging to any utterance *as a whole.* Let us call the significance of a whole utterance its *theme.*[1] The theme must be unitary, otherwise we would have no basis for talking about any one utterance. The theme of an utterance itself is individual and unreproducible, just as the utterance itself is individual and unreproducible. The theme is the expression of the concrete, historical situation that engendered the utterance. The utterance "What time is it?" has a different meaning each time it is used, and hence, in accordance with our terminology, has a different theme, depending on the concrete historical situation ("historical" here in microscopic dimensions) during which it is enunciated and of which, in essence, it is a part.

---

1. The term is, of course, a provisional one. *Theme* in our sense embraces its implementation as well; therefore, our concept must not be confused with that of a theme in a literary work. The concept of "thematic unity" would be closer to what we mean.

It follows, then, that the theme of an utterance is determined not only by the linguistic forms that comprise it—words, morphological and syntactic structures, sounds, and intonation—but also by extraverbal factors of the situation. Should we miss these situational factors, we would be as little able to understand an utterance as if we were to miss its most important words. The theme of an utterance is concrete—as concrete as the historical instant to which the utterance belongs. *Only an utterance taken in its full, concrete scope as an historical phenomenon possesses a theme.* That is what is meant by the theme of an utterance.

However, if we were to restrict ourselves to the historical unreproducibility and unitariness of each concrete utterance and its theme, we would be poor dialecticians. Together with theme or, rather, within the theme, there is also the *meaning* that belongs to an utterance. By meaning, as distinguished from theme, we understand all those aspects of the utterance that are *reproducible* and *self-identical* in all instances of repetition. Of course, these aspects are abstract: they have no concrete, autonomous existence in an artificially isolated form, but, at the same time, they do constitute an essential and inseparable part of the utterance. The theme of an utterance is, in essence, indivisible. The meaning of an utterance, on the contrary, does break down into a set of meanings belonging to each of the various linguistic elements of which the utterance consists. The unreproducible theme of the utterance "What time is it?" taken in its indissoluble connection with the concrete historical situation, cannot be divided into elements. The meaning of the utterance "What time is it?"—a meaning that, of course, remains the same in all historical instances of its enunciation—is made up of the meanings of the words, forms of morphological and syntactic union, interrogative intonations, etc., that form the construction of the utterance.

Theme is a complex, dynamic system of signs that attempts to be adequate to a given instant of generative process. Theme is reaction by the consciousness in its generative process to the generative process of existence. Meaning is *the technical apparatus for the implementation of theme.* Of course, no absolute, mechanistic boundary can be drawn between theme and meaning. There is no theme without meaning and no meaning without theme . Moreover, it is even impossible to convey the meaning of a particular word (say, in the course of teaching another person a foreign language) without having made it an element of theme, i.e., without having constructed an "example" utterance. On the other hand, a theme must base itself on some kind of fixity of meaning; otherwise it loses its connection with what came before and what comes after—i.e., it altogether loses its significance.

The study of the languages of prehistoric peoples and modern semantic paleontology have reached a conclusion about the so-called "complex-ness" of prehistoric thinking. Prehistoric man used one word to denote a wide variety of phenomena that, from our modern point of view, are in no way related to one another. What is more, the same word could be used to denote diametrically opposite notions—top and bottom, earth and sky, good and bad, and so on. Declares Marr:

> Suffice it to say that contemporary paleontological study of language has given us the possibility of reaching, through its investigations, back to an age when a tribe had only one word at its disposal for usage in all the meanings of which mankind was aware.[2]

"But was such an all-meaning word in fact a word?" we might be asked. Yes, precisely a word. If, on the contrary, a certain sound complex had only one single, inert, and invariable meaning, then such a complex would not be a word, not a sign, but only a signal.[3] *Multiplicity of meanings is the constitutive feature of word.* As regards the all-meaning word of which Marr speaks, we can say the following: *such a word, in essence, has virtually no meaning; it is all theme.* Its meaning is *inseparable from the concrete situation of its implementation.* This meaning is different each time, just as the situation is different each time. Thus the theme, in this case, subsumed meaning under itself and dissolved it before meaning had any chance to consolidate and congeal. But as language developed further, as its stock of sound complexes expanded, meaning began to congeal along lines that were basic and most frequent in the life of the community for the thematic application of this or that word.

Theme, as we have said, is an attribute of a whole utterance only; it can belong to a separate word only inasmuch as that word operates in the capacity of a whole utterance. So, for instance, Marr's all-meaning word always operates in the capacity of a whole (and has no fixed meanings precisely for that reason). Meaning, on the other hand, belongs to an element or aggregate of elements in their relation to the whole. Of course, if we entirely disregard this relation to the whole (i.e., to the utterance), we shall entirely forfeit meaning. That is the reason why a sharp boundary between theme and meaning cannot be drawn.

The most accurate way of formulating the interrelationship between theme and meaning is in the following terms. Theme is the *upper, actual limit of linguistic significance;* in essence, only theme means something definite. Meaning is the *lower limit* of linguistic significance. Meaning, in essence, means nothing; it only possesses potentiality—the possibility of having a meaning within a concrete theme. Investigation of the meaning of one or another linguistic element

---

2. N. Ja. Marr, *Japhetic Theory*, (1926), p. 278.

3. It is clear that even that earliest of all words, about which Marr speaks, is not in any way like a signal (to which a number of investigators endeavor to reduce language). After all, a signal that meant everything would be minimally capable of carrying out the function of a signal. The capacity of a signal to adapt to the changing conditions of a situation is very low. By and large, change in a signal means replacement of one signal by another.

can proceed, in terms of our definition, in one of two directions: either in the direction of the upper limit, toward theme, in which case it would be investigation of the contextual meaning of a given word within the conditions of a concrete utterance; or investigation can aim toward the lower limit, the limit of meaning, in which case it would be investigation of the meaning of a word in the system of language or, in other words, investigation of a dictionary word.

A distinction between theme and meaning and a proper understanding of their interrelationship are vital steps in constructing a genuine science of meanings. Total failure to comprehend their importance has persisted to the present day. Such discriminations as those between a word's *usual* and *occasional* meanings, between its central and lateral meanings, between its denotation and connotation, etc., are fundamentally unsatisfactory. The basic tendency underlying all such discriminations—the tendency to ascribe greater value to the central, usual aspect of meaning, presupposing that that aspect really does exist and is stable—is completely fallacious. Moreover, it would leave theme unaccounted for, since theme, of course, can by no means be reduced to the status of the occasional or lateral meaning of words.

The distinction between theme and meaning acquires particular clarity in connection with the *problem of understanding*, which we shall now briefly touch upon.

We have already had occasion to speak of the philological type of passive understanding, which excludes response in advance. Any genuine kind of understanding will be active and will constitute the germ of a response. Only active understanding can grasp theme—a generative process can be grasped only with the aid of another generative process.

To understand another person's utterance means to orient oneself with respect to it, to find the proper place for it in the corresponding context. For each word of the utterance that we are in process of understanding, we, as it were, lay down a set of our own answering words. The greater their number and weight, the deeper and more substantial our understanding will be.

Thus each of the distinguishable significative elements of an utterance and the entire utterance as a whole entity are translated in our minds into another, active and responsive, context. *Any true understanding is dialogic in nature.* Understanding is to utterance as one line of a dialogue is to the next. Understanding strives to match the speaker's word with a *counter word.* Only in understanding a word in a foreign tongue is the attempt made to match it with the "same" word in one's own language.

Therefore, there is no reason for saying that meaning belongs to a word as such. In essence, meaning belongs to a word in its position between speakers; that is, meaning is realized only in the process of active, responsive understanding. Meaning does not reside in the word or in the soul of the speaker or in the soul of the listener. Meaning is the *effect of interaction between speaker and listener produced via the material of a particular sound complex.* It is like an electric spark that occurs only when two different terminals are hooked together. Those who ignore theme (which is accessible only to active, responsive understanding) and who, in attempting to define the meaning of a word, approach its lower, stable, self-identical limit, want, in effect, to turn on a light bulb after having switched off the current. Only the current of verbal intercourse endows a word with the light of meaning.

Let us now move on to one of the most important problems in the science of meanings, the problem of the *interrelationship between meaning and evaluation.*

Any word used in actual speech possesses not only theme and meaning in the referential, or content, sense of these words, but also value judgment: i.e., all referential contents produced in living speech are said or written in conjunction with a specific *evaluative accent.* There is no such thing as word without evaluative accent.

What is the nature of this accent, and how does it relate to the referential side of meaning?

The most obvious, but, at the same time, the most superficial aspect of social value judgement incorporated in the word is that which is conveyed with the help of *expressive intonation.* In most cases, intonation is determined by the immediate situation and often by its most ephemeral circumstances. To be sure, intonation of a more substantial kind is also possible. Here is a classic instance of such a use of intonation in real-life speech. Dostoevskij, in *Diary of a Writer,* relates the following story.

One Sunday night, already getting on to the small hours, I chanced to find myself walking alongside a band of six tipsy artisans for a dozen paces or so, and there and then I became convinced that all thoughts, all feelings, and even whole trains of reasoning could be expressed merely by using a certain noun, a noun, moreover, of utmost simplicity in itself [Dostoevskij has in mind here a certain widely used obscenity.—*V. V.*]. Here is what happened. First, one of these fellows voices this noun shrilly and emphatically by way of expressing his utterly disdainful denial of some point that had been in general contention just prior. A second fellow repeats this very same noun in response to the first fellow, but now in an altogether different tone and sense—to wit, in the sense that he fully doubted the veracity of the first fellow's denial. A third fellow waxes indignant at the first one, sharply and heatedly sallying into the conversation and shouting at him that very same noun, but now in a pejorative, abusive sense. The second fellow, indignant at the third for being offensive, himself sallies back in and cuts the latter short to the effect: "What the hell do you think you're doing, butting in like that?! Me and Fil'ka were having a nice quiet talk and just like that you come along and start cussing him out!" And in fact, this whole train of thought he conveyed by emitting just that very same time-honored word, that same extremely laconic designation of a certain item, and nothing more, save only that he also raised his hand and grabbed the second fellow by the shoulder. Thereupon, all of a sudden a fourth fellow, the youngest in the crowd, who had remained silent all this while, apparently having just struck upon the solution to the problem that had originally occasioned the dispute, in a tone of rapture, with one arm half-raised, shouts—What do you think: "Eureka!"? "I found it, I found it!"? No, nothing at all like "Eureka," nothing like "I found it." He merely repeats that very same unprintable noun, just that one single word, just that one word alone, but with rapture, with a squeal of ecstacy, and apparently somewhat excessively so, because the sixth fellow, a surly character and the oldest in the bunch, didn't think it seemly and in a trice stops the young fellow's rapture cold by turning on him and repeating in a gruff and expostulatory bass—yes, that very same noun whose usage is forbidden in the company of ladies, which, however, in this case clearly and precisely denoted: "What the hell are you shouting for, you'll burst a blood vessel!" And so, without having uttered one other word, they repeated just this one, but obviously beloved, little word of theirs six times in a row, one after the other, and they understood one another perfectly.[4]

All six "speech performances" by the artisans are different, despite the fact that they all consisted of one and the same word. That word, in this instance, was essentially only a vehicle for intonation. The conversation was conducted in intonations expressing the value judgments of the speakers. These value judgments and their corresponding intonations were wholly determined by the immediate social situation of the talk and therefore did not require any referential support. In living speech, intonation often does have a meaning quite independent of the semantic composition of speech. Intonational material pent up inside us often does find outlet in linguistic constructions completely inappropriate to the particular kind of intonation involved. In such a case, intonation does not impinge upon the intellectual, concrete, referential significance of the construction. We have a habit of expressing our feelings by imparting expressive and meaningful intonation to some word that crops up in our mind by chance, often a vacuous interjection or adverb. Almost everybody has his favorite interjection or adverb or sometimes even a semantically full-fledged word that he customarily uses for purely intonational resolution of certain trivial (and sometimes not so trivial) situations and moods that occur in the ordinary business of life. There are certain expressions like "so-so," "yes-yes," "now-now," "well-well" and so on that commonly serve as "safety valves" of that sort. The doubling usual in such expressions is symptomatic; i.e., it represents an artificial prolongation of the sound image for the purpose of allowing the pent up intonation to expire fully. Any one such favorite little expression may, of course, be pronounced in an enormous variety of intonations in keeping with the wide diversity of situations and moods that occur in life.

In all these instances, theme, which is a property of each utterance (each of the utterances of the six artisans had a theme proper to it), is implemented en-

4. *Polnoe sobranie sočinenij F. M. Dostoevskogo* [The Complete Works of F. M. Dostoevskij], Vol. IX, pp. 274-275, 1906.

tirely and exclusively by the power of expressive intonation without the aid of word meaning or grammatical coordination. This sort of value judgment and its corresponding intonation cannot exceed the narrow confines of the immediate situation and the small, intimate social world in which it occurs. Linguistic evaluation of this sort may rightly be called an accompaniment, an accessory phenomenon, to meaning in language.

However, not all linguistic value judgments are like that. We may take any utterance whatsoever, say, an utterance that encompasses the broadest possible semantic spectrum and assumes the widest possible social audience, and we shall still see that, in it, an enormous importance belongs to evaluation. Naturally, value judgment in this case will not allow of even minimally adequate expression by intonation, but it will be the determinative factor in the choice and deployment of the basic elements that bear the meaning of the utterance. No utterance can be put together without value judgment. Every utterance is above all an *evaluative orientation.* Therefore, each element in a living utterance not only has a meaning but also has a value. Only the abstract element, perceived within the system of language and not within the structure of an utterance, appears devoid of value judgment. Focusing their attention on the abstract system of language is what led most linguists to divorce evaluation from meaning and to consider evaluation an accessory factor of meaning, the expression of a speaker's individual attitude toward the subject matter of his discourse.[5]

In Russian scholarship, G. Špett has spoken of evaluation as the *connotation* of a word. Characteristically, he operates with a strict division between referential denotation and evaluative connotation, locating this division in various spheres of reality. This sort of disjuncture between referential meaning and evaluation is totally inadmissible. It stems from failure to note the more profound functions of evaluation in speech. Referential meaning is molded by evaluation; it is evaluation, after all, which determines that a particular referential meaning may enter the purview of speakers—both the immediate purview and the broader social purview of the particular social group. Furthermore, with respect to changes of meaning, it is precisely evaluation that plays the creative role. A change in meaning is, essentially, always a *reevaluation:* the transposition of some particular word from one evaluative context to another. A word is either advanced to a higher rank or demoted to a lower one. The separation of word meaning from evaluation inevitably deprives meaning of its place in the living social process (where meaning is always permeated with value judgment), to its being ontologized and transformed into ideal Being divorced from the historical process of Becoming.

---

5. That is how Anton Marty defines evaluation, and it is Marty who gives the most acute and detailed analysis of word meanings; see his *Untersuchungen zur Grundlegung der allgemeinen Grammatik und Sprachphilosophie* (Halle, 1908).

Precisely in order to understand the historical process of generation of theme and of the meanings implementing theme, it is essential to take social evaluation into account. The generative process of signification in language is always associated with the generation of the evaluative purview of a particular social group, and the generation of an evaluative purview—in the sense of the totality of all those things that have meaning and importance for the particular group—is entirely determined by expansion of the economic basis. As the economic basis expands, it promotes an actual expansion in the scope of existence which is accessible, comprehensible, and vital to man. The prehistoric herdsman was virtually interested in nothing, and virtually nothing had any bearing on him. Man at the end of the epoch of capitalism is directly concerned about everything, his interests reaching the remotest corners of the earth and even the most distant stars. This expansion of evaluative purview comes about dialectically. New aspects of existence, once they are drawn into the sphere of social interest, once they make contact with the human word and human emotion, do not coexist peacefully with other elements of existence previously drawn in, but engage them in a struggle, reevaluate them, and bring about a change in their position within the unity of the evaluative purview. This dialectical generative process is reflected in the generation of semantic properties in language. A new significance emanates from an old one, and does so with its help, but this happens so that the new significance can enter into contradiction with the old one and restructure it.

The outcome is a constant struggle of accents in each semantic sector of existence. There is nothing in the structure of signification that could be said to transcend the generative process, to be independent of the dialectical expansion of social purview. Society in process of generation expands its perception of the generative process of existence. There is nothing in this that could be said to be absolutely fixed. And that is how it happens that meaning—an abstract, self-identical element—is subsumed under theme and torn apart by theme's living contradictions so as to return in the shape of a new meaning with a fixity and self-identity only for the while, just as it had before.

PART III

TOWARD A HISTORY OF FORMS OF UTTERANCE IN LANGUAGE CONSTRUCTIONS

(Study in the Application of the
Sociological Method to Problems of Syntax)

CHAPTER 1

Theory of Utterance
and Problems of Syntax

*The significance of problems of syntax. Syntactic categories
and utterance as a whole. The problem of paragraphs. Forms
of reported speech.*

Traditional principles and methods in linguistics do not provide grounds for
a productive approach to problems of syntax. This is particularly true of abstract
objectivism where the traditional methods and principles have found their most
distinct and most consistent expression. All the fundamental categories of modern linguistic thought, with their development stemming primarily from Indo-
European comparative linguistics, are thoroughly *phonetic* and *morphological*
categories. As the product of comparative phonetics and morphology, such
thought is incapable of viewing other phenomena of language except through
the spectacles of phonetic and morphological forms. It attempts to view syntax
in the same way, and this has led to the morphologization of syntactic problems.[1]
In consequence, the study of syntax is in a very bad state, a fact that even the
majority of representatives of the Indo-European school openly admit.

This is perfectly understandable once we recall the basic features characterizing perception of a dead and alien language—perception governed by the overriding needs to decipher such a language and instruct others in it.[2]

1. As a consequence of this covert tendency to morphologize syntactic form, the study
of syntax is dominated by scholastic thinking to a degree unmatched in any other branch
of linguistics.

2. Added to this are the special aims of comparative linguistics: the establishment of a
family of languages, of their genetic order, and of a protolanguage. These aims further rein-
force the primacy of phonetics in linguistic thought. The problem of comparative linguistics,
a very important one in contemporary philosophy of language owing to the massive position
it occupies in modern linguistics, unfortunately had to be left untouched within the scope of
our study. It is a problem of great complexity, and even superficial treatment of it would
have necessitated enlarging our book considerably.

Meanwhile, problems of syntax have immense importance for the proper understanding of language and its generative process. In point of fact, of all the forms of language, *the syntactic forms are the ones closest to the concrete forms of utterance,* to forms of concrete speech performances. All syntactic analyses of speech entail analyzing the living body of an utterance and, therefore, powerfully resist relegation to the abstract system of language. Syntactic forms are more concrete than morphological or phonetic forms and are more closely associated with the real conditions of discourse. Therefore, our point of view, which deals with the living phenomena of language, must give precedence to syntactic forms over morphological and phonetic ones. But, as we have also made clear, productive study of syntactic forms is only possible on the grounds of a fully elaborated theory of utterance. As long as the utterance, in its wholeness, remains *terra incognita* for the linguist, it is out of the question to speak of a genuine, concrete, and not scholastic kind of understanding of syntactic forms.

We have already indicated that the issue of whole utterances is a matter very poorly off in linguistics. We can go so far as to say that *linguistic thinking has hopelessly lost any sense of the verbal whole.* A linguist feels most sure of himself when operating at the center of a phrase unit. The further he approaches the peripheries of speech and thus the problem of the utterance as a whole, the more insecure his position becomes. He has no way at all of coping with the whole. Not a single one of the categories of linguistics is of any value for defining a whole linguistic entity.

The fact of the matter is that all linguistic categories, per se, are applicable only on the inside territory of an utterance. All morphological categories, for instance, are of value exclusively as regards the constituents of an utterance and cease being serviceable when it comes to defining the whole. The same is true of syntactic categories, the category of "sentence," for example: the category of sentence is merely a definition of the sentence as a unit-element within an utterance, and not by any means as a whole entity.

For proof of this "elementariness" in principle of all linguistic categories, one need only take any finished utterance (relatively speaking, of course, since any utterance is part of a verbal process) consisting of a single word. If we apply all the categories used by linguistics to this word, it will immediately become apparent that these categories define the word exclusively in terms of a potential element of speech and that none encompasses the whole utterance. That extra something that converts this word into a whole utterance remains outside the scope of the entire set of linguistic categories and definitions. Were we to develop this word into a full-fledged sentence by filling in all the basic constituents (following the prescription: "not stated, but understood"), we would obtain a simple sentence and not at all an utterance. No matter which of the linguistic categories we would try to apply to this sentence, we would never find just what it is that converts it into a whole utterance. Thus if we remain within the confines of the grammatical categories with which contemporary linguistics supplies us, the verbal whole will be forever elusive and beyond our grasp. The effect of these linguistic categories is to draw us relentlessly away from the utterance and its concrete structure into the abstract system of language.

This failure of linguistic definition applies not only to the utterance as a whole entity, but even to units within a monologic utterance that have some claim to being regarded as complete units. A case in point involves units set off from one another in writing by indentation that we call *paragraphs*. The syntactic composition of paragraphs is extremely diverse. Paragraphs may contain anything from a single word to a whole array of complex sentences. To say that a paragraph is supposed to consist of a complete thought amounts to saying absolutely nothing. What is needed, after all, is definition from the standpoint of language, and under no circumstances can the notion of "complete thought" be regarded a linguistic definition. Even if it is true, as we believe, that linguistic definitions cannot be completely divorced from ideological definitions, still, neither can they be used to substitute for one another.

Were we to probe deeper into the linguistic nature of paragraphs, we would surely find that in certain crucial respects paragraphs are analogous to exchanges in dialogue. The paragraph is something like a *vitiated dialogue worked into the body of a monologic utterance.* Behind the device of partitioning speech in units, which are termed paragraphs in their written form, lie orientation toward listener or reader and calculation of the latter's possible reactions. The weaker this orientation and calculation are, the less organized, as regards paragraphs, our speech will be. The classic types of paragraphs are: question and answer (where question is posed and answer given by the same author); supplementation; anticipation of possible objections; exposition of seeming discrepancies or illogicalities in one's own argument, and so forth.[3] Very commonly, we make our own speech or some part of it (for example, the preceding paragraph) the object of discussion. In such a case, a shift occurs in the speaker's attention from the referent of his speech to the speech itself (reflection over one's own words). But even this shift in verbal intentions is conditioned by the addressee's interest. If we could imagine speech that absolutely ignored the addressee (an impossible kind of speech, of course), we would have a case of speech with organic partition reduced to the minimum. Needless to say, we are not thinking here of certain special types of partition shaped by the particular aims and purposes of specific ideological fields—for instance, the strophic partition of speech in verse or the

---

3. We, of course, merely sketch out the problem of paragraphs here. The assertions we make must sound dogmatic, since we present them without proof and appropriate supporting material. Moreover, we have simplified the problem. Widely different ways of partitioning monologic speech may be conveyed by the written form of paragraphs. Here we mention only one of the more important of such types—a type of partitioning that takes the addressee and his active understanding into decisive account.

purely logical partition of speech of the type: premise, conclusion; thesis, anti-thesis, and the like.

Our study of the forms of verbal communication and the corresponding forms of whole utterances can shed light on the system of paragraphing and all analogous problems. As long as linguistics continues to orient itself toward the isolated, monologic utterance, it will remain devoid of any organic approach to all these questions. Even treatment of the more elementary problems of syntax is possible only on the grounds of verbal communication. All the basic categories of linguistics should be closely reexamined along these lines. The interest in intonation that has arisen recently in syntactic studies and the attempts, in conjunction with that interest, to revise definitions of syntactic wholes via a more subtle and differentiated consideration of intonation, do not strike us as very productive. They can become productive only if they are combined with a proper understanding of the bases of verbal communication.

We shall now devote the remaining chapters of our study to one of the special problems of syntax.

It is sometimes extremely important to expose some familiar and seemingly already well-studied phenomenon to fresh illumination by reformulating it as a problem, i.e., to illuminate new aspects of it with the aid of a set of questions that have a special bearing upon it. It is particularly important to do so in those fields where research has become bogged down in masses of meticulous and detailed—but utterly pointless—descriptions and classifications. In the course of such a reformulation of a problem, it may turn out that what had appeared to be a limited and secondary phenomenon actually has meaning of fundamental importance for the whole field of study. An apt posing of a problem can make the phenomenon under scrutiny reveal the methodological potentialities embedded in it.

We believe that one such highly productive, "pivotal" phenomenon is that of so-called *reported speech*, i.e., the syntactic patterns (direct discourse, indirect discourse, quasi-direct discourse), the modifications of those patterns and the variants of those modifications, which we find in a language for the reporting of other persons' utterances and for incorporating those utterances, as the utterances of others, into a bound, monologic context. The extraordinary methodological interest inherent in these phenomena has gone totally unappreciated to the present day. No one was able to discern in this issue of syntax, in what superficial examination held to be a secondary matter, problems of enormous general linguistic and theoretical significance.[4] It is precisely when emplaced in sociologically oriented scientific concern with language that the whole significance, the whole hermeneutic power of this phenomenon is disclosed.

4. For example, in A. M. Peškovskij's study of syntax, this phenomenon has a mere four pages devoted to it. See his *Russkij sintaksis v naučnom osveščenii* [Russian Syntax in a Scientific Light] (2nd ed., Moscow, 1920), pp. 465-468; (3rd ed., 1928, pp. 552-555).

To take the phenomenon of reported speech and postulate it as a problem from a sociological orientation—that is the task we undertake in the remainder of our study. On the material of this problem we shall attempt to map out the sociological method in linguistics. We do not presume to establish major, positive conclusions of a specifically historical kind. The very nature of the material we have chosen, while adequate for purposes of expositing the problem and making evident the necessity of treating it along sociological lines, is far from adequate for drawing broad historical generalizations. Such historical generalizations as do occur are of merely a provisional and hypothetical order.

CHAPTER 2

Exposition of the
Problem of Reported Speech

Definition of reported speech. The problem of active reception
of reported speech in connection with the problem of dialogue.
The dynamics of the interrelationship of authorial context and
reported speech. The "linear style" of reporting speech. The
"pictorial style" of reporting speech.

Reported speech is speech within speech, utterance within utterance, and at the same time also *speech about speech, utterance about utterance.*

Whatever we talk about is only the content of speech, the themes of our words. Such a theme—and it is only a theme—might be, for instance, "nature," "man," or "subordinate clause" (one of the themes of syntax). A reported utterance, however, is not just a theme of speech: it has the capacity of entering on its own, so to speak, into speech, into its syntactic makeup, as an integral unit of the construction. In so doing, it retains its own constructional and semantic autonomy while leaving the speech texture of the context incorporating it perfectly intact.

What is more, a reported utterance treated solely as a theme of speech may be characterized only superficially at best. If its content is to be had to the full, it must be made part of a speech construction. When limited to the treatment of reported speech in thematic terms, one can answer questions as to "how" and "about what" so-and-so spoke, but "what" he said could be disclosed only by way of reporting his words, if only in the form of indirect discourse.

However, once it becomes a constructional unit in the author's speech, into which it has entered on its own, the reported utterance concurrently becomes a theme of that speech. It enters into the latter's thematic design precisely as reported, an utterance with its own autonomous theme: the autonomous theme thus becomes a theme of a theme.

Reported speech is regarded by the speaker as an utterance belonging to *someone else*, an utterance that was originally totally independent, complete in its construction, and lying outside the given context. Now, it is from this independent existence that reported speech is transposed into an authorial context while retaining its own referential content and at least the rudiments of its own linguistic integrity, its original constructional independence. The author's utterance, in incorporating the other utterance, brings into play syntactic, stylistic, and compositional norms for its partial assimilation—that is, its adaptation to the syntactic, compositional, and stylistic design of the author's utterance, while preserving (if only in rudimentary form) the initial autonomy (in syntactic, compositional, and stylistic terms) of the reported utterance, which otherwise could not be grasped in full.

Certain modifications of indirect discourse and, in particular, of quasi-direct discourse in modern languages evince a disposition to transpose the reported utterance from the sphere of speech construction to the thematic level—the sphere of content. However, even in these instances, the dissolution of the reported utterance in the authorial context is not—nor can it be—carried out to the end. Here, too, aside from indications of a semantic nature, the reported utterance perseveres as a construction—the body of the reported speech remains detectable as a self-sufficient unit.

Thus, what is expressed in the forms employed for reporting speech is an *active relation* of one message to another, and it is expressed, moreover, not on the level of the theme but in the stabilized constructional patterns of the language itself.

We are dealing here with words reacting on words. However, this phenomenon is distinctly and fundamentally different from dialogue. In dialogue, the lines of the individual participants are grammatically disconnected; they are not integrated into one unified context. Indeed, how could they be? *There are no syntactic forms with which to build a unity of dialogue.* If, on the other hand, a dialogue is presented as embedded in an authorial context, then we have a case of direct discourse, one of the variants of the phenomenon with which we are dealing in this inquiry.

The attention of linguists nowadays is drawn more and more to the problem of dialogue; indeed, it sometimes becomes their central concern.[1] This makes

1. In Russian scholarship, only one study devoted to the problem of dialogue from the linguistic point of view has appeared: L. P. Jakubinskij, "O dialogičeskoj reči" [On Dialogic Speech], *Russkaja reč'* (Petrograd, 1923). Interesting comments of a semilinguistic nature on the problem of dialogue are contained in V. Vinogradov, *Poèzija Anny Axmatovoj* [The Poetry of Anna Axmatova] (Leningrad, 1925); see the chapter "Grimasy dialoga" [Dialogue Gesticulations]. In German scholarship, the problem is currently under intensive treatment by the Vossler school. See, especially, Gertraud Lerch, "Die uneigentliche direkte Rede, *Festschrift für Karl Vossler* (1922).

perfectly good sense, for, as we now know, the real unit of language that is implemented in speech (*Sprache als Rede*) is not the individual, isolated mono-logic utterance, but the interaction of at least two utterances—in a word, dialogue. The productive study of dialogue presupposes, however, a more profound inves-tigation of the forms used in reported speech, since these forms reflect basic and constant tendencies in the *active reception of other speakers' speech,* and it is this reception, after all, that is fundamental also for dialogue.

How, in fact, is another speaker's speech received? What is the mode of existence of another's utterance in the actual, inner-speech consciousness of the recipient? How is it manipulated there, and what process of orientation will the subsequent speech of the recipient himself have undergone in regard to it?

What we have in the forms of reported speech is precisely an objective docu-ment of this reception. Once we have learned to decipher it, this document pro-vides us with information, not about accidental and mercurial subjective psycho-logical processes in the "soul" of the recipient, but about steadfast social tenden-cies in an active reception of other speakers' speech, tendencies that have crystallized into language forms. The mechanism of this process is located, not in the individual soul, but in society. It is the function of society to select and to make grammatical (adapt to the grammatical structure of its language) just those factors in the active and evaluative reception of utterances that are socially vital and constant and, hence, that are grounded in the economic existence of the particular community of speakers.

There are, of course, essential differences between the active reception of another's speech and its transmission in a bound context. These differences should not be overlooked. Any type of transmission—the codified variety in par-ticular—pursues special aims, appropriate to a story, legal proceedings, a scholarly polemic, or the like. Furthermore, transmission takes into account a third per-son—the person to whom the reported utterances are being transmitted. This pro-vision for a third person is especially important in that it strengthens the impact of organized social forces on speech reception. When we engage in a live dialogue with someone, in the very act of dealing with the speech received from our part-ner, we usually omit those words to which we are answering. We repeat them only in special and exceptional circumstances, when we want to check the correctness of our understanding, or trip our partner up with his words, or the like. All these specific factors, which may affect transmission, must be taken into account. But the essence of the matter is not changed thereby. The circumstances under which transmission occurs and the aims it pursues merely contribute to the implementa-tion of what is already lodged in the tendencies of active reception by one's inner-speech consciousness. And these tendencies, for their part, can only develop within the framework of the forms used to report speech in a given language.

We are far from claiming that syntactic forms—for instance those of indirect or direct discourse—directly and unequivocally express the tendencies and forms of an active, evaluative reception of another's utterance. Our speech reception does not, of course, operate directly in the forms of indirect and direct discourse. These forms are only standardized patterns for reporting speech. But, on the one hand, these patterns and their modifications could have arisen and taken shape only in accordance with the governing tendencies of speech reception; on the other hand, once these patterns have assumed shape and function in the language, they in turn exert an influence, regulating or inhibiting in their development, on the tendencies of an evaluative reception that operate within the channel prescribed by the existing forms.

Language reflects, not subjective, psychological vacillations, but stable social interrelationships among speakers. Various linguistic forms of these interrelationships, and various modifications of these forms, prevail in different languages at different periods of time within different social groups and under the effect of different contextual aims. What this attests to is the relative strength or weakness of those tendencies in the social interorientation of a community of speakers, of which the given linguistic forms themselves are stabilized and age-old crystallizations. Should it happen that circumstances conspire to disparage some particular form (for example, certain modifications of indirect discourse, such as the "dogmatic-rationalistic" type in the modern Russian novel), then this may be taken as evidence that the dominant tendencies in understanding and evaluating the messages to be reported are not properly manifested by that particular form—that it is too unaccommodating, too hampering.

Everything vital in the evaluative reception of another's utterance, everything of any ideological value, is expressed in the material of inner speech. After all, it is not a mute, wordless creature that receives such an utterance, but a human being full of inner words. All his experiences—his so-called apperceptive background—exist encoded in his inner speech, and only to that extent do they come into contact with speech received from outside. Word comes into contact with word. The context of this inner speech is the locale in which another's utterance is received, comprehended, and evaluated; it is where the speaker's active orientation takes place. This active inner-speech reception proceeds in two directions: first, the received utterance is framed within a context of factual commentary (coinciding in part with what is called the apperceptive background of the words), the visual signs of expression, and so on; second, a reply (*Gegenrede*) is prepared. Both the preparation of the reply (*internal retort*) and the *factual commentary*[2] are organically fused in the unity of active reception, and these can be isolated only in abstract terms. Both lines of reception find their expression, are objectified, in the "authorial" context surrounding the reported speech. Regardless of the functional orientation of the given context—whether it is a work of fiction, a polemical article, a defense attorney's summation, or the like—we clearly discern

2. The term is borrowed from L. P. Jakubinskij (see the article cited above).

these two tendencies in it: that of commenting and that of retorting. Usually one of them is dominant. Between the reported speech and the reporting context, dynamic relations of high complexity and tension are in force. A failure to take these into account makes it impossible to understand any form of reported speech.

Earlier investigators of the forms of reported speech committed the fundamental error of virtually divorcing the reported speech from the reporting context. That explains why their treatment of these forms is so static and inert (a characterization applicable to the whole field of syntactic study in general). Meanwhile, the true object of inquiry ought to be precisely the dynamic interrelationship of these two factors, the speech being reported (the other person's speech) and the speech doing the reporting (the author's speech). After all, the two actually do exist, function, and take shape only in their interrelation, and not on their own, the one apart from the other. The reported speech and the reporting context are but the terms of a dynamic interrelationship. This dynamism reflects the dynamism of social interorientation in verbal ideological communication between people (within, of course, the vital and steadfast tendencies of that communication).

In what direction may the dynamism of the interrelationship between the authorial and the reported speech move?

We see it moving in two basic directions.

In the first place, the basic tendency in reacting to reported speech may be to maintain its integrity and authenticity; a language may strive to forge hard and fast boundaries for reported speech. In such a case, the patterns and their modifications serve to demarcate the reported speech as clearly as possible, to screen it from penetration by the author's intonations, and to condense and enhance its individual linguistic characteristics.

Such is the first direction. Within its scope we must rigorously define to what extent a given language community differentiates the social reception of the speech to be reported and to what extent the expressiveness, the stylistic qualities of speech, its lexical coloration, and so forth, are felt as distinct and socially important values. It may be that another's speech is received as one whole block of social behavior, as the speaker's indivisible, conceptual position—in which case only the "what" of speech is taken in and the "how" is left outside reception. This content conceptualizing, and (in a linguistic sense) depersonalizing way of receiving and reporting speech predominates in Old and Middle French (in the latter with a considerable development of the depersonalizing modifications of indirect discourse).[3] The same type is found in the literary monuments of Old

---

3. See below concerning special features of Old French in this connection. On reported speech in Middle French, see Gertraud Lerch, "Die uneigentliche direkte Rede," in *Festschrift für Karl Vossler* (1922), pp. 112ff, and, also, K. Vossler, *Frankreichs Kultur im Spiegel seiner Sprachentwicklung* (1913).

Russian—though here the pattern of indirect discourse is almost completely lacking. The dominant type in this case was that of the depersonalized (in the linguistic sense) direct discourse.[4]

Within the scope covered by the first direction, we must also define the degree of authoritarian reception of an utterance and the degree of its ideological assurance—its dogmatism. The more dogmatic an utterance, the less leeway permitted between truth and falsehood or good and bad in its reception by those who comprehend and evaluate, the greater will be the depersonalization that the forms of reported speech will undergo. In point of fact, given the situation in which all social value judgments are divided into wholesale, clearcut alternatives, we have simply no room for a positive and observant attitude toward all those factors which give another speaker's utterance its individual character. Authoritarian dogmatism of that type characterizes Middle French and Old Russian writings. The 17th century in France and the 18th century in Russia were characterized by a rationalistic type of dogmatism that likewise tended to curb the individualization of reported speech, though in different ways. In the sphere of rationalistic dogmatism, the dominant forms were the content-analyzing modifications of indirect discourse and the rhetorical modifications of direct discourse.[5] Here the explicitness and inviolability of the boundaries between authorial and reported speech reach the utmost limits.

We may call this first direction in which the dynamism of the interorientation between reporting and reported speech moves the *linear style (der lineare stil)* of speech reporting (borrowing the term from Wölfflin's study of art). The basic tendency of the linear style is to construct clear-cut, external contours for reported speech, whose own internal individuality is minimized. Wherever the entire context displays a complete stylistic homogeneity (in which the author and his characters all speak exactly the same language), the grammatical and compositional manipulation of reported speech achieves a maximal compactness and plastic relief.

The processes we observe in the second direction in which the dynamism of the interorientation between reporting and reported speech moves are exactly opposite in nature. Language devises means for infiltrating reported speech with authorial retort and commentary in deft and subtle ways. The reporting context strives to break down the self-contained compactness of the reported speech, to resolve it, to obliterate its boundaries. We may call this style of speech reporting *pictorial*. Its tendency is to obliterate the precise, external contours of

---

4. For instance, in *Slovo o polku Igoreve* [The Lay of Igor's Campaign], there is not a single instance of indirect discourse despite the abundance of other speakers' words in this monument. Indirect discourse in the Old Russian chronicles is extremely rare. Reported speech is incorporated everywhere as a compact, impermeable block with little or no individualization.

5. Indirect discourse is virtually nonexistent in Russian neoclassicism.

reported speech; at the same time, the reported speech is individualized to a much greater degree—the tangibility of the various facets of an utterance may be subtly differentiated. This time the reception includes not only the referential meaning of the utterance, the statement it makes, but also all the linguistic peculiarities of its verbal implementation.

A number of diverse types may be placed within the scope of this second direction. The impetus for weakening the peripheries of the utterance may originate in the author's context, in which case that context permeates the reported speech with its own intonation—humor, irony, love or hate, enthusiasm or scorn. This type characterizes the Renaissance (especially in the French language), the end of the 18th century, and virtually the entire 19th century. It involves a severe debilitation of both the authoritarian and the rationalistic dogmatism of utterance. Social value judgments were then ruled by a relativism supplying extremely favorable grounds for a positive and sensitive reception of all individualized verbal nuances of thought, belief, feeling. These grounds even encouraged the growth of a "decorative" trend in treating reported speech, leading sometimes to a neglect of the meaning of an utterance in favor of its "color"—for example, in the Russian "natural school." Indeed, in Gogol''s case, characters' speech sometimes loses almost all its referential meaning and becomes decor instead, on a par with clothing, appearance, furnishings, etc.

A rather different type is also possible: the verbal dominant may shift to the reported speech, which in that case becomes more forceful and more active than the authorial context framing it. This time the reported speech begins to resolve, as it were, the reporting context, instead of the other way around. The authorial context loses the greater objectivity it normally commands in comparison with reported speech. It begins to perceive itself— and even recognizes itself—as subjective, "other person's" speech. In works of fiction, this is often expressed compositionally by the appearance of a narrator who replaces the author (in the usual sense of the word). The narrator's speech is just as individualized, colorful, and nonauthoritative as is the speech of the characters. The narrator's position is fluid, and in the majority of cases he uses the language of the personages depicted in the work. He cannot bring to bear against their subjective position a more authoritative and objective world. Such is the nature of narration in Dostoevskij, Andrej Belyj, Remizov, Sologub, and more recent Russian writers of prose.[6]

6. There is a fairly large literature on the role of the narrator in the novel. The basic work up to the present has been: K. Friedmann, *Die Rolle des Erzählers in der Epik* (1910). In Russia it was the "formalists" who aroused interest in the problem of the narrator. V. V. Vinogradov defines narrator's speech in Gogol' as "zigzagging from the author to the characters." (see his *Gogol' i natural'naja škola* [Gogol' and the Natural School]). According to Vinogradov, the language style of Dostoevskij's narrator in *Dvojnik* [The Double] occu-

While the incursion of an authorial context into reported speech is typical of speech reception in the moderate variety of both idealism and collectivism, the dissolution of the authorial context testifies to a relativistic individualism in speech reception. In the latter, the subjective reported utterance stands in opposition to a commenting and retorting authorial context that recognizes itself to be equally subjective.

The entire second direction is characterized by an exceptional development of mixed forms of speech reporting, including quasi indirect discourse and, in particular, quasi direct discourse, in which the boundaries of the message reported are maximally weakened. Also, among modifications of indirect and direct discourse, the predominant ones are those which show the greatest flexibility and are the most susceptible to permeation by authorial tendencies (for example, disseminated direct discourse, texture-analyzing forms of indirect discourse, and others).

Inquiry into all these tendencies shown in the actively responsive reception of speech must take into account every peculiarity of the linguistic phenomena under scrutiny. The teleology of the authorial context is especially important. In this respect, it is verbal art that most keenly implements all the permutations in sociolingual interorientation. As distinct from verbal art, rhetoric, owing simply to its teleology, is less free in its handling of other speakers' utterances. Rhetoric requires a distinct cognizance of the boundaries of reported speech. It is marked by an acute awareness of property rights to words and by a fastidiousness in matters of authenticity.

---

pies a like position with respect to the style of the hero, Goljadkin. See Vinogradov's "Stil' peterburgskoj poèmy, *Dvojnik*" [The style of the Petersburg epic, *The Double*], *Dostoevskij*, edited by Dolinin, I, 1923, pp. 239, 241 (the resemblance between the language of the narrator and the language of the hero had already been noted by Belinskij). B. M. Èngel'gardt points out quite correctly that "one cannot find any so-called objective description of the external world in Dostoevskij. . . . Owing to this fact there arose in the literary work of art a multistratification of reality that has led to a unique dissolution of being in the case of Dostoevskij's successors." Èngel'gardt sees evidence of this "dissolution of being" in Sologub's *Melkij bes* [Petty Demon] and A. Belyj's *Petersburg*. See B. M. Èngel'gardt, "Ideologičeskij roman Dostoevskogo" [Dostoevskij's Ideological Novel], *Dostoevskij*, edited by Dolinin, II, 1925, p. 94. *Cf.* Bally's description of Zola's style:

> Personne plus que Zola n'a usé et abusé du procédé qui consiste à faire passer tous les événements par le cerveau de ses personnages, à ne décrir les paysages que par leurs yeux, à n'enoncer des idées personelles que par leur bouche. Dans ses derniers romans, ce n'est plus une manière: c'est un tic, c'est une obsession. Dans *Rome*, pas un coin de la ville éternelle, pas une scène qu'il ne voie par les yeux de son abbé, pas une idée sur la religion qu'il ne formule par son intermédiaire [quoted from E. Lorck, *Die "Erlebte Rede,"* p. 64].

An interesting article devoted to the problem of the narrator is Il'ja Gruzdev's "O priemax xudožestvennogo povestvovani ja" [On Devices of Narration in Literary Art], *Zapiski Peredvižnogo Teatra* (Petrograd, 1922), Nos. 40, 41, 42. Nowhere, however, is the linguistic problem of reported speech formulated in these studies.

Judicial language intrinsically assumes a clear-cut discrepancy between the verbal subjectivism of the parties to a case and the objectivity of the court—between a ruling from the bench and the entire apparatus of judicial-interpretative and investigative commentary. Political rhetoric presents an analogous case. It is important to determine the specific gravity of rhetorical speech, judicial or political, in the linguistic consciousness of the given social group at a given time. Moreover, the position that a specimen of speech to be reported occupies on the social hierarchy of values must also be taken into account. The stronger the feeling of hierarchical eminence in another's utterance, the more sharply defined will its boundaries be, and the less accessible will it be to penetration by retorting and commenting tendencies from outside. So, for instance, it was possible within the neoclassical sphere for the low genres to display striking deviations from the rationalistic, dogmatic, linear style of speech reporting. It is symptomatic that quasi-direct discourse achieved its first powerful development precisely there—in the fables and tales of La Fontaine.

In summarizing all we have said of the various possible tendencies in the dynamic interrelationship of reported and reporting speech, we may mark out the following chronological sequence:

1. *Authoritarian dogmatism,* characterized by the linear, impersonal, monumental style of reported speech transmission in the Middle Ages;
2. *Rationalistic dogmatism,* with its even more pronounced linear style in the 17th and 18th centuries;
3. *Realistic and critical individualism,* with its pictorial style and its tendency to permeate reported speech with authorial retort and commentary (end of the 18th century and early 19th century); and finally
4. *Relativistic individualism,* with its decomposition of the authorial context (the present period).

Language exists not in and of itself but only in conju..iction with the individual structure of a concrete utterance. It is solely through the utterance that language makes contact with communication, is imbued with its vital power, and becomes a reality. The conditions of verbal communication, its forms, and its methods of differentiation are dictated by the social and economic prerequisites of a given period. These changing sociolingual conditions are what in fact determines those changes in the forms of reported speech brought out in our analysis. We would even venture to say that in the forms by which language registers the impressions of received speech and of the speaker the history of the changing types of socioideological communication stands out in particularly bold relief.

CHAPTER 3

Indirect Discourse, Direct Discourse, and Their Modifications

Patterns and modifications; grammar and stylistics. The general nature of speech reporting in Russian. The pattern of indirect discourse. The referential-analytical modification of indirect discourse. The impressionistic modification of indirect discourse. The pattern of direct discourse. Preset direct discourse. Particularized direct discourse. Anticipated, disseminated, and concealed direct discourse. The phenomenon of speech interference. Rhetorical questions and exclamations. Substituted direct discourse. Quasi-direct discourse.

We have now outlined the basic directions of the dynamism characterizing the interorientation of the author's and another person's speech. This dynamism finds its concrete linguistic expression in the patterns of reported speech and in the modifications of those patterns—which may be said to be the indices of the balance between reporting and reported messages achieved at any given time in the development of a language.

Let us now turn to a brief characterization of these patterns and their principal modifications from the standpoint of the tendencies already pointed out.

First, a few words must be said about the relation of the modifications to the pattern. This relation is analogous to the relation of the actuality of rhythm to the abstraction of meter. A pattern may be implemented only in the form of its specific modification. Changes within modifications build up over periods of time, whether centuries or decades, and new habits of active orientation toward the speech to be reported take hold—to crystallize later as regular linguistic formations in syntactic patterns. The position of the modifications is on the borderline between grammar and stylistics. From time to time, disputes arise as to whether a given form of speech transmission is a pattern or a modification, a

125

matter of grammar or a matter of style. An example of such a dispute was the one waged over the question of quasi-direct discourse in French and German, with Bally taking one side and Kalepky and Lorck the other. Bally refused to recognize a legitimate syntactic pattern in quasi-direct discourse and regarded it as nothing more than a stylistic modification. The same argument might be applied to quasi indirect discourse in French. From our point of view, the demarcation of a strict borderline between grammar and style, between a grammatical pattern and its stylistic modification, is methodologically unproductive and in fact impossible. This borderline is fluid because of the very mode of existence of language, in which, simultaneously, some forms are undergoing grammaticization while others are undergoing degrammaticization. It is precisely these ambiguous, borderline forms that are of the greatest interest to the linguist: this is precisely where the developmental tendencies of a language may be discerned.[1]

We shall keep our brief characterization of the patterns of direct and indirect discourse confined to the standard Russian literary language, and even so, with no intention of covering all their possible modifications. We are here concerned exclusively with the methodological aspect of the problem.

In Russian, as is well known, the syntactic patterns for reporting speech are very poorly developed. Aside from quasi-direct discourse (which in Russian lacks clear-cut syntactic markers, as is also true of German), we have two patterns: direct and indirect discourse. But these two patterns are not so strictly delimited from one another as in other languages. The hallmarks of indirect discourse are weak, and in colloquial language they easily combine with those of direct discourse.[2]

A lack of *consecutio temporum* and the subjunctive mood deprives indirect discourse in Russian of any distinctive character of its own. Thus there is no

---

1. One very frequently hears Vossler and the Vosslerites accused of concerning themselves more with stylistics than with linguistics in the strict sense. Actually, the Vossler school directs its interest to issues on the border between the two, in full realization of the methodological and heuristic significance of such issues; and therein lie the great advantages of this school, as we see it. Regrettably, the Vosslerites, as we know, focus primary attention on subjective psychological factors and on individual intentions in their explanations of these phenomena. Due to this fact, language does at times become a mere plaything of individual taste.

2. In many other languages, indirect discourse has distinct syntactic differentiation from direct discourse (special usage of tenses, moods, conjunctions, personal forms), resulting in a special, complex *pattern* for the indirect reporting of speech. In Russian, however, even those few distinguishing marks we have just mentioned very often lose their effect, so that indirect discourse mixes with direct discourse. For instance, in Gogol''s *Revizor* [The Inspector General], Osip says: "The innkeeper said *that I* won't give *you* anything to eat until you pay for what you've had. (Example taken from Peškovskij, *Russian Syntax* (3rd ed), p. 553, with Peškovskij's italics).

favorable ground for the wide development of certain modifications that are particularly important and interesting from our point of view. On the whole, one must acknowledge the unqualified primacy of direct discourse in Russian. The history of the Russian language knows no Cartesian, rationalistic period, during which an objective "authorial context," self-confident in its power of reason, had analyzed and dissected the referential structure of the speech to be reported and created complex and remarkable devices for the indirect transmission of speech.

All these peculiarities of the Russian language create an extremely favorable situation for the pictorial style of speech reporting—though, granted, of a somewhat loose and flaccid kind, that is, without that sense of boundaries forced and resistance overcome that one feels in other languages. An extraordinary ease of interaction and interpenetration between reporting and reported speech is the rule. This is a circumstance connected with the negligible role (in the history of the Russian literary language) played by rhetoric, with its clear-cut linear style of handling utterances to be reported and its wholesale, but distinct and single-minded, intonation.

Let us first of all describe the characteristics of indirect discourse, the pattern least elaborated in Russian. And let us begin with a brief criticism of the claims made by the grammarian, A. M. Peškovskij. After noting that forms of indirect discourse in Russian are underdeveloped, Peškovskij makes the following exceedingly peculiar declaration:[3]

> To convince oneself that the Russian language is naturally uncongenial to reporting indirect speech, one need only try rendering any piece of direct discourse, even just slightly exceeding a simple statement, into indirect discourse. For example: The Ass, bowing his head to the ground, says to the Nightingale *that not bad, that no kidding, it's nice listening to him sing, but that what a shame he doesn't know their Rooster, that he could sharpen up his singing quite a bit, if he'd take some lessons from him.*

If Peškovskij had performed the same experiment of mechanically transposing direct discourse into indirect discourse, using the French language and observing only the grammatical rules, he would have had to come to exactly the same conclusions. If, for instance, he had attempted translating into forms of indirect discourse La Fontaine's use of direct discourse or even of quasi-direct discourse in his fables (in which instances of the latter form are very common), the results obtained would have been just as grammatically correct and stylistically inadmissible as in the example given. And this would have happened despite the fact

---

3. *Ibid.*, p. 554. [The "piece of direct discourse" Peškovskij uses for his example is from the well-known fable by Ivan Krylov, *The Ass and the Nightingale.* In the fable, the Ass says to the Nightingale, after the latter's demonstration of his art: "Not bad! No kidding, it's nice listening to you sing. But what a shame you don't know our Rooster! You could sharpen up your singing quite a bit if you'd take some lessons from him." Peškovskij makes a purely mechanical rendition of this statement in indirect discourse. The result is awkward; indeed, impossible. The English translation aims at mirroring this result.—*Translators.]*

that quasi-direct discourse in French is extremely close to indirect discourse (the same shift of tenses and persons occurs in both). There are whole sets of words, idioms, and turns of speech appropriate in direct and quasi-direct discourse that would sound weird if transposed into an indirect discourse construction.

Peškovskij makes a typical grammarian's error. His mechanical, purely grammatical mode of translating reported speech from one pattern into another, without the appropriate stylistic reshaping, is nothing but a bogus and highly objectionable way of manufacturing classroom exercises in grammar. This sort of implementation of the patterns of speech reporting has nothing even remotely to do with their real existence in a language. The patterns express some tendency in one person's active reception of another's speech. Each pattern treats the message to be reported in its own creative fashion, following the specific direction proper to that pattern alone. If, at some given stage in its development, a language habitually perceives another's utterance as a compact, indivisible, fixed, impenetrable whole, then that language will command no other pattern than that of primitive, inert direct discourse (the monumental style). It is exactly this conception of the immutability of an utterance and the absolute literalness of its transmission that Peškovskij asserts in his experiment; yet, at the same time, he tries to apply the pattern of indirect discourse. The results of that experiment do not by any means prove that the Russian language is naturally uncongenial to reporting indirect speech. On the contrary, they prove that, however weakly developed its pattern, indirect discourse in Russian has enough character of its own so that not every case of direct discourse lends itself to literal translation.[4]

This singular experiment of Peškovskij's makes evident his complete failure to recognize the linguistic essence of indirect discourse. That essence consists in the analytical transmission of someone's speech. An analysis simultaneous with and inseparable from transmission constitutes the obligatory hallmark of all modifications of indirect discourse whatever. They may differ only with respect to the degree and direction of the analysis.

The analytical tendency of indirect discourse is manifested by the fact that all the emotive-affective features of speech, in so far as they are expressed not in the content but in the form of a message, do not pass intact into indirect discourse. They are translated from form into content, and only in that shape do they enter into the construction of indirect discourse, or are shifted to the main clause as a commentary modifying the *verbum dicendi*.

Thus, for example, the direct utterance, "Well done! What an achievement!" cannot be registered in indirect discourse as, "He said that well done and what an achievement." Rather, we expect: "He said that that had been done very well and was a real achievement." Or: "He said, delightedly, that that had been done

---

4. This error of Peškovskij's which we have been examining once again testifies to the methodological perniciousness of divorcing grammar and stylistics.

well and was a real achievement." All the various ellipses, omissions, and so on, possible in direct discourse on emotive-affective grounds, are not tolerated by the analyzing tendencies of indirect discourse and can enter indirect discourse only if developed and filled out. The Ass's exclamation, "Not bad!" in Peškovskij's example cannot be mechanically registered in indirect discourse as: "He says that not bad. . . ." but only as "He says that it was not bad. . . ." or even "He says that the nightingale sang not badly."

Neither can the "no kidding" be mechanically registered in indirect discourse, nor can "What a shame you don't know. . ." be rendered as, "but that what a shame he doesn't know. . ."

It is obvious that the same impossibility of a mechanical transposition from direct into indirect discourse also applies to the original form of any compositional or compositional-inflectional means that the speaker being reported used in order to convey his intention. Thus the compositional and inflectional peculiarities of interrogative, exclamatory, and imperative sentences are relinquished in indirect discourse, and their identification depends solely on the content.

Indirect discourse "hears" a message differently; it actively receives and brings to bear in transmission different factors, different aspects of the message than do the other patterns. That is what makes a mechanical, literal transposition of utterances from other patterns into indirect discourse impossible. It is possible only in instances in which the direct utterance itself was somewhat analytically constructed—insofar as direct discourse will tolerate such analysis. Analysis is the heart and soul of indirect discourse.

A closer scrutiny of Peškovskij's "experiment" reveals that the lexical tint of expressions such as "not bad" and "sharpen up" does not fully harmonize with the analytical spirit of indirect discourse. Such expressions are too colorful; they not only convey the exact meaning of what was said but they also suggest the manner of speech (whether individual or typological) of the Ass as protagonist. One would like to replace them with a synonym (such as "good" or "well" and "perfect/his singing/") or, if these "catchy" terms are to be retained in indirect discourse, at least to enclose them within quotation marks. If we were to read the resulting case of indirect discourse aloud, we would speak the expressions within quotation marks somewhat differently, as if to give notice through our intonation that they are taken directly from another person's speech and that we want to keep our distance.

Here we come up against the necessity of distinguishing between the two directions which the analyzing tendency of indirect discourse can take, and, accordingly, the necessity of distinguishing its two basic modifications.

The analysis involved in a construction of indirect discourse may indeed go in two directions or, more precisely, it may focus attention on two fundamentally different objects. An utterance may be received as a certain particular ideational position of the speaker. In that case, its exact referential makeup (what the speaker said) is transmitted analytically by the agency of the indirect discourse construction. Thus in the example we have been using, it is possible to transmit precisely the referential meaning of the Ass's evaluation of the Nightingale's singing. On the other hand, an utterance may be received and analytically transmitted as an expression characterizing not only the referent but also, or even more so, the speaker himself—his manner of speech (individual, or typological, or both); his state of mind as expressed not in the content but in the forms of his speech (disconnectedness, pauses between words, expressive intonation, and the like); his ability or lack of ability to express himself, and so on.

These two objects of analysis by the transmission of indirect discourse are profoundly and fundamentally different. In the one case, meaning is dissected into its constitutent, ideational, referential units, while in the other the utterance per se is broken down into the various stylistic strands that compose its verbal texture. The second tendency, carried to its logical extreme, would amount to a technical linguistic analysis of style. However, simultaneously with what would appear to be stylistic analysis, a referential analysis of the speech to be reported also takes place in this type of indirect discourse, with a resulting dissection of the referential meaning and of its implementation by the verbal envelope.

Let us term the first modification of the pattern of indirect discourse as the *referent-analyzing* modification, and the second, the *texture-analyzing* modification. The referent-analyzing modification receives an utterance on the purely thematic level and simply does not "hear" or take in whatever there is in that utterance that is without thematic significance. Those aspects of the formal verbal design which do have thematic significance—which are essential to an understanding of the speaker's ideational position—may be transmitted thematically by this variant or may be incorporated into the authorial context as characterization on the author's part.

The referent-analyzing modification provides a wide opportunity for the retorting and commenting tendencies of authorial speech, while at the same time maintaining a strict and clear-cut separation between reporting and reported utterance. For that reason, it makes an excellent means for the linear style of speech reporting. It unquestionably has a built-in tendency to thematicize another speaker's utterance, and thus it preserves the cohesiveness and autonomy of the utterance, not so much in constructional terms as in terms of meaning (we have seen how an expressive construction in a message to be reported can be rendered thematically). These results are achieved, however, only at the price of a certain depersonalization of the reported speech.

The development of the referent-analyzing modification to any appreciable extent occurs only within an authorial context that is somewhat rationalistic and dogmatic in nature—one at any rate in which the focus of attention is strongly ideational and in which the author shows through his words that he himself, in his own right, occupies a particular ideational position. Where this does not hold true, where either the author's language is itself colorful and particularized, or where the conduct of speech is directly handed over to some narrator of the appropriate type, this modification will have only a very secondary and occasional significance (as it does, for instance, in Gogol', Dostoevskij, and others).

On the whole, this modification is only weakly developed in Russian. It is found primarily in discursive or rhetorical contexts (of a scientific, philosophical, political, or similar nature), in which the author must deal with the problem of explaining, comparing, and putting into perspective the opinions of other people on the topic being discussed. Its occurrence in verbal art is rare. It takes on a certain stature only in works by writers who are not loath to have their own say with its special ideational aim and weight, such as Turgenev, for instance, or more especially, Tolstoj. Even in these cases, however, we do not find this modification in that richness and diversity of variation we observe in French or German.

Let us now turn to the texture-analyzing modification. It incorporates into indirect discourse words and locutions that characterize the subjective and stylistic physiognomy of the message viewed as expression. These words and locutions are incorporated in such a way that their specificity, their subjectivity, their typicality are distinctly felt; more often than not they are enclosed in quotation marks. Here are four examples:

> About the deceased, Grigorij remarked, making the sign of the cross, that he was a good hand at a thing or two, but was thick-headed and *scourged by his sickness,* and a *disbeliever to boot,* and that it was Fedor Pavlovič and the eldest son who had taught him his *disbelief* [Dostoevskij, *The Brothers Karamazov;* italics added].

> The same thing happened with the Poles: they appeared with a show of pride and independence. They loudly testified that, in the first place, they were both *"in the service of the Crown"* and that *"Pan Mitja"* had offered to buy their honor for 3000, and that they themselves had seen large sums of money in his hands (*ibid.*).

> Krasotkin proudly parried the accusation, giving to understand that it would indeed have been shameful *"in our day and age"* to play make-believe with his contemporaries, other 13 year-olds, but that he did it for the "chubbies" because he was fond of them, and no one had any business calling him to account for his feelings (*ibid.*).

> He found Nastas'ja Filippovna in a state similar to utter derangement: she continually cried out, trembled, shouted that Rogožin was hidden in the garden, in their very house, that she had just seen him, that he would *murder her . . . cut her throat!* [Dostoevskij, *The Idiot.* Here the indirect-discourse construction retains the expressive intonation of the original message. Italics added].

The words and expressions, incorporated into indirect discourse with their own specificity detectable (especially when they are enclosed in quotation marks), are being "made strange," to use the language of the Formalists, and made strange precisely in the direction that suits the author's needs: they are particularized, their coloration is heightened, but at the same time they are made to accommodate shadings of the author's attitude—his irony, humor, and so on.

It is advisable to keep this modification separate from cases of unbroken transition from indirect to direct discourse, although both types have virtually identical functions. In the latter, when direct discourse continues indirect discourse, the subjectivity of speech acquires a heightened definition and moves in the direction that suits the author's needs. For example:

> Try as he might to be evasive, nevertheless, Trifon Borisovič, once the peasants had been interrogated about the thousand ruble note, made his confession, adding only that right then and there he had scrupulously returned and remitted everything to Dmitrij Fedorovič *"out of the strictest sense of honor,"* and that *"only, you see, the gentleman himself, having been at the time dead drunk, cannot recall it"* [Dostoevskij, *The Brothers Karamazov;* italics added].

> Though filled with the profoundest respect for the memory of his ex-master, he nevertheless, among other things, declared that he had been negligent toward Mitja and had *"brought the children up wrong. The little child without me would have been eaten alive by lice,"* he added, recounting episodes from Mitja's earliest years [*ibid.;* italics added].

Such an instance, in which direct discourse is prepared for by indirect discourse and emerges as if from inside it—like those sculptures of Rodin's, in which the figure is left only partially emerged from stone—is one of the innumerable modifications of direct discourse treated pictorially.

Such is the nature of the texture-analyzing modification of the indirect discourse construction. It creates highly original pictorial effects in reported speech transmission. It is a modification that presupposes the presence in the linguistic consciousness of a high degree of individualization of other speakers' utterances and an ability to perceive differentially the verbal envelope of an utterance and its referential meaning. None of that is congenial either to the authoritarian or the rationalistic type of reception of other speakers' utterances. As a viable stylistic device, it can take root in a language only on the grounds of critical and realistic individualism, whereas the referent-analyzing modification is characteristic of the rationalistic kind of individualism. In the history of the Russian literary language, the latter period hardly existed. And that explains the absolute preeminence of the texture-analyzing modification over the referent-analyzing modification in Russian. Also, the development of the texture-analyzing modification benefited to a high degree from the lack of *consecutio temporum* in Russian.

We see, therefore, that our two modifications, despite their liaison through the common analytical tendency of the pattern, express profoundly different linguistic conceptions of the reported addresser's words and the speaker's individuality. For the first modification, the speaker's individuality is a factor only as it occupies some specific ideational position (epistemological, ethical, existential, or behavioral), and beyond that position (which is transmitted in strictly referential terms) it has no existence for the reporter. There is no wherewithal here for the speaker's individuality to congeal into an image.

The opposite is true of the second modification, in which the speaker's individuality is presented as subjective manner (individual or typological), as manner of thinking and speaking, involving the author's evaluation of that manner as well. Here the speaker's individuality congeals to the point of forming an image.

Still a third and not inconsiderable modification of the indirect discourse construction in Russian may be pointed out. It is used mainly for reporting the internal speech, thoughts, and experiences of a character. It treats the speech to be reported very freely; it abbreviates it, often only highlighting its themes and dominants, and therefore it may be termed the impressionistic modification. Authorial intonation easily and freely ripples over its fluid structure. Here is a classic example of the impressionistic modification from Puškin's *Bronze Horseman:*

> What were the thoughts he pondered then? That he was poor; that he perforce must labor to achieve respect, security; that God just might have granted him more brains and money. That goodness knows, there are those idle lucky dogs with little brains, those loungers, *for whom life is just a lark!* That he had been in service in all two years; his thoughts remarked as well that the weather wasn't calming down; that the river kept on rising; that the bridges over the Neva were all most likely up and that he would be two days or three cut off from his Paraša. Thus went his pondering [italics added].

Judging from this example, we note that the impressionistic modification of indirect discourse lies somewhere midway between the referent-analyzing and the texture-analyzing modifications. In this or that instance, a referential analysis has quite definitely taken place. Certain words and locutions have clearly originated from the mind of the hero, Evgenij (though no emphasis is put on their specificity). What comes through most is the author's irony, his accentuation, his hand in ordering and abbreviating the material.

Let us now turn to the pattern of *direct discourse,* which is extremely well worked out in the Russian literary language and commands an immense assortment of distinctively different modifications. From the cumbersome, inert, and indivisible blocks of direct discourse in Old Russian literary monuments to the modern, elastic, and often ambiguous modes of its incorporation into the authorial context stretches the long and instructive path of its historical development. But here we must refrain from examining that historical development; nor can we inventory the existing modifications of direct discourse in the literary language. We shall limit ourselves only to those modifications which display a mutual exchange of intonations, a sort of reciprocal infectiousness between the reporting context and the reported speech. Furthermore, within those limits, our concern lies not so much with those instances in which the author's speech advances upon the reported message and penetrates it with its own intonations, but rather with instances in which, on the contrary, elements of the reported message creep into and are dispersed throughout the entire authorial context, making it fluid and ambiguous. It is true, however, that a sharp dividing line cannot always be drawn between these two types of instances: often it is indeed a matter of a reciprocity of effect.

The first direction of the dynamic interrelationship, characterized by the author's "imposition," may be termed *preset direct discourse.*[5]

The case of direct discourse emerging out of indirect discourse (with which we are already familiar) belongs in this category. A particularly interesting and widespread instance of this modification is the emergence of direct discourse out of quasi-direct discourse. Since the nature of the latter discourse is half narration and half reported speech, it presets the apperception of the direct discourse. The basic themes of the impending direct discourse are anticipated by the context and are colored by the author's intonations. Under this type of treatment, the boundaries of the reported utterance become extremely weak. A classic example of this modification is the portrayal of Prince Myškin's state of mind on the verge of an epileptic fit, which takes up almost the entire fifth chapter of Part II of Dostoevskij's *Idiot* (magnificent specimens of quasi-direct discourse are also to be found there). In this chapter, Prince Myškin's directly reported speech resounds within his self-enclosed world, since the author narrates within the confines of his, Prince Myškin's, purview. Half the apperceptive background created for the "other speaker's" utterance here belongs to that other speaker (the hero), and half to the author. However, it is made perfectly clear to us that a deep penetration of authorial intonations into direct discourse is almost always accompanied by a weakening of objectivity in the authorial context.

Another modification in the same direction may be termed *particularized direct discourse.* The authorial context here is so constructed that the traits the author used to define a character cast heavy shadows on his directly reported speech. The value judgments and attitudes in which the character's portrayal is steeped carry over into the words he utters. The referential weight of the reported utterances declines in this modification but, in exchange, their characterological significance, their picturesqueness, or their time-and-place typicality, grows more intense. Similarly, once we recognize a comic character on stage by his style of makeup, his costume, and his general bearing, we are ready to laugh even before we catch the meaning of his words. Such is the way direct discourse is usually handled by Gogol' and by representatives of the so-called "natural school." As a matter of fact, Dostoevskij tried to reanimate this particularized treatment of reported utterances in his first work, *Poor Folk.*

5. We shall disregard the more primitive devices for authorial retort and commentary in direct discourse, e.g., the author's use of italics in direct discourse (shift of accent), interpolation of parenthetical remarks of various kinds, or simply of exclamation or question marks or such conventional notations as (sic!), etc. Of crucial significance in overcoming the inertness of direct discourse are the various possible positionings of the reporting verb in conjunction with commentary and retort.

The presetting of the reported speech and the anticipation of its theme in the narrative, its judgments, and accents may so subjectivize and color the author's context in the tints of his hero that that context will begin to sound like "reported speech," though a kind of reported speech with its authorial intonations still intact. To conduct the narrative exclusively within the purview of the hero himself, not only within its dimensions of time and space but also in its system of values and intonations, creates an extremely original kind of apperceptive background for reported utterances. It gives us the right to speak of a special modification: *anticipated and disseminated reported speech* concealed in the authorial context and, as it were, breaking into real, direct utterances by the hero.

This modification is very widespread in contemporary prose, especially that of Andrej Belyj and the writers under his influence (for instance, in Erenburg's *Nikolaj Kurbov*). However, the classical specimens must be sought in Dostoevskij's work of his first and second periods (in his last period, this modification is encountered less often). Let us look at his *Skvernyj anekdot [A Nasty Story]*.

One might enclose the whole narrative in quotation marks as narration by a "narrator," though no such narrator is denoted, either thematically or compositionally. However, the situation within the narrative is such that almost every epithet, or definition, or value judgment might also be enclosed in quotation marks as originating in the mind of one or another character.

Let us quote a short passage from the beginning of the story:

> Once in winter, on a cold and frosty evening—very late evening, rather, it being already the twelfth hour—three *extremely distinguished* gentlemen were sitting in a *comfortable*, even sumptuously appointed, room inside a *handsome* two-story house on Petersburg Island and were occupied in *weighty* and *superlative* talk on an *extremely remarkable* topic. All three gentlemen were officials of the rank of general. They were seated around a small table, each in a *handsome* upholstered chair, and during pauses in the conversation they *comfortably* sipped champagne [italics added].

If we disregarded the remarkable and complex play of intonations in this passage, it would have to be judged as stylistically wretched and banal. Within the few lines of print, the epithets "handsome" and "comfortable" are used twice, and others are "sumptuously," "weighty," "superlative," and "extremely distinguished"!

Such style would not escape our severest verdict if we took it seriously as description emanating from the author (as we would in the case of Turgenev or Tolstoj) or even as a narrator's description, provided the narrator be of the monolithic *Ich-Erzählung* variety.

However, it is impossible to take this passage in that way. Each of these colorless, banal, insipid epithets is an arena in which *two* intonations, *two* points of view, *two* speech acts converge and clash.

Let us look at a few more excerpts from the passage characterizing the master of the house, Privy Councilor Nikiforov:

> A few words about him: he had begun his career as a minor official, had contentedly fiddle-faddled his way through the next 45 years or so. . . . He particularly despised untidiness and excitability, considering the latter moral untidiness, and toward the end of his life he submerged himself completely in a state of *sweet and relaxed comfort* and systematic solitude. . . . His *appearance was that of an extremely respectable and well-shaven* man who seemed younger than his years, was well preserved, showed promise of living for a long time to come, and abided by the *most exalted gentlemanly code.* His position was a quite comfortable one: he was the head of something and put his signature on something from time to time. *In short, he was considered to be a most excellent man.* He had only one passion or, rather, one ardent wish: to own his own house—one, moreover, built along manorial, not tenement, lines. His wish at last came true [italics added].

Now we see clearly where the first passage derived its banal and monotonous epithets (but with their banal monotony pointedly *sustained*). They originated not in the author's mind but in the mind of the general savoring his comfort, his very own house, his situation in life, his rank—the mind of Privy Councilor Nikiforov, a man who has "come up in the world." Those words might be enclosed in quotation marks as "another's speech," the reported speech of Nikiforov. But they belong not only to him. After all, the story is being told by a narrator, who would seem to be in solidarity with the "generals," who fawns upon them, adopts their attitude in all things, speaks their language, but nonetheless provocatively overdoes it and thus thoroughly exposes all their real and potential utterances to the author's irony and mockery. By each of these banal epithets, the author, through his narrator, makes his hero ironic and ridiculous. This is what creates the complex play of intonations in the passage cited—a play of intonations virtually unproducible if read aloud.

The remaining portion of the story is constructed entirely within the purview of another main character, Pralinskij. This portion, too, is studded with the epithets and value judgments of the hero (his hidden speech), and against that background, steeped in the author's irony, his actual, properly punctuated, internal and external direct speech arises.

Thus almost every word in the narrative (as concerns its expressivity, its emotional coloring, its accentual position in the phrase) figures simultaneously in two intersecting contexts, two speech acts: in the speech of the author-narrator (ironic and mocking) and the speech of the hero (who is far removed from irony). This simultaneous participation of two speech acts, each differently oriented in its expressivity, also explains the curious sentence structure, the twists and turns of syntax, the highly original style, of the story. If only one of the two speech acts had been used, the sentences would have been structured otherwise, the style would have been different. We have here a classic instance of a linguistic phenomenon almost never studied—the phenomenon of *speech interference.*

In Russian, this phenomenon of speech interference may take place to a certain extent in the texture-analyzing modification of indirect discourse, in those comparatively rare instances in which the reported clause contains not only some of the original words and expressions but also the expressive structure of the message reported. We have seen an example of this above, one in which indirect discourse incorporated the exclamatory structure—granted, it was somewhat toned down—of the original message. What resulted was a certain counterpoint between the calm, businesslike, narrational intonation of the author's analytical transmission and the emotional, hysterical intonation of his half-crazed heroine. This also accounts for the peculiar disfigurement of the syntactic physiognomy of the clause—a clause serving two masters, participating simultaneously in two speech acts. Indirect discourse, however, does not supply the grounds for anything like a distinctive and durable stylistic expression for this phenomenon of speech interference.

The most important and, in French at least, the most syntactically standardized case of an interferential merging of two differently oriented speech acts is *quasi-direct discourse.* In view of its extraordinary importance, we shall devote the entire next chapter to the question of quasi-direct discourse. There we shall also examine how the question has been treated in Romance and Germanic linguistics. The controversy over quasi-direct discourse and the various stands taken on the issue, especially by members of the Vossler school, comprise material of considerable methodological interest and, therefore, ought to be subjected to our critical analysis.

Within the scope of the present chapter, we shall be concerned with examining a few other phenomena related to quasi-direct discourse, which probably, in Russian, are to be identified as the basis for its inception and formation.

In our exclusive concern with dualistic, duplex modifications of direct discourse in its pictorial treatment, we have neglected one of the most important of the *linear* modifications of direct discourse: *rhetorical direct discourse.* This "persuasive" modification with its several variants has great sociological significance. We cannot dwell on these forms but shall focus some attention on certain phenomena associated with rhetoric.

There is in social intercourse what is called the *rhetorical question,* or the *rhetorical exclamation.* Certain instances of this phenomenon are especially interesting because of the problem of their localization in context. They would seem to be situated on the very boundary between authorial and reported speech (usually, internal speech) and often they slide directly into one or the other. Thus they may be interpreted as a question or exclamation on the part of the author or, equally, as a question or exclamation on the part of the hero, addressed to himself.

Here is an example of such a question:

> But who is approaching, stealthy footed, by moonlit path, amid deepest stillness? The
> Russian suddenly comes to. Before him stands, with tender, wordless greeting, the
> Circassian maid. He gazes at her silently and thinks: this is some lying dream, the
> hollow play of flagging feelings. . . [Puškin, *The Captive of the Caucasus*].

The hero's concluding (internal) words seem to respond to the rhetorical question posed by the author, and that rhetorical question may be interpreted as part of the hero's own internal speech.

Here is an example of rhetorical exclamation:

> All, all, the dreadful sound betrayed. The world of nature dimmed before him. Fare-
> well, blessed freedom! He is a slave! [*ibid.*].

A particularly frequent occurrence in prose is the case in which some such question as "What is to be done now?" introduces the hero's inner deliberations or the recounting of his actions—the question being equally the author's and also one the hero poses to himself in a predicament.

It will surely be claimed that in these and similar questions and exclamations the author's initiative takes the upper hand, and that that is why they never appear enclosed in quotation marks. In these particular instances, it is the author who steps forward, but he does so on his hero's behalf—he seems to speak for him

Here is an interesting example of this type:

> The Cossacks, leaning on their pikes, gaze over the rushing water of the river, while
> unnoticed by them, blurred in fog, a villain and his weapon float past. . . What are
> you thinking, Cossack? Are you recalling battles of bygone years? . . . . Farewell,
> free frontier villages, paternal home, the quiet Don, and war, and pretty girls. The
> unseen enemy has reached the bank, an arrow leaves the quiver—takes flight—and
> down the Cossack falls from the bloodied rampart [*ibid.*].

Here the author stands in for his hero, says in his stead what the hero might or should have said, says what the given occasion calls for. Puškin bids farewell to the Cossack's homeland for him (naturally, something the Cossack himself could not have done).

This talking in another's stead comes very close to quasi-direct discourse. Let us term this case *substituted direct discourse*. Such a substitution presupposes a *parallelism of intonations*, the intonations of the author's speech and the substituted speech of the hero (what he might or should have said), both running in the same direction. Therefore, no interference takes place here.

When a complete solidarity in values and intonations exists between the author and his hero within the framework of a rhetorically constructed context, the author's rhetoric and that of the hero begin to overlap: their voices merge; and we get protracted passages that belong simultaneously to the author's narrative and to the hero's internal (though sometimes also external) speech. The result obtained is almost indistinguishable from quasi-direct discourse; only interference is missing. It was on the grounds of the young Puškin's Byronic rhetoric that quasi-direct discourse (presumably for the first time) took shape in Russian. In *The Captive of the Caucasus,* the author shares a complete solidarity in values and intonations with his hero. The narrative is forged in the hero's tones, and the hero's utterances in the author's tones. We find the following, for instance:

> There, mountain peaks, each one alike, stretch out in line; a lonely track among them winds and fades in gloom. . . . *Oppressive thoughts* beset the captive youth's tormented breast. . . . The distant track leads back to Russia, land where his ardent youth began, so proud, so free of care: where he knew early joy, where he found so much to love, where he embraced dire suffering, where he destroyed delight, desire, and hope in stormy life. . . . The world and its ways he fathomed, and he knew the price of a faithless life. In people's hearts he found betrayal, in dreams of love, a mad illusion. . . . Freedom! For *you alone* he kept the quest in this sublunar world. . . . It came to pass . . . . Now he sees nothing in the world on which to set his hopes, and even *you,* his last fond dream, *you,* too, are gone from him. He is a slave [*ibid.*; italics added].

Here, clearly, it is the captive's own "oppressive thoughts" that are being transmitted. It is *his* speech, but it is being formally delivered by the author. If the personal pronoun "he" were changed everywhere to "I," and if the verb forms were adjusted accordingly, no dissonance or incongruity, whether in style or otherwise, would result. Symptomatically enough, this speech contains apostrophes in the second person (to "freedom," to "dreams"), which all the more underscore the author's identification with his hero. This instance of the hero's speech does not differ in style or ideas from the rhetorical direct discourse reported as delivered by the hero in the second part of the poem:

> "Forget me! I am unworthy of your love, your heart's delight. . . . Bereft of rapture, empty of desire, I wither, passion's victim. . . . O why did not my eyes behold you long ago, in days when still I laid my trust in hope and rapturous dreams! But now it is too late! To happiness I am no more alive, the phantom Hope has flown away. . . ." [*ibid.*].

All writers on quasi-direct discourse (perhaps with the single exception of Bally) would acknowledge the passage in question a perfectly genuine specimen.

We, however, are inclined to regard it as a case of substituted direct discourse. True, only one step is needed to turn it into quasi-direct discourse. And Puškin took that step when he succeeded in standing apart from his heroes and brought to bear the contrast of a more objective authorial context with its own values and intonations. The example cited above still lacks any interference between the author's speech and the character's speech. Consequently, it also lacks the grammatical and stylistic features that such interference generates and which characterize quasi-direct discourse, differentiating it from the surrounding authorial context. The fact is that in our example we recognize the speech of the "captive" only by purely semantic indications. We do not sense here the merging of two *differently* oriented speech acts; we do not sense the *integrity and resistance* of the reported message behind the author's transmission.

Finally, to demonstrate what we regard as real quasi-direct discourse, we reproduce below a remarkable specimen from Puškin's *Poltava*. With this we will end this chapter.

> But his rage for action Kočubej hid deep within his heart. "His thoughts had now, all woebegone, addressed themselves to death. No ill-will did he bear Mazeppa—his daughter was alone to blame. But he forgave his daughter, too: Let her answer to God, now that she had plunged her family into shame, had Heaven and the laws of man forgot. . ." But meanwhile he scanned his household with an eagle eye, seeking for himself bold, unswerving, incorruptible companions.

CHAPTER 4

Quasi-Direct Discourse in French, German, and Russian

Quasi-direct discourse in French: Tobler; Kalepky; Bally. Criticism of Bally's hypostasizing abstract objectivism. Bally and the Vosslerites. Quasi-direct discourse in German. Eugen Lerch's conception. Lorck's conception. Lorck's theory concerning the role of fantasy in language. Gertraud Lerch's conception. Reported speech in Old French. Reported speech in Middle French. The Renaissance. Quasi-direct discourse in La Fontaine and La Bruyère. Quasi-direct discourse in Flaubert. The emergence of quasi-direct discourse in German. Criticism of the hypostasizing individualistic subjectivism of the Vosslerites.

Various writers have proposed various nomenclatures for the phenomenon of quasi-direct discourse in French and German. Each of the writers on the subject has, in effect, proposed his or her own term. We have been using and shall continue to use Gertraud Lerch's term, "uneigentliche direkte Rede," [quasi-direct discourse] as the most neutral of all the terms proposed and the one entailing the least amount of theory. As regards Russian and German, the term is beyond reproach; with respect to French, however, its usage may arouse some misgivings.[1]

1. Here are some examples of quasi-direct discourse in French:

   1. Il protesta: *Son père la haïssait!*
      In direct discourse that would be:
      Il protesta et s'écria: *"Mon père te haït!"*
      In indirect discourse:
      Il protesta et s'écria que son père la haïssait.
      In quasi-indirect discourse:
      Il protesta: *"son père, s'écria-t-il, la haïssait!"*
      (Example from Balzac as cited by G. Lerch.)

(*Continued on next page*)

The first mention of quasi-direct discourse as a special form for reporting an utterance, on a par with direct and indirect discourse, was made by Tobler in 1887 (*Zeitschrift für romanische Philologie, XI, 437*).

Tobler defined quasi-direct discourse as a "peculiar mixture of direct and indirect discourse" [*eigentümliche Mischung direkter und indirekter Rede*]. This mixed form, according to Tobler, derives its *tone* and *word order* from direct discourse and its *verbal tenses* and *persons* from indirect discourse.

As pure description, this definition may be considered acceptable. Indeed, from the superficial viewpoint of the comparative description of features, Tobler has accurately indicated the resemblances and differences between the form in question and direct and indirect discourse.

But the word "mixture" in the definition is completely unacceptable, since it entails a genetic explanation—"formed from a mixture of"—which can hardly be proved. And even in its purely descriptive way, the definition is faulty inasmuch as what we have in quasi-direct discourse is not a simple mechanical mixture or arithmetical sum of two forms but a completely *new*, positive tendency in active reception of another person's utterance, a *special direction* in which the dynamics of the interrelationship between reporting and reported speech moves. But Tobler is deaf to dynamics and registers only the abstract features of patterns.

So much for Tobler's definition. Now, how does he explain the emergence of the form?

A speaker, relating past events, cites another person's utterance in an autonomous form just as it sounded in the past. In the process, the speaker changes the *present* tense of the original utterance to the *imperfect* in order to show that the utterance is contemporaneous with the past events being related. He then makes some additional changes (persons of the verbs and pronouns) so that the utterance not be mistaken for the relator's own.

Tobler's explanation is built on a faulty but old and very widespread linguistic way of arguing: if the speaker had consciously and premeditatedly planned to introduce the new form, what would his reasoning and motivation have been?

(*Footnote 1—Continued*)

2. Tout le jour, il avait l'oeil au guet; et la nuit, si quelque chat faisait du bruit, *le chat prenait l'argent* [La Fontaine].

3. En vain il (le colonel) parla de la sauvagerie du pays et de la difficulté pour une femme d'y voyager: elle (Miss Lydia) *ne craignait rien; elle aimait par-dessus tout à voyager à cheval; elle se faisait une fête de coucher au bivac; elle menaçait d'aller en Asie Mineure.* Bref, elle avait réponse à tout, car *jamais Anglaise n'avait été en Corse; donc elle devait y aller* [P. Mérimée, *Colomba*].

4. Resté seul dans l'embrasure de la fenêtre, le cardinal s'y tint immobile, un instant encore. . . . Et ses bras frémissants se tendirent, en un geste d'imploration: "*O Dieu! puisque ce médecin s'en allait ainsi, hereux de sauver l'embarras de son impuissance, ô Dieu! que ne faisiez-vous un miracle, pour montrer l'éclat de votre pouvoir sans bornes! Un miracle, un miracle!* Il le demandait du fond de son âme de croyant [Zola, *Rome*].

(Examples three and four are cited and discussed by Kalepky, Bally, and Lorck.)

Even if such a way of arriving at explanations were admissible, still, the motives of Tobler's "speaker" are not quite convincing or clear: If he wants to preserve the autonomy of the utterance as it actually sounded in the past, would it not be better to report it in direct discourse? Its belonging to the past and to the reported, not the reporting, addresser would then be beyond any possible doubt. Or, if the *imperfect* and the *third* person are what is at stake, wouldn't it be easier simply to use indirect discourse? The trouble is that what is *basic* to our form—*that entirely new interelationship between reporting and reported speech which it achieves*—is just exactly what Tobler's motives fail to express. For Tobler, it is simply a matter of two old forms out of which he wants to paste together a new form.

In our opinion, what can at best be explained by this type of argument about speakers' motives is merely the use in one or another concrete instance of an *already available* form, but under no circumstances will it do to explain the composing of a *new* form in language. The individual motives and intentions of a speaker can take meaningful effect only within limits imposed by current grammatical possibilities on the one hand, and within the limits of the conditions of socioverbal intercourse that predominate in his group on the other. These possibilities and these conditions are *given quantities*—they are what circumscribe the speaker's linguistic purview. It is beyond the speaker's individual power to force that purview open.

No matter what the intentions the speaker means to carry out, no matter what errors he may commit, no matter how he analyzes forms or mixes them or combines them, he will not create a new pattern in language and he will not create a new tendency in socioverbal intercourse. His subjective intentions will bear a creative character only to the extent that there is something in them that coincides with tendencies in the socioverbal intercourse of speakers that are in process of formation, of generation; and these tendencies are dependent upon socioeconomic factors. Some displacement, some shift had to have occurred within socioverbal intercourse and with regard to the mutual orientation of utterances in order for that essentially new manner of perceiving another person's words, which found expression in the form of quasi-direct discourse, to have been established. As it took shape, this new form began penetrating into that field of linguistic possibilities only within the confines of which can the individual verbal intentions of speakers find definition, motivation, and productive implementation.

The next writer on the subject of quasi-direct discourse was Th. Kalepky (*Zeitschrift für romanische Philologie*, XIII, 1899, 491-513). He recognized in quasi-direct discourse a completely autonomous third form of reported speech and defined it as *concealed* or *veiled* discourse (*verschleierte Rede*). The stylistic point of the form consisted in the necessity of guessing who the speaker is. And indeed, there is a puzzle: from the standpoint of abstract grammar, it is the author who speaks; from the standpoint of the actual sense of the whole context, it is a character who speaks.

Kalepky's analysis contains an undoubted step forward in investigation of the question concerning us. Instead of mechanically coupling the abstract features of two patterns, Kalepky attempts to descry the *new*, positive stylistic bearing of the form. In addition, he correctly understood the *double-faced* nature of quasi-direct discourse. However, he incorrectly defined it. Under no conditions can we agree with Kalepky that quasi-direct discourse is "masked" discourse and that the point of the device consists in guessing who the speaker is. No one, after all, starts off the process of understanding with abstract grammatical considerations. Therefore, it is clear to everyone from the very start that, in terms of the *sense* of what is said, it is the character speaking. Difficulties arise only for grammarians. Furthermore, our form does not at all contain an "either/or" dilemma; its *specificum* is precisely a matter of *both* author *and* character speaking at the same time, a matter of a single linguistic construction within which the accents of two differently oriented voices are maintained. We have already seen that the phenomenon of genuinely concealed reported speech does take place in language. We have seen how the insidious effect of another person's speech secreted in the author's context can cause that context to manifest special grammatical and stylistic features. But that is one of the modifications of direct discourse. Quasi-direct discourse, however, is an *overt* type of discourse, notwithstanding the fact that it is double-faced, like Janus.

The chief methodological deficiency in Kalepky's approach is his interpreting a linguistic phenomenon within the framework of the *individual consciousness*, his attempting to discover its psychic roots and subjective-aesthetic effects. We shall return to a fundamental criticism of this approach when we examine the views of the Vosslerites (Lorck, E. Lerch, and G. Lerch).

Bally spoke out on our topic in 1912 (*Germanisch-romanische Monatsschrift*, IV, 549 ff, 597 ff). In 1914, in response to Kalepky's polemic, he returned once again to the question with an article on its fundamentals entitled "Figures de pénsée et formes linguistiques" (*Germanisch-romanische Monatsschrift*, VI, 1914, 405 ff, 456 ff).

The gist of Bally's views amounts to the following: he considers quasi-direct discourse a new, later variant of the classical form of indirect discourse. He traces its formation through the series: il disait qu'il était malade > il disait: il était malade > il était malade (disait-il).[2] The dropping of the conjunction *que* is explained, according to Bally, by a more recent tendency inherent in language to prefer paratactic coordination of clauses to hypotactic subordination. Bally points out, furthermore, that this variant of indirect discourse—which he appropriately enough terms *style indirect libre*—is not an inert form but a form in

---

2. The intermediate (transitional) form is, of course, a linguistic fiction.

motion, moving toward direct discourse as its furthest extreme. In particularly intensive cases, Bally claims, it is sometimes difficult to say where *style indirect libre* leaves off and *style direct* begins. That is how, incidentally, he regards the passage from Zola quoted in our fourth example [see footnote 1, pp. 141-142]. The difficulty arises precisely at the point where the cardinal addresses God: "Ô Dieu! que ne faisiez-vous un miracle!," which apostrophe contains simultaneously a feature of indirect discourse (the imperfect) and the use of the second person as in direct discourse. Bally considers as analogous to French *style indirect libre* that form of German indirect discourse which omits the conjunction and keeps the word order as in direct discourse (the second type in Bally's analysis).

Bally makes a strict distinction between *linguistic forms* ("formes linguistiques") and *figures of thought* ("figures de pensée"). He understands by the latter devices of expression which are illogical from the standpoint of language and in which the normal interrelationship between the linguistic sign and its usual meaning is violated. Figures of thought cannot be acknowledged linguistic phenomena in the strict sense: indeed, there are no specific, stable linguistic features which might express them. On the contrary, the linguistic features involved have a meaning in language which is pointedly other than the meaning imposed upon them by figures of thought. To figures of thought Bally relegates quasi-direct discourse in its pure forms. After all, from a strictly grammatical point of view, it is the author's speech, whereas according to the sense of it, it is the character's speech. But this "sense of it" is not represented by any special linguistic sign. Consequently, what we are dealing with is, according to Bally, an extra-linguistic phenomenon.

Such is Bally's conception in basic outline. He is the linguist who at the present time most outstandingly represents linguistic abstract objectivism. Bally hypostasizes and vivifies forms of language obtained by way of abstraction from concrete speech performances (speech performances in the spheres of practical life, literature, science, etc.). This process of abstraction has been carried out by linguists, as we have already indicated, for purposes of deciphering a dead, alien language and for the practical purposes of teaching it. And now Bally comes along and endows these abstractions with life and momentum: a modification of indirect discourse begins to pursue a course toward the pattern of direct discourse, and on the way quasi-direct discourse is formed. A creative role in the composition of the new form is ascribed to the dropping of the conjunction *que* and the reporting verb. In actual fact, however, the abstract system of language, where Bally's *formes linguistiques* are to be found, is devoid of any movement, any life, any achievement. Life begins only at the point where utterance crosses utterance, i.e., where verbal interaction begins, be it not even "face-to-face" verbal interaction, but the mediated, literary variety.[3]

3. On mediated and unmediated forms of verbal interaction, see the already cited study by L. P. Jakubinskij.

It is not a matter of one abstract form moving toward another, but a matter of the mutual orientation of two utterances changing on the basis of a change in the active perception by the linguistic consciousness of the "speaking personality," of its ideational, ideological autonomy, of its verbal individuality. The dropping of the conjunction *que* brings together, not two abstract forms, but two utterances in all their ideational fullness. The dike ruptures, as it were, and authorial intonations freely stream into the reported speech.

A methodological divorce between linguistic forms and figures of thought, between "langue" and "parole," also results from this kind of hypostasizing objectivism. In point of fact, the linguistic forms Bally has in mind exist only in grammar books and dictionaries (where, to be sure, their existence is perfectly legitimate), but in the living reality of language they are immersed deeply in what, from the abstract grammatical point of view, is the irrational element of "figures de pensée."

Bally is also wrong in taking the German indirect discourse construction of his second type to be analogous to French quasi-direct discourse.[4] It is an extremely symptomatic mistake. Bally's analogy is irreproachable from the standpoint of abstract grammar, but from the standpoint of socioverbal tendency, the comparison cannot hold up under criticism. After all, one and the same social-verbal tendency (dictated by identical socioeconomic conditions) in different languages may, in accordance with the grammatical structures of those languages, appear with different outer features. In any particular language, what begins to undergo modification in a certain specific direction is precisely that pattern which turns out to be the most adaptable in the necessary regard. In French it was the pattern of indirect discourse, in German and Russian—direct discourse.

Let us now turn to an examination of the point of view of the Vosslerites. These linguists shift the dominant in their investigations from grammar to stylistics and psychology, from "language forms" to "figures of thought." Their disagreements with Bally are, as we already know, fundamental and far reaching. Lorck in his criticism of the Geneva linguist contrasts, in Humboldtian terms, Bally's outlook on language as *ergon* with his outlook on language as *energeia*. Thus, the basic premises of individualistic subjectivism are brought directly to bear against Bally's point of view on the particular question at hand. What now enter the lists as factors to explain quasi-direct discourse are: affect in language, fantasy in language, empathy, linguistic taste, and the like.[5]

4. Kalepky pointed out this mistake to Bally, who, in his second study, does partially correct it.

5. Before proceeding to an analysis of the Vosslerites' view, we shall supply three examples of quasi-direct discourse in German:

1. Der Konsul ging, die Hände auf dem Rücken, umher und bewegte nervös die Schultern.

Er hatte keine Zeit. Er war bei Gott überhäuft. Sie sollte sich gedulden und sich gefälligst noch fünfzig mal besinnen! [Thomas Mann, *Buddenbrooks*].

Also in 1914—the year of the Kalepky-Bally polemics—Eugen Lerch came forward with his assessment of quasi-direct discourse (*G-r.M.*, VI, 470). His definition of quasi-direct discourse was "speech as fact" (*Rede als Tatsache*). Reported speech is transmitted by this form in such a way as if its content were a fact that the author himself is communicating. Contrasting direct, indirect, and quasi-direct discourse in terms of the degrees of realness inherent in the content of each, Lerch came to the conclusion that the most real of them is quasi-direct discourse. He also evinced a stylistic preference for quasi-direct discourse over indirect discourse in regard to the vividness and concreteness of the impression produced. That is what Lerch's definition amounts to.

A detailed study of quasi-direct discourse was furnished by E. Lorck in 1921 in a small volume under the title *Die "Erlebte Rede."* The book was dedicated to Vossler. In it, Lorck dwells at some length on the history of the issue in question.

Lorck defined quasi-direct discourse as "experienced speech" (*erlebte Rede*) in contradistinction to direct discourse, defined as "repeated speech" (*gesprochene Rede*), and indirect discourse—"communicated speech" (*berichtete Rede*).

Lorck expounds his definition in the following way. Let us suppose Faust on stage speaking his monologue: "Habe nun, ach! Philosophie, Juristerei. . . durchaus studiert mit heissem Bemühn. . ." What the hero utters in the first person, a member of the audience experiences in the third person. And this transposition, occurring in the very depths of the experience of reception, stylistically aligns the experienced discourse with narrative.

Now, if the listener should want to transmit the speech of Faust, which he had heard and experienced, to another, a third person, he will either quote it in direct form or in indirect form. But if he should desire to summon up for himself in his own mind the living impression of the scene experienced, he will recall it as: "Faust hat nun, ach! Philosophie. ." or, inasmuch as it is a case of impressions in the past, "Faust hatte nun, ach!. . ."

Thus, according to Lorck, quasi-direct discourse is a form for the direct depiction of the experiencing of another's speech, a form for summoning up a living

---

2. *Herrn Gosch ging es schlecht:* mit einer schönen und grossen Armbewegung wies er die Annahme zurück, er könne zu den Glücklichen gehören. *Das beschwerliche Greisenalter nahte heran, es war da, wie gesagt, seine Grube war geschaufelt. Er konnte abends kaum noch sein Glas Grog zum Munde führen, ohne die Hälfte zu verschütten, so machte der Teufel seinen Arm zittern. Da nützte kein Fluchen. . . Der Wille triumphierte nicht mehr* [*Ibid.*].

3. Nun kreutzte Doktor Mantelsack im Stehen die Beine und blätterte in seinem Notizbuch. Hanno Buddenbrook sah vornüber gebeugt und rang unter dem Tisch die Hände. *Das B, der Buchstabe B war an der Reihe! Gleich würde sein Name ertönen, und er würde einen Skandal geben, eine laute, schreckliche Katastrophe, so guter Laune der Ordinarius auch sein mochte. . . Die Sekunden dehnten sich martervoll. "Buddenbrook.".* . . Jetzt sagte er *"Buddenbrook.".* . .

"Edgar" sagte Doktor Mantelsack. . . [*Ibid.*].

impression of that speech and, on that account, of little use for conveying that speech to a third person. Indeed, if quasi-direct discourse were used for that purpose, the reporting act would lose its communicative character and would make it appear as if the person were talking to himself or hallucinating. Hence, as one would expect, quasi-direct discourse is unusable in conversational language and meant only to serve aims of artistic depiction. There, in its proper function, quasi-direct discourse has enormous stylistic significance.

Indeed, for an artist in process of creation, the figures of his fantasies are the realest of realities; he not only sees them, he hears them, as well. He does not make them speak (as in direct discourse), he hears them speaking. And this living impression of voices heard as if in a dream can be directly expressed only in the form of quasi-direct discourse. It is fantasy's own form. And that explains why it was in the fable world of La Fontaine that the form was first given tongue and why it is the favorite device of such artists as Balzac and especially Flaubert, artists wholly able to immerse and lose themselves in the created world of their own fantasies.

And the artist, when he uses this form, also addresses himself only to the reader's fantasy. It is not his aim to communicate facts or the content of thought with its help; he desires only to convey his impressions directly, to arouse in the reader's mind living figures and representations. He addresses himself not to the reader's intellect, but to his imagination. Only the reasoning and analyzing intellect can take the position that the author is speaking in quasi-direct discourse; for the living fantasy, it is the hero who speaks. Fantasy is the mother of the form.

Lorck's basic idea, an idea he expatiates upon in other works of his,[6] amounts to the point that *the creative role in language belongs not to the intellect but to fantasy.* Only forms that fantasy has already created and that are finished, inert products abandoned by its living spirit come under the command of the intellect. The intellect itself creates nothing.

Language, in Lorck's view, is not ready-made being (*ergon*) but eternal becoming and living occurrence (*energeia*). Language is not a means or an instrument for achieving extralinguistic goals but a living organism with its own goal, which it bears within itself and which it realizes also within itself. And this creative self-sufficiency of language is implemented by linguistic fantasy. In language, fantasy feels itself at home, in its vital native element. Language, for fantasy, is not a means, but flesh of its flesh and blood of its blood. The play of language for the sake of play suffices for fantasy. Writers such as Bally approach language from the angle of the intellect and, therefore, are incapable of understanding those forms which are still alive in language, in which the pulse of becoming still

6. *Passé défini, imparfait, passé indéfini.* Eine grammatischpsychologische Studie von E. Lorck.

beats and which have not yet been transformed into a means for intellectual use. That is why Bally failed to grasp the uniqueness of quasi-direct discourse and, discovering no logical coherence in it, excluded it from language.

Lorck attempts to understand and interpret the form of the imperfect tense in quasi-direct discourse from the point of view of fantasy. He distinguishes "Défini-Denkakte" and "Imparfait-Denkakte." The distinction between these acts runs not along lines of their conceptual content, but along lines of the very form of their effectuation. With the *Défini*, our view projects outward into the world of conceived artifacts and contents; with the *Imparfait* our view plunges inward—into the world of thought in process of generation and formation.

"Défini-Denkakten" bear a character of factual ascertainment; "Imparfait-Denkakten"—that of felt experience, impression. Through them, fantasy itself recreates the living past.

Lorck analyzes the following example:

> L'Irlande poussa un grand cri de soulagement, mais la Chambre des lords, six jours plus tard, *repoussait* le bill: Gladstone *tombait* [*Revue des deux Mondes*, 1900, Mai, p. 159].

If, he says, the two cases of the imperfect were to be replaced by the definite past, we would be very sensible of a difference. *Gladstone tombait* is colored in an emotive tone, whereas *Gladstone tomba* would have the sound of a dry businesslike communiqué. In the first case, thought lingers, as it were, over its object and over itself. But what fills the consciousness here is not the idea of Gladstone's fall, but a sense of the momentousness of what has happened. "La Chambre des lords repoussait le bill" is a different matter. Here a sort of anxious suspense about the consequences of the event is established: the imperfect in "repoussait" expresses tense expectation. One need only utter the whole sentence aloud to detect these special features in the psychic orientation of the speaker. The last syllable of "repoussait" is pronounced with high pitch expressing tension and expectation. This tension finds resolution and release, as it were, in "Gladstone tombait." The imperfect in both instances is emotively colored and permeated with fantasy; it does not so much establish the fact of, but rather lingeringly experiences and recreates, the action denoted. Herein consists the significance of the imperfect for quasi-direct discourse. In the atmosphere created by the form, the definite past would have been impossible.

Such is Lorck's conception; he himself calls his analysis investigation in the field of the linguistic psyche (*Sprachseele*). This field (*"das Gebiet der Sprachseelenforschung"*) was, according to Lorck, opened up by Karl Vossler. And it was in Vossler's footsteps that Lorck followed in his study.

Lorck examined the question in its static, psychological dimensions. Gertraud Lerch, in an article published in 1922, using the same Vosslerite grounds, endeavors to establish its broad historical perspectives. Her study contains a number of extremely valuable observations, and we shall, therefore, stop to consider it in some detail.

The role assigned to fantasy in Lorck's conception is played by empathy (*Einfühlung*) in Lerch's. It is empathy that finds adequate expression in quasi-direct discourse. A reporting verb ("said," "thought," and the like) is a prerequisite in direct and indirect discourse. In this way, the author places the responsibility for what is said on his character. Thanks to the fact that such a verb is omitted in quasi-direct discourse, the author is able to present the utterances of his characters in a way suggesting that he himself takes them seriously, and that what is at stake is not merely something that was said or thought, but actual facts. This is possible, Lerch claims, only on the basis of the poet's empathy with the creations of his own fantasy, on the basis of his identifying himself with them.

How did this form come about historically? What were the essential historical features underlying its development?

In Old French, psychological and grammatical constructions were far from being as sharply distinguished as they are now. Paratactic and hypotactic components could still be mixed together in a great many different ways. Punctuation was still in its embryonic stage. Therefore, no clearly marked boundaries between direct discourse and indirect discourse existed then. The Old French storyteller was as yet unable to separate the figures of his fantasy from his own "I." He participated in their words and actions from within, operating as their intercessor and advocate. He had not as yet learned to transmit another person's words in their literal, outward shape, eschewing personal involvement and interference. The Old French temperament still stood far removed from dispassionate, cogitative observation and objective judgment. However, this dissolving of narrator into his characters in Old French was not only the result of the storyteller's free choice, but also came about of necessity: firm logical and syntactic forms for distinct, mutual demarcation were lacking. And so, quasi-direct discourse first appears in Old French on the basis of this grammatical deficiency and not as a free stylistic device. Quasi-direct discourse in this instance is the result of the simple grammatical incapacity of the author to separate his own point of view, his own position, from that of his characters.[7]

---

7. Here is a curious passage from *Canticle to St. Eulalie* (second half of the 9th century):

Ell'ent adunet lo suon element;
melz sostendreiet les empedementz
qu'elle perdesse sa Virginitet.
Poros furer morte a grand honestet.

("She gathers her strength: *better that she undergo tortures than lose her virginity.* Thus she died with great honor.")

Here, Lerch asserts, the saint's staunch, unshakable decision chimes with ("klingt zusammen"), the author's passionate stand on her behalf.

In the Middle French of the late Middle Ages, this immersion of oneself in the minds and feelings of others no longer holds true. In the historical writings of the time, very rarely is the *praesens historicum* encountered, and the standpoint of the narrator is kept distinctly apart from the standpoints of the persons depicted. Emotion gives way to the intellect. Reported speech becomes impersonal and colorless, and the narrator's voice is now heard more distinctly in it than the voice of the reported speaker.

After this depersonalizing period comes the heavily marked individualism of the Renaissance. Reported speech once again endeavors to become intuitive. The storyteller once again tries to align himself with his character, to take a more intimate stand in his regard. Characteristic of Renaissance style is the free, fluctuating, psychologically colored, capricious concatenation of grammatical tenses and moods.

In the 17th century, the linguistic irrationalism of the Renaissance was counteracted by the initiation of firm rules governing tense and mood in indirect discourse (thanks especially to Oudin, 1632). A harmonious balance was established between the objective and subjective sides of thought, between referential analysis and expression of personal attitudes. All this did not come about without pressure on the part of the Academy.

The appearance of quasi-direct discourse as a free, consciously used stylistic device was possible only after a background had been created, thanks to the establishment of *consecutio temporum*, against which it could be distinctly perceived. As such, it first appears in La Fontaine and maintains, in the form in which he used it, an equilibrium between the objective and the subjective, as was characteristic for the age of neoclassicism.

The omission of the reporting verb indicates the identification of the narrator with his character and the use of the imperfect (in contrast to the present tense of direct discourse) and the choice of pronouns appropriate to indirect discourse indicate that the narrator maintains his own independent position, that he does not utterly dissolve into his character's experiences.

The device of quasi-direct discourse, which so neatly surmounted the dualism of abstract analysis and unmediated impression, bringing them into harmonious consonance, proved very suitable for the fabulist La Fontaine. Indirect discourse was too analytical and inert. Direct discourse, though able to recreate another person's utterance dramatically, was incapable of creating, at the same time, a stage for that utterance, a mental and emotional milieu for its perception.

While the device served La Fontaine's purpose of congenial empathizing, La Bruyère was able to extract from it acute satirical effects. He depicted his characters neither in the land of fable nor with mild-mannered humor—he invested quasi-direct discourse with his animosity toward them, his superiority over them. He recoils from the creatures he depicts. All of La Bruyère's figures come out ironically refracted through the medium of his mock objectivism.

In Flaubert's case, the device reveals an even more complex nature. Flaubert unflinchingly fixes his regard upon precisely those things which disgust and repel him. But even then he is able to empathize, to identify himself with the hateful and despicable things he portrays. Quasi-direct discourse in Flaubert becomes just as ambivalent and just as turbulent as his own standpoint vis-à-vis his creations: his inner position oscillates between admiration and revulsion. Quasi-direct discourse, with its capacity for conveying simultaneously identification with and independence, distance from one's creations, was an extremely suitable means for embodying this love-hate relation Flaubert maintained toward his characters.

Such are Gertraud Lerch's interesting deliberations on our topic. To her historical sketch of the development of quasi-direct discourse in French, let us add the information supplied by Eugen Lerch about the time of the appearance of this device in German. Quasi-direct discourse is an extremely late development in German. As a deliberate and full-fledged device, it is used for the first time by Thomas Mann in his novel *Buddenbrooks* (1901), apparently under the direct influence of Zola. This "family epic" is narrated by the writer in emotional tones suggesting one of the unassuming members of the Buddenbrook clan who reminisces about, and in reminiscing vividly reexperiences, the whole history of the family. To this we may add our own remark that in his latest novel, *Der Zauberberg* (1924), Thomas Mann provides us with a still subtler and more profound utilization of the device.

To our knowledge, nothing new and nothing else of any weight has been said on the issue under investigation here. Let us now turn to a critical analysis of the views expressed by Lorck and Lerch.

In the studies of both Lorck and Lerch, a consistent and emphatic individualistic subjectivism is pitted against Bally's hypostasizing objectivism. The individual, subjective critical awareness of speakers underlies the notion of linguistic psyche. Language in all its manifestations becomes expression of individual psychic forces and individual ideational intentions. The generation of language turns out to be the process of generation of mind and soul in individual speakers.

The Vosslerites' individualistic subjectivism in explanation of our concrete phenomenon is just as unacceptable as Bally's abstract objectivism. The fact is, after all, that the speaking personality, its subjective designs and intentions, and its conscious stylistic stratagems do not exist outside their material objectification in language. Without a way of revealing itself in language, be it only in inner speech, personality does not exist either for itself or for others; it can illuminate and take cognizance in itself of only that for which there is objective, illuminating material, the materialized light of consciousness in the form of established words, value judgments, and accents. The inner subjective personality with its own self-awareness does not exist as a material fact, usable as a basis for causal explanation, but it exists as an ideologeme. The inner personality, with all its subjective intentions and all its inner depths, is nothing but an ideologeme—an

ideologeme that is vague and fluid in character until it achieves definition in the
more stable and more elaborated products of ideological creativity. Therefore,
it is nonsense to try to explain ideological phenomena and forms with the aid
of subjective psychic factors and intentions: that would mean explaining an ideologeme of greater clarity and precision with another ideologeme of a vaguer,
more muddled character. Language lights up the inner personality and its con-
sciouness; language creates them and endows them with intricacy and profundity—and it does not work the other way. Personality is itself generated through
language, not so much, to be sure, in the abstract forms of language, but rather
in the ideological themes of language. Personality, from the standpoint of its
inner, subjective content, is a theme of language, and this theme undergoes development and variation within the channel of the more stable constructions of
language. Consequently, *a word is not an expression of inner personality; rather,*
inner personality is an expressed or inwardly impelled word. And the word is an
expression of social intercourse, of the social interaction of material personalities,
of producers. The conditions of that thoroughly material intercourse are what
determine and condition the kind of thematic and structural shape that the inner
personality will receive at any given time and in any given environment; the ways
in which it will come to self-awareness; the degree of richness and surety this
self-awareness will achieve; and how it will motivate and evaluate its actions. The
generation of the inner consciousness will depend upon the generative process
of language, in terms, of course, of language's grammatical and concrete ideological structure. The inner personality is generated along with language, in the comprehensive and concrete sense of the word, as one of its most important and
most profound themes. The generation of language, meanwhile, is a factor in the
generative process of social communication, a factor inseparable from that communication and its material base. The material base determines differentiation
in a society, its sociopolitical order; it organizes society hierarchically and de-
ploys persons interacting within it. Thereby are the place, time, conditions, forms,
and means of verbal communication determined and, by the same token, the
vicissitudes of the individual utterance in any given period in the development of
language, the degree of its inviolability, the degree of differentiality in perception of its various aspects, the nature of its ideational and verbal individualization. And this finds expression above all in stable constructions of language, in
language patterns and their modifications. Here the speaking personality exists
not as an amorphous theme but as a more stable construction (to be sure, concretely this theme is inextricably bound up with the specific thematic content
appropriate to it). Here, in the forms of reported speech, language itself reacts
to personality as the bearer of the word.

But what do the Vosslerites do? They provide explanations that merely put
the comparatively stable structural reflection of speaking personality into loose
thematic terms that translate events of social generation, events of history, into

the language of individual motivations, extremely subtle and genuine though they may be. They provide an ideology of ideology. However, the objective, material factors in these ideologies—both in forms of language and in the subjective motivations for their usage—remain outside their field of investigation. We do not contend that the endeavor to ideologize ideology is completely worthless. On the contrary, sometimes it is very important to thematicize a formal construction in order to gain access to its objective roots—those roots, after all, are common to both aspects. The keen and animated interest in ideology that the idealist Vosslerites have introduced into linguistics does help elucidate certain aspects of language that had turned inert and opaque in the hands of abstract objectivism. And we owe them gratitude for that. They teased and worried the ideological nerve in language when language had at times, in the hands of certain linguists, begun to resemble inanimate nature. However, they did not find their way to a real, objective explanation of language. They came close to the life of history, but not to an explanation of history; they approached the ever-seething, ever-moving surface of history, but not its deep, underlying motive forces. It is symptomatic that Lorck, in a letter to Eugen Lerch that is appended to his book, goes so far as to make the following somewhat surprising statement. After having described the inertness and intellectualist sclerosis of French, he adds the comment: "There is only one possibility for its rejuvenation: the proletariat must take over command of the word from the bourgeoisie (Für sie gibt es nur eine Möglichkeit der Verjüngung: anstelle des Bourgeois muss der Proletarier zu Worte kommen)."

How is this to be connected with the overriding, creative role of fantasy in language? Is a member of the proletariat such a fantasizer, then?

Surely Lorck had something else in mind. He probably means that the proletariat will bring with it new forms of socioverbal intercourse, new forms of verbal interaction of speakers, and a whole new world of social intonations and accents. It will also bring with it a new linguistic truth. Probably that or something like it was what Lorck had in mind when he made his assertion. But there is no reflection of this in his theory. As for fantasizing, a bourgeois is no worse a hand at it than a proletarian, and has more spare time for it, to boot.

Lorck's individualistic subjectivism in application to our concrete question makes itself felt in the incapacity of his conception to reflect the dynamics of the interrelationship between reporting and reported speech. By no means does quasi-direct discourse express a passive impression received from another's utterance. It expresses, instead, an active orientation, and not one that merely amounts to a shift of person from first to third, but one that imposes upon the reported utterance its own accents, which collide and interfere with the accents in the reported utterance. Nor can we agree with Lorck in his contention that quasi-direct discourse is the form of reported speech closest to direct reception and experience of another person's speech. Each form of reported speech perceives the speech to be reported in its own particular way. Gertraud Lerch seems to have some grasp of the dynamics involved, but she expresses it in terms of subjective psychology. Both writers, therefore, attempt to flatten out a three-dimensional phenomenon, as it were. In the objective linguistic phenomenon of quasi-direct discourse, we have a combination not of empathy and distancing within the confines of an individual psyche, but of the character's accents (empathy) and the author's accents (distancing) within the confines of one and the same linguistic construction.

Both Lorck and Lerch alike fail to take into account one factor of extreme importance for the understanding of our phenomenon: the value judgment inherent in every living word and brought out by the accentuation and expressive intonation of an utterance. Message in speech does not exist outside its living and concrete accentuation and intonation. In quasi-direct discourse, we recognize another person's utterance not so much in terms of its message, abstractly considered, but above all in terms of the reported character's accentuation and intonation, in terms of the evaluative orientation of his speech.

We perceive the author's accents and intonations being interrupted by these value judgments of another person. And that is the way, as we know, in which quasi-direct discourse differs from substituted discourse, where no new accents vis-à-vis the surrounding authorial context appear.

Let us now return to examples of quasi-direct discourse from Russian literature.

Here is a sample of an extremely characteristic type in this regard, again from Puškin's *Poltava*:

> Pretending grief, Mazeppa raises loud his humble voice unto the Tsar. *"God knows and all the world can see, he, hapless hetman, twenty years has served the Tsar with loyal heart; bestrewn with boundless favours and most wondrously advanced. . . . What blindness, what folly animosity would be! Is it thinkable that he, who stands upon the threshold to the tomb, would now commence to school himself in treason and becloud his honest name? And did not he indignantly refuse his aid to Stanislaw; appalled, reject the Ukrainian crown and send the Tsar the pact and letters of the plot, as was his duty? Did not he turn a deaf ear unto the blandishments of Khan and Tsargrad Sultan? Aflame with zeal, he gladly plied his mind and sword in contests with the White Tsar's foes, he spared no pains nor life itself, and now a vicious enemy his old grey hairs has covered all in shame. And who? Iskra and Kočubej! Who were so long his friends!. ."* And with bloodthirsty tears, in icy insolence, the villain demands their punishment. . . Whose punishment? Implacable old man! Whose daughter is in his embrace? But the murmurings of his heart he coldly stills. . . [italics added].

Syntax and style in this passage, on the one hand, are determined by the evaluative tones of Mazeppa's humility and tearful plea and, on the other hand, this "tearful plea" is subjected to the evaluative orientation of the author's context, his narrative accents which, in the given instance, are colored in tones of indignation that eventually erupts in the rhetorical question: "Whose punishment? Implacable old man! Whose daughter is in his embrace?"

It would be entirely possible to recite this passage aloud and convey the double intonation of each of its words, i.e., indignantly reveal the hypocrisy of Mazeppa's plea through the very reading of it. What we have here is a fairly simple case with its rhetorical, somewhat primitive and sharply etched intonations. In most cases, however, and especially in that area where quasi-direct discourse has become a massively used device—the area of modern prose fiction—transmission by voice of evaluative interference would be impossible. Furthermore, the very kind of development quasi-direct discourse has undergone is bound up with the transposition of the larger prose genres into a silent register, i.e., for silent reading. Only this "silencing" of prose could have made possible the multileveledness and voice-defying complexity of intonational structures that are so characteristic for modern literature.

An example of this kind of interference of two speech acts which cannot be conveyed adequately by voice is the following passage from Dostoevskij's *The Idiot:*

> And why did he [Prince Myškin] avoid going straight up to him and turn away as if he didn't notice anything, although their eyes had met. (Yes, their eyes had met! And they had looked at one another.) Didn't he himself, after all, want not long ago to take him by the arm and go with him *there?* Didn't he himself, after all, want to go to him tomorrow and say that he had been to see her? Didn't he himself, after all, renounce his demon on his way there, in mid-course, when suddenly joy flooded his soul? Or was there indeed something or other in Rogožin, that is, in *today's* whole image of the man, in the sum total of his words, gestures, behavior, looks, that might justify the prince's terrible forebodings and the infuriating insinuations of his demon? Something or other of the sort that makes itself felt but is difficult to analyze and relate, something impossible to pin down with sufficient reasons. But something nevertheless that produces, despite all the difficulty and the impossibility, a perfectly cogent and irresistible impression that unwittingly turns into the most absolute conviction. Conviction that what? (Oh, how the prince was tormented by the monstrosity, the "baseness" of that conviction, of "that vile foreboding," and how he reproached himself!).

Let us now devote a few words to a consideration of the very important and interesting problem of the *phonic embodiment of reported speech displayed by the author's context.*

The difficulty of evaluative, expressive intonation consists here in the constant shifting from the evaluative purview of the author to that of the character and back again.

In what cases and to what limits can an author act out his character? The absolute of acting out we understand to be not only a change of expressive intonation—a change equally possible within the confines of a single voice, a single consciousness—but also a change of voice in terms of the whole set of features individualizing that voice, a change of persona ("mask") in terms of a whole set of individualizing traits of facial expression and gesticulation, and, finally, the complete self-consistency of this voice and persona throughout the entire acting out of the role. After all, into that self-enclosed, individual world there can no longer be any infusion or spillover of the author's intonations. As a result of the self-consistency of the other voice and persona, there is no possibility for gradation in shifting from the author's context to reported speech and from reported speech to author's context. The reported speech will begin to sound as if it were in a play where there is no embracing context and where the character's lines confront other lines by other characters without any grammatical concatenation. Thus relations between reported speech and authorial context, via absolute acting out, take a shape analogous to the relations between alternating lines in dialogue. Thereby the author is put on a level with his character, and their relationship is dialogized. From all this, it necessarily follows that the absolute acting out of reported speech, where a work of fiction is read aloud, is admissible only in the rarest cases. Otherwise an inevitable conflict arises with the basic aesthetic design of the context. It goes without saying that these exceedingly rare cases can involve only linear and moderately picturesque modifications of the direct discourse construction. If the author's retorting remarks intersect the direct discourse or if too dense a shadow from the author's evaluative context falls upon it, absolute acting out is impossible.

However, another possibility is partial acting out (without transformation), which permits making gradual intonational transitions between authorial context and reported speech and, in some cases, given double-faced modifications, permits accomodating all intonations within one voice. To be sure, such a possibility is viable only in cases analogous to the ones we have cited. Rhetorical questions and exclamations often carry out the function of switching from one tone to another.

It remains only for us to sum up our analysis of quasi-direct discourse and, at the same time, to sum up the whole third section of our study. We shall be brief: the substance of the matter is in the argument itself, and we shall refrain from rehashing it.

We have conducted an inquiry into the chief forms of reported speech. We were not concerned with providing abstract grammatical descriptions; we endeavored instead to find in those forms a document of how language at this or that period of its development has perceived the words and personality of another addresser. The point we had in mind throughout was that the vicissitudes of utterance and speaking personality in language reflect the social vicissitudes of verbal interaction, of verbal-ideological communication, in their most vital tendencies.

The word as the ideological phenomenon par excellence exists in continuous generation and change; it sensitively reflects all social shifts and alterations. In the vicissitudes of the word are the vicissitudes of the society of word-users. But the dialectical generation of the word is susceptible of investigation by various routes. One can study the *generation of ideas,* that is, the history of ideology in the exact sense—the *history of knowledge,* as the history of the generation of truth (since truth is eternal only as eternally generated truth); the *history of literature,* as the generation of artistic veracity. That is one route. Another, intimately connected and in close collaboration with the first, is the study of the *generation of language itself,* as *ideological material,* as the *medium for ideological reflection of existence,* since the reflection of the refraction of existence in the human consciousness comes about only in and through the word. The generation of language cannot be studied, of course, in complete disregard of the social existence refracted in it and of the refracting powers of the socioeconomic conditions. The generation of the word cannot be studied in disregard of the generation of truth and artistic veracity in the word and of the human society for whom that truth and veracity exist. Thus these two routes, in their constant interaction with one another, study the *reflection and refraction of the generation of nature and history in the generation of the word.*

But there is still another route: the *reflection of the social generation of word in word itself,* with its two branches: the *history of the philosophy of the word* and *the history of word in word.* It is precisely in this latter direction that our own study lies. We are perfectly well aware of the shortcomings of our study and can only hope that the very posing of the problem of the word in word has crucial importance. The history of truth, the history of artistic veracity, and the history of language can benefit considerably from a study of the refractions of their basic phenomenon—the *concrete utterance*—in constructions of language itself.

And now a few additional words in conclusion about quasi-direct discourse and the social tendency it expresses.

The emergence and development of quasi-direct discourse must be studied in close association with the development of other picturesque modifications of direct discourse and indirect discourse. We shall then be in a position to see that quasi-direct discourse lies on the main road of development of the modern European languages, that it signalizes some crucial turning point in the social vicissitudes of the utterance. The victory of extreme forms of the picturesque style in reported speech is not, of course, to be explained in terms either of psychological factors or the artist's own individual stylistic purposes, but is explainable in terms of the *general, far-reaching subjectivization of the ideological word-utterance.* No longer is it a monument, nor even a document, of a substantive ideational position; it makes itself felt only as expression of an adventitious, subjective state. Typifying and individualizing coatings of the utterance have reached such an intense degree of differentiation in the linguistic consciousness that they have completely overshadowed and relativized an utterance's ideational core, the responsible social position implemented in it. The utterance has virtually ceased to be an object for serious ideational consideration. The categorical word, the word "from one's own mouth," the *declaratory* word remains alive only in scientific writings. In all other fields of verbal-ideological creativity, what predominates is not the "outright" but the "contrived" word. All verbal activity in these cases amounts to piecing together "other persons' words" and "words seemingly from other persons." Even the humanities have developed a tendency to supplant responsible statements about an issue with a depiction of the issue's contemporary state of affairs, including computation and inductive adducing of "the prevailing point of view at the present time," which is sometimes even taken as the most solid kind of "solution" to the issue. All this bespeaks an alarming instability and uncertainty of ideological word. Verbal expression in literature, rhetoric, philosophy, and humanistic studies has become the realm of "opinions," of out and out opinions, and even the paramount feature of these opinions is not *what* actually is "opined" in them but *how*—in what individual or typical way—the "opining" is done. This stage in the vicissitudes of the word in present-day bourgeois Europe and here in the Soviet Union (in our case, up to very recent times) can be characterized as the stage of *transformation of the word into a thing*, the stage of *depression in the thematic value of the word*. The ideologues of this process, both here and in Western Europe, are the formalistic movements in poetics, linguistics, and philosophy of language. One hardly need mention here what the underlying social factors explaining this process are, and one hardly need repeat Lorck's well-founded assertion as to the only ways whereby a revival of the ideological word can come about—the word with its theme intact, the word permeated with confident and categorical social value judgment, the word that really means and takes responsibility for what it says.

On the First Russian Prolegomena to Semiotics

Ladislav Matejka

1. Modern philosophical speculation about the nature of signs and about their role in social communication has a tradition in Graeco-Roman civilization going back to remote antiquity. This tradition embraces both Platonic and Aristotelian reasoning on the relationship between language sounds and the human mind. It involves the Stoics and their dialectical approach to the opposition between the signifying and the signified, and, furthermore, it maintains a vital connection with the medieval semiotics, which regarded signs as something material standing for something spiritual and considered human words as the most important signs among signs.

In Russia, the modern inquiry into the nature of verbal signs was stimulated by the brilliant linguists of the Kazan school, particularly by Baudouin de Courtenay, whose phenomenological observations about the systematic connection between sound and meaning found many talented followers in the major Russian academic centers at the beginning of the 20th century. Moreover, the Russian science of signs was given a solid base by the scholarly, as well as pedagogical, contributions of the prominent Moscow professor, F. F. Fortunatov, for whom the notion that human language is a system of signs was one of the most fundamental concepts of linguistics. Also the classic English empiricist, John Locke, whose doctrine on signs subsequently influenced American semiotics, has to be considered a powerful intellectual source in prerevolutionary Russia, where the Anglo-Saxon philosophers found many attentive students among both Marxists and non-Marxists. However, the most decisive impact on modern Russian semiotics was, no doubt, produced by Ferdinand de Saussure, the spiritual founder of the Geneva school of linguistics.

Young Russian linguists in the years just prior to the revolution became acquainted with Saussure not only through his posthumous *Cours de linguistique générale* [*Course in General Linguistics*], but also through the interpretation of

Saussurian teaching by Sergej Karcevskij, who returned to Russia in 1917 after several years of study in Geneva. As Roman Jakobson recollects in his *Selected Writings,*

> It was in those years that students of psychology and linguistics in our university were passionately discussing the philosophers' newest attempts toward a phenomenology of language and of signs in general; we learned to sense the delicate distinction between the *signatum* (the signified) and the *denotatum* (the referred-to); hence to assign an intrinsically linguistic position, first to the *signatum* and then, by inference, to its inalienable counterpart as well—that is, to the *signans.*[1]

Russian linguistics in the early 1920s clearly reflects the impact of various aspects of Saussure's *Course.* References to Saussure and to his influence appear, critically filtered, in Jakobson's book on Czech versification published in 1923. The same year, references to Saussure and his Geneva school were made repeatedly in *Russkaja rěc'* [Russian language], a compendium of studies by several young Russian linguists mutually associated (as the editor of the volume, Lev Ščerba, suggests in his introductory footnote) by their common dependence on the linguistic teaching of Baudouin de Courtenay.[2] Moreover, in 1923, the young syntactician, M. N. Peterson, published a lucid outline of Saussure's fundamental concepts in the journal *Pečat' i revoljucija* [The press and the revolution].[3] During the 1920s, the impact of Saussure, particularly on the students, and the students of the students, of Baudouin de Courtenay, dominated to such an extent that V. N. Vološinov was apparently very close to the truth when he stated: "It can be claimed that the majority of Russian thinkers in linguistics are under the determinative influence of Saussure and his disciples, Bally and Sechehaye."

In Saussure's *Course,* as we know, the concept of sign is viewed as the very pivot of verbal communication and of any communication of meaning in general. "Language," he says, "is a system of signs that express ideas."[4] Although Saussure distinguishes various sign systems, human language is for him the most important of them all. In his interpretation, the semiotic nature of human language necessarily implies its social character. Language as a system is a social institution. As Saussure puts it, "It exists only by virtue of a sort of contract signed by the members of a community; the individual must always serve an apprenticeship in order to learn the functioning of language; a child assimilates it only gradually."[5] Since language is only one among several semiotic systems, Saussure considers linguistics a branch of the general science of signs.[6] Using Greek

1. "Retrospect," *Selected Writings,* I. p. 631. 's-Gravenhage: Mouton, 1962.
2. Edited by L. V. Ščerba, *Russkaja rec'* (Petrograd, 1923), p. 11.
3. M. N. Peterson, "Obščaja linguistika," *Pečat' i revoljucija,* 6, (1923), pp. 26-32.
4. Ferdinand de Saussure, *Course in General Linguistics,* translated by Wade Baskin, p. 16. McGraw-Hill, New York, 1959.
5. *Ibid.,* p. 14.
6. *Ibid.,* p. 77.

sēmeîon (sign) as his derivational base, he calls the envisaged science of signs *semiology*, as distinct from John Locke's term *semiotic,* subsequently adapted and ingeniously developed by Charles Sanders Peirce.

There can hardly be any doubt that Saussure's emphasis on the semiotic nature of human language and on its intrinsically social character found, in Valentin Vološinov, a mightily impressed albeit critical reader. As a matter of fact, the essential part of Vološinov's *Marxism and the Philosophy of Language* could be considered the first extensive Russian prolegomenon to semiotics, enthusiastically elaborating the binary concept of sign and the notion of the social basis of semiotics in general. "Everything ideological possesses meaning," claims Vološinov in the opening chapter of his book. "It represents, depicts, or stands for something lying outside itself; in other words, it is a sign; without signs, there is no ideology." Consequently, the study of signs is for Vološinov a study of ideology, and the philosophy of language is a philosophy of sign.

Developing Saussure's observations about the origin of language in the community of speakers ("masse parlante"), Vološinov insists that signs can arise only on an interindividual territory. "It is essential," he says, "that they [the individuals] compose a group (a social unit); only then can the medium of signs take shape between them." In sharp distinction from Saussure, however, he does not consider signs as being basically psychological in nature. While for Saussure language "is a system of signs in which the only essential thing is the union of meaning and sound images, and in which both parts of the sign are psychological,"[7] for Vološinov "a sign is a phenomenon of the external world." In his view, the localization of signs in the psyche would change semiotic into the study of consciousness and its laws. He is unwilling to neglect the physical properties of the sign and to treat them as if they were "merely technical means for the realization of the inner effect, which is understanding." While Saussure regards his semiology as "a part of social psychology and consequently of general psychology,"[8] for Vološinov the study of signs "does not depend on psychology to any extent and need not be grounded in it." On the contrary, he is convinced that objective psychology has to be grounded in the study of signs. In his dialectical approach, the binary character of each sign implies that the physical and meaningful aspects are inseparable and cannot be studied in isolation from one another, precisely because the unity of the binary opposition is the basis of semioticity.

Ferdinand de Saussure, faithfully following the spirit of Cartesian dualism, emphatically insists on a clear-cut separation between the actual speech act and the abstract system of norms internalized by the linguistic competence of the speakers. "In separating language from speaking," he says, "we are at the same time separating (1) what is social from what is individual, and (2) what is essen-

7. *Ibid.,* p. 15.
8. *Ibid.,* p. 16.

tial from what is accessory and more or less accidental.''[9] The epistemological implications of such an analytic divorce of language system (*la langue*) from speech act (*la parole*) became a major challenge for the Russian students of Saussure. Not all of them were willing to embrace the methodological consequences of the two routes that resulted from Saussure's divorcing language from speaking. In obvious opposition to Saussure's insistence that "we must choose between two routes that cannot be followed simultaneously."[10] Jurij Tynjanov and Roman Jakobson in 1928 proposed that the principle *relating* these two categories (i.e., *la langue* and *la parole*) must be elaborated.[11] Also Vološinov, applying his dialectical approach, regarded the speech act and the language system as an indivisible coupling that cannot be studied by isolating one pole from the other. Throughout his entire book he makes it clear that the concrete utterance cannot be adequately handled without simultaneously taking into account the system of language. And conversely, the language system, in his opinion, cannot be analytically grasped without the simultaneous consideration of concrete utterances. Or, as he puts it, "the actual reality of language-speech is not the abstract system of linguistic forms, not the isolated monologic utterance, and not the psychophysiological act of its implementation, but the social event of verbal interaction implemented in an utterance or utterances." Thus linguistic inquiry is placed by Vološinov into a sociological framework where not only the opposition between language and speech has to be taken into account, but also the opposition between speaker and hearer. Within such a complex analytic model, neither the speaker's nor the hearer's role is favored; they have to be considered complementary and mutually dependent in the process whereby the abstract language system is deployed to execute the concrete utterance. While Saussure's dualism breaks the complexity of the semiotic operation apart in order to facilitate its analysis, Vološinov's dialectical predilection is to try to supersede the inner duality by a single unifying structure. In explicit opposition to Saussure's divorce between system and utterance, Vološinov insists that:

1. Ideology may not be divorced from the material reality of sign (i.e., by locating it in the "consciousness" or other vague and elusive regions).
2. Sign may not be divorced from the concrete forms of social intercourse (seeing that sign is part of organized social intercourse and cannot exist, as such, outside it, reverting to a mere physical artifact).
3. Communication and the forms of communication may not be divorced from their material basis.

9. *Ibid.*, p. 14.
10. *Ibid.*, p. 19.
11. Cf., Jurij Tynjanov and Roman Jakobson, "Problemy izučenija literatury i jazyka," *Novyj Lef*, **12** (1928), p. 36 ["Problems in the Study of Literature and Language," *Readings in Russian Poetics*, edited by L. Matejka and K. Pomorska, p. 79. MIT Press, Cambridge, 1971.]

Saussure's systematic language versus speech bifurcation virtually implied the necessity of imposing strict boundaries between the synchronic aspect of a language system and the history of the language. "The opposition between the two viewpoints, the synchronic and diachronic," he says, "is absolute and allows no compromise."[12] Accordingly, the study of language is divided by Saussure into two distinct parts, defined in the *Course* as follows:

> *Synchronic linguistics* will be concerned with the logical and psychological relations that bind together coexisting terms and form a system in the collective mind of speakers.
>
> *Diachronic linguistics*, on the contrary, will study relations that bind together successive terms not perceived by the collective mind but substituted for each other without forming a system.[13]

It was precisely this separation of synchronic and diachronic linguistics that became a major topic of methodological controversy in Russia in the 1920s. In 1922, Sergej Karcevskij applied the Saussurian synchronic approach to the description of the Russian verbal system and used as the epigraph to his article Saussure's dictum: "La langue est un système dont toutes les parties peuvent et doivent être considerées dans leur solidarité synchronique."[14] The following year, in 1923, V. V. Vinogradov, acknowledging the methodological stimulus of Saussure, Baudouin de Courtenay, and Karcevskij, proposed the application of a rigorous synchronic method to the analysis of style in verbal art. In his proposal, the primary task of every stylistic analysis is to inquire into the specific system of linguistic means and their organization as used by a given writer; such a task categorically requires, according to Vinogradov, a classification of elements and an exhaustive description of the stylistic forms and their functions.[15] Hence, the very center of Vinogradov's attention is a literary text that is viewed as a concrete corpus of data representing a certain linguistic type and characterizing a special social group (a dialect). The proposed description and classification are, as Vinogradov admits, inevitably static. From this position, which strictly adheres to Saussure's dichotomy of synchrony and diachrony, Vinogradov attacked those followers of the so-called formal method who were unwilling to embrace Saussure's dualistic separation and had insisted that a true explanatory approach had "to overcome statics and discard the absolute."[16]

Among the responses to Saussure's dualistic fallacy and its Russian application, the most outspoken rejection appeared in 1927 in a set of polemic theses,

12. *Course*, p. 83.

13. *Ibid.*, p. 99-100.

14. S. Karcevskij, "Études sur le système verbal du russe contemporain," *Slavia*, 1, (1922), p. 242.

15. Cf., V. V. Vinogradov, O zadačax stilistiki *"Russkaja reč,"* (Petrograd, 1923), p. 286.

16. Roman Jakobson, "Futurizm," *Iskusstvo*, Aug. 2, 1919; cf. his *Selected Writings*, I, p. 651 (1962).

signed by Jurij Tynjanov and Roman Jakobson. "Pure synchronism now proves to be an illusion," the authors assert. "Every synchronic system has its past and its future as inseparable structural elements of the system." While Saussure claims that "everything that relates to the static side of our science is synchronic and everything that has to do with evolution is diachronic,"[17] Tynjanov and Jakobson proclaim:

> The opposition between synchrony and diachrony was an opposition between the concept of system and the concept of evolution; it loses its importance in principle as soon as we recognize that every system necessarily exists as evolution, whereas, on the other hand, evolution is inescapably of a systematic nature.[18]

For Jakobson, the rejection of Saussure's fallacy became one of the recurrent themes of his scholarly career. In 1928, he renewed his attack on Saussure's fallacious dualism by stating:

> F. de Saussure and his school broke a new trail in static linguistics, but as to the field of language history, they remained in the neogrammarian rut. Saussure's teaching that sound changes are destructive factors, fortuitous and blind, limits the active role of the speech community to sensing each given stage of deviations from the customary linguistic pattern as an orderly system. This antinomy between synchronic and diachronic linguistic studies should be overcome by a transformation of historical phonetics into the history of the phonemic system."[19]

The tenor of this argument reappears, essentially unchanged, 40 years later in Jakobson's "Retrospect" to the second volume of his *Selected Writings* (1971)

> According to Saussure's *Cours*, the inner duality of synchrony and diachrony threatens linguistics with particular difficulties and calls for a complete separation of the two facets: what can be investigated is either the coexistent relations within the linguistic system "d'où tout intervention du temps est exclue" or single successive changes without any reference to the system. In other words, Saussure anticipated and announced a new, structural approach to linguistic synchrony but followed the old, atomizing, neogrammarian dogma in historical linguistics. His fallacious identification of two oppositions—synchrony versus diachrony, and statics versus dynamics—was refuted by post-Saussurian linguistics.[20]

It must be said that not all post-Saussurian linguistics has rejected Saussure's dichotomy of synchrony and diachrony and statics versus dynamics. It certainly prevails in the present revival of Saussurian semiotics in France, particularly in the school of Claude Lévi-Strauss, who himself embraces Saussurian synchrony without reservations. Also, in the United States, Saussure's synchronic approach

17. *Course*, p. 81.
18. *Readings in Russian Poetics*, p.80.
19. *Časopis pro moderní filologii*, XIV (Prague, 1928); *cf.* "The concept of the sound law and the teleological criterion," *Selected Writings*, I, p. 1-2.
20. "Retrospect," *Selected Writings*, II, p. 721, The Hague, 1971.

still dominates linguistic structuralism whether post-Bloomfieldian or neo-Saussurian. On the other hand, the rejection of Saussure's dualism by representatives of the Russian school of formalism was fully adopted by the Prague school of structuralism and became a characteristic trait of their semiotic studies. The rejection of Saussure's dualism also became typical for Vološinov's philosophy of language and for Baxtin's Leningrad school in general.

While Saussure suggests that the synchronic system exists in the collective mind of speakers, for Vološinov a synchronic system is not a real entity at all. "From an objective point of view," he asserts, "no such system exists at any real instant of historical time." A synchronic system is in his opinion nothing more than a descriptive construct of an analyst which is handy for the bookkeeping of his observations:

> "That system is merely an abstraction arrived at with a good deal of trouble and with a definite cognitive and practical focus of attention; the system of language is the product of deliberation on language, and deliberation by no means of the kind carried out by the consciousness of the native speaker and by no means of the kind carried out for the immediate purpose of speaking."

The static nature of Saussure's synchronic model and its artificial separation from the ceaslessly changing continuum of the creative flow of language was correctly interpreted by Vološinov as the revival of the Cartesian spirit in the area of linguistic investigation. As a dialectician, he objected to the segregating tendency of Cartesian dualism and tried to see evolutionary forces and systematization as a continuous interaction which is indivisible, albeit antithetic. At the same time, however, Vološinov was fully aware of the impact of Saussure's Cartesianism on his contemporaries. "Saussure's views on history," he readily admits, "are extremely characteristic for the spirit of rationalism that continues to hold sway in the philosophy of language and that regards history as an irrational force distorting the logical purity of the language system."

2. The static nature of an abstract system of norms, featured in the formalism of Cartesian linguistics, found a persuasive critic in Wilhelm von Humboldt, for whom language was a continuous, incessantly changing generative process. While the tradition of Cartesian linguistics tended to consider every language as a closed, stable system of rules, as a ready-made normative instrument inherited from preceding generations, Humboldt saw it as a natural creative activity of mankind. Although various aspects of Humboldt's observations about language are not fully discernible in the twilight of his grandiose generalizations, nevertheless he was often regarded as a coryphaeus of the Romantic reaction against the era of rationalism, which dominated 17th- and 18th-century linguistics.[21] In Russia, the tradition of Humboldtian linguistics was commonly viewed

21. A diametrically opposite interpretation of von Humboldt appears in Noam Chomsky's *Cartesian Linguistics.* Harper and Row, New York, 1966. See, for example, p. 19: "The Cartesian emphasis on the creative aspect of language use, as the essential and defining char-

as an opposition to the tradition of Cartesian linguistics. Characteristically, the most outspoken follower of the Humboldtian trend in the history of Russian linguistics was the syntactician Alexander Potebnja, the leading theorist of the Russian symbolic movement and the principal target of the generation inspired by Ferdinand de Saussure. In the 1920s, the tradition of Humboldtian linguistics was viewed in direct contrast to the modern trends in linguistics as pointed out by the Moscow linguist, R. Šor, who in 1927 in "Crisis in contemporary linguistics" arrived at the following conclusion:

> "Language is not an artifact (*ergon*) but a natural and congenital activity of mankind"—
> so claimed the romanticist linguistics of the 19th century. Theoretical linguistics of
> modern times claims otherwise: "Language is not individual activity (*energeia*) but a
> cultural-historical legacy of mankind (*ergon*)."[22]

Thus the Humboldtian emphasis on the creative aspect of human language was identified as a typical expression of romanticism in direct opposition to modern linguistics. For Vološinov, likewise, von Humboldt was an antithesis to Descartes and, in effect, the most prominent antipode of abstract objectivism in European philosophy of language. In distinction from R. Šor, however, Vološinov did not consider the Humboldtian focus on the creative aspect of human language as something irrelevant to linguistic investigation; on the contrary, he conceived it as one of the most important concepts of his own philosophy of language.

In contradistinction to the tradition of the Cartesian linguistics, the Humboldtian linguistics encompasses, according to Vološinov, the need for the true explanation of linguistic phenomena, while descriptive and classifying procedures are viewed as preliminary at best. The Humboldtian emphasis on the creative aspect as the fundamental characteristic of human language is, as Vološinov sees it, in direct contradiction to interest in the inner logic of the system of sign itself, taken as in algebra without adequate relation to the actual reality or to the participants of the communication. The systematic presentation of the grammar, lexicon, and phonetics is for Vološinov nothing more than deliberation on language and speculative exercises in logic, segmentation, classification, abstracting, and algebraization.

Thus, the primary target of linguistic investigation should be exactly that which reveals the creative aspect of human language; and such a task, in Vološinov's view, cannot be fulfilled without adequate study of utterances, that is to

22. R. Šor, "Krizis sovremennoj lingvistiki," *Jafetičeskij sbornik*, V (1927) p. 71 (as quoted by V. N. Vološinov).

---

acteristic of human language, finds its most forceful expression in Humboldt's attempt to develop a comprehensive theory of general linguistics." Also see Chomsky's note 36 (p. 86): "Considered against the background that we are surveying here, it [Humboldt's treatise] seems to mark the terminal point of the development of Cartesian linguistics rather than the beginning of a new era of linguistic thought."

say, without accounting for the creative aspect of human language in its social function. As Vološinov says,

> The task of identifying the real object of study in the philosophy of language is by no means an easy one; with each attempt to delimit the object of investigation, to reduce it to a compact subject-matter complex of definitive and inspectable dimensions, we forfeit the very essence of the thing we are studying—its semiotic and ideological nature.

The semiotic nature of human communication cannot be grasped, as Vološinov sees it, if the novelty of the speech act and its relevance are disregarded as superficial phenomena, as "merely fortuitous refraction and variations or plain and simple distortions of normatively identical forms." In Cartesian linguistics and in the school of abstract objectivism in general, according to Vološinov, the factor of stable self-identity in linguistic forms takes precedence over their mutability, the abstract over the concrete, systematicity over historicity, the forms of isolated components over the property of the entire structure. In Vološinov's view, Cartesian linguistics and its continuation in abstract objectivism rejected the speech act and the resulting utterance as something individual because the abstract system of rules and norms was promoted to the exclusive object of linguistic investigation.

On the other hand, Humboldtian linguistics and its continuation in idealistic subjectivism rejected the static, normative system of rules as artificial deliberation on language and promoted the creative novelty, the stylistic variability of the speech act, to the primary focus of attention. Although Vološinov agrees with the followers of the Humboldtian trend that the study of utterance deserves the full attention of linguistic investigation, he disagrees with the emphasis on the individual character of the utterance and with the attempts to explain the creative aspect of human language in terms of the individual psychic life of the speaker. And precisely for that reason, he rejects certain followers of the Humboldtian tradition, particularly the Vossler school:

> In point of fact, the speech act, or more accurately, its product—the utterance, cannot under any circumstances be considered an individual phenomenon in the precise meaning of the word, and cannot be explained in terms of the individual psychological or psychophysiological conditions of the speaker.

Thus neither Cartesian linguistics nor Humboldtian linguistics and their followers are fully embraced by Vološinov. In his attempt to operate as a dialectician, he sees individualistic subjectivism and abstract objectivism as thesis and antithesis and proposes a dialectical synthesis beyond these opposing trends, a synthesis that would constitute a negation of both thesis and antithesis alike. The true center of linguistic reality for Vološinov is the meaningful speech act, viewed as a social structure in all its aspects vital for semiotic operation.

Dialogue in a broader sense is for Vološinov an exemplary case of verbal interaction displaying, as it does, the most essential features of semiotic operation: not only the speech event with its physical and semantic aspects in relation to another speech event but also the opposition of the participants of the speech event and the conditions of their verbal contact in a given context.

3. Although Vološinov had many harsh comments to make about the Vossler school, he certainly shared with the Vosslerites some of their basic views, including the notion of importance of dialogue as an approach to a more correct understanding of verbal interaction. He particularly singled out Leo Spitzer's book on the Italian conversational language, appreciating its emphasis on the role of speaker and listener in actual conversation.[23] Also Mixail M. Baxtin, whose intellectual bond with Vološinov in the late 1920s was strikingly close, highly prized Spitzer's observations on the essential role of the participants of the speech event in the structure of the utterance. In his study of discourse typology, Baxtin quotes Spitzer:

> When we reproduce in our own speech a portion of what our conversational partner said, a change of tone inevitably occurs if for no other reason than that the addressers have been shifted around: the words of the "other" in our mouths always sound like something foreign, very often with a mocking, exaggerated, and derisive intonation. . . In this connection I should like to make a special point of the funny or sharply ironic repetition of the verb of our partner's question in our subsequent reply. In such a situation it may be seen that we often resort, not only to grammatically incorrect, but even to very daring, sometimes completely impossible constructions for the sole purpose of somehow repeating a part of our partner's speech and giving it an ironic twist.[24]

The framework of dialogue naturally brought forward the crucial role of intonation for semantics and the inadequacy of grammatical analysis confined within the boundaries of a single, complete and so-called well-formed sentence. The focus on the binary character of a verbal exchange implied an urgent need for taking into account syntactic units that were either more comprehensive or less comprehensive than a single complete sentence. The problem of correctness and incorrectness of sentence formation was shown in a new light. The incompleteness of sentences, the dependence on the antecedent, and the concept of utterance as a whole appeared as stimulating challenges for syntactic inquiry. At the same time, it became apparent that morphologized syntax was a poor tool for handling an utterance as a whole, the syntactic interdependence of utterance structure and, in general, the multifarious manifestations of verbal interaction.

In Russian linguistic scholarship, the theoretical importance of the dialogue framework was outlined in modern terms as early as 1915 by Baudouin de

23. Leo Spitzer, *Italienische Umgangssprache* (Leipzig, 1922).
24. M. M. Baxtin, "Discourse Typology in Prose," *Readings in Russian Poetics*, edited by L. Matejka and K. Pomorska, pp. 186-187. MIT Press, Cambridge, 1971.

Courtenay's student, Lev Ščerba, in his study on East-Lusatian dialects. Developing Ščerba's observations about the naturalness of dialogue and the artificiality of monologue, Lev Jakubinskij, a prominent theoretician of the Russian school of Formalism, devoted a comprehensive study to the problem of dialogue which was published in Ščerba's *Russkaja reč'* [Russian Language] in 1923.

In Jakubinskij's view, dialogue provides a natural framework for linguistic inquiry into verbal interaction, which is for him one of the most fundamental linguistic concepts. The study of dialogue implies the necessity of considering verbal communication in its social setting. The relationship of the opposing partners in the verbal interchange is shown by Jakubinskij as a basis for an adequate interpretation of utterances in semantic terms as well as for the study of incomplete sentences and their dependence on various types of antecedents. Jakubinskij's observations about "speech by hints" dramatically revealed the insufficiencies of syntactic procedures originally developed only for the analysis of isolated, monological sentences. Phonological and morphological criteria, however sophisticated, proved to be inadequate points of departure for analysis of the semantic consequences of verbal interaction displayed in a dialogue.

Inquiry into verbal interaction shifted focus of attention to the crucial importance of intonation or, as Jakubinskij puts it, to "the communicative role played by the relationship of the dynamic, intonational, and timbre systems in the perception of speech." To illustrate the meaningful function of intonation, Jakubinskij quotes the famous passage from Dostoevskij's *Diary of a Writer* about the "unprintable noun" of the drunkards who suddenly made the writer realize "that all thoughts, all feelings, and even whole trains of reasoning" can be expressed by means of intonational variants in pronouncing a single obscenity. Subsequently, the same passage from Dostoevskij was quoted by Vološinov in his discussion of the interrelationship between intonation and meaning; curiously enough, it was also used in Lev Vygotskij's *Myšlenie i reč'* [*Thought and language*] (1934), a suggestive Russian contribution to psychology that in many respects brings to mind not only Jakubinskij's study of dialogue but also Vološinov's philosophy of language. In general, it appears that the formalist, Lev Jakubinskij, more than any other investigators of dialogue and the speech act, exercised an important impact on the Russian intellectual élite in the 1920s and early 1930s, shortly before the Marxist mechanists and reflexologists began to dominate intellectual life in the Soviet Union.

The study of dialogue not only provided a new approach to the structural characteristics of an utterance but, for both Vološinov and Vygotskij, became a basis from which to venture into the mysteries of inner speech and its relationship to human thoughts. "Only by ascertaining the forms of whole utterances and, especially, the forms of dialogue speech," Vološinov argues, "can light be shed on the forms of inner speech and on the peculiar logic of their concatenation in the stream of inner speech." Lev Vygotskij's observations display the same disposition of mind:

> Our experiments convinced us that inner speech must be regarded, not as speech minus
> sound, but as an entirely separate speech function. Its main distinguishing trait is its
> peculiar syntax. Compared with external speech, inner speech appears disconnected
> and incomplete.[25]

Vološinov came to the conclusion that inner speech was profoundly different
from its implementation in utterances. "It is clear from the outset," he claims,
"that without exception all categories worked out by linguistics for the analysis
of the forms of external language-speech (the lexicological, the grammatical, the
phonetic) are inapplicable to the analysis of inner speech, or if applicable, are
applicable only in thoroughly and radically revised versions." And Vygotskij in
obvious agreement with Vološinov says:

> All our observations indicate that inner speech is an autonomous speech function. We
> can confidently regard it as a distinct plane of verbal thought. It is evident that the
> transition from inner to external speech is not a simple translation from one language
> into another. It cannot be achieved by merely vocalizing silent speech. It is a complex,
> dynamic process involving the transformation of the predicative, idiomatic structure
> of inner speech into syntactically articulated speech intelligible to others.[26]

Utterance and dialogue also played a fundamental role in the semiotic analyses of M. M. Baxtin, who obviously held many views on verbal communication
in common with V. N. Vološinov and was capable of elaborating some of them
with admirable lucidity. In his book on the verbal art of Dostoevskij (*Problemy
tvorčestva Dostoevskogo*, Leningrad, 1929), Baxtin demonstrated that the various types of relationship of one speech act with another were of pivotal importance for the understanding of verbal art—prose fiction in particular. In the introduction to the theoretical part of his book, Baxtin writes:

> A set of certain verbal devices used in literary art has recently attracted the special at-
> tention of investigators. This set comprises stylization, parody, *skaz* (in its strict sense,
> the oral narration of a narrator), and dialogue. Despite the fundamental differences
> among them, all these devices have one feature in common: in all of them discourse
> maintains a double focus, aimed at the referential object of speech, as in ordinary dis-
> course, and simultaneously at a second context of discourse, a second speech act by
> another addresser. If we remain ignorant of this second context, if we accept styliza-
> tion or parody as we accept ordinary speech with its single focus on its referential ob-
> ject, then we shall fail to grasp these devices for what they really are: we shall take
> stylization for straight style and read parody as poor writing.[27]

The role of dialogue, of verbal interaction, and of doubly oriented discourse
continued to be a productive standpoint for Baxtin after several decades of bru-
tally enforced silence. In his book, *Tvorčestvo Fransua Rable,* [*Rabelais and his*

25. Lev Semenovich Vygotskij, *Thought and Language,* translated by E. Hanfmann and
G. Vakar, p. 138. MIT Press, Cambridge, 1962.
26. *Ibid.*, p. 148.
27. *Readings in Russian Poetics*, p. 176.

world]²⁸ published first in 1965, Baxtin employed the analytic framework of dialogue and verbal interaction to illuminate Rabelais' ingenious creativity, still convinced, as he had always been, that the analysis of verbal art offered the best opportunity for illustrating the creative aspect of language usage and, implicitly, the most fundamental characteristics of verbal semiotic.

4. Although Vološinov in his book, *Marxism and the Philosophy of Language*, used lengthy references to N. Ja. Marr's thoughts about language and anthropology, he was in apparent disagreement with the Marristic dogma about the class character of language and about the causal relationship between language and class struggle. In his book, Vološinov argues that "class does not coincide with sign community" that "various different classes will use one and the same language" and that "the word is neutral with respect to a specific ideological function." In contradistinction, N. Ja. Marr, in his discussion of Marxism and Japhetic theory in 1930, apodictically repeats that human language has been a class language from its very origin and that there is no human language which is classless. And, as a matter of fact, one could speculate that the discrepancy between Marr's Marxism and Vološinov's Marxism might have been one of the reasons for Vološinov's downfall.

The mechanists, reflexologists, and Marrists, who in the 1930s gained absolute control over all aspects of humanistic studies in the Soviet Union, were hardly flattered by Vološinov's assertion that linguistics remained "at a stage of pre-dialectical, mechanistic materialism, one expression of which is the continued hegemony of mechanistic causality in all domains of ideological studies." The powerful guardians of official Marxism were obviously not ready to accept with equanimity Vološinov's dictum, "The range of application for the categories of mechanical causality is extremely narrow, and even within the natural sciences themselves it grows constantly narrower, the further and more deeply dialectics takes hold in the basic principles of these sciences." It is apparent that Vološinov was unable to persuade his powerful opponents about the true Marxist nature of his dialectical synthesis which, like a rainbow, arched over the polar opposition of Cartesian and Humboldtian linguistics. His combination of the binary concept of sign with the incessant, immanent flow of the generative process of language became a suspicious concept in principle. Vološinov's special emphasis on the social character of sign, on the social character of language, on the social character of the individual consciousness, and on the social character of inner speech and human thinking in general were all to no avail. In the 1930s in the Soviet Union, the binary nature of the sign and the incessant generative process of language creativity became subjects too dangerous to tackle if one wanted to survive. Although the details are obscure and will probably remain obscure forever, it is clear that Vološinov did not survive. He disappeared in the 1930s and,

28. Mikhail Baxtin, *Rabelais and His World*, translated by H. Iswolsky. MIT Press, Cambridge, 1968.

together with him, his *Marxism and the Philosophy of Language,* as well as his *Freudianism,* were doomed to sink into oblivion. The prolegomena to semiotics became a prolegomenon to an intellectual tragedy. For decades, the concept of the sign was taboo. In the 1950s, when it became apparent that the technological advances of data processing devices were intrinsically related to the achievements of modern semiotics linguistics, logic, and applied algebra, the conservative guardians of Marxist "Truth" loosened their grip to allow the Soviet Union to catch up with the West in the application of sophisticated data processing to industrialization, to the exploration of the universe, and, of course, to modern warfare. Still, in 1959, in a programmatic article published by several authors in the *Izvestija Akademii Nauk* U.S.S.R., the official publication of the Soviet Academy of Sciences, the linguist V. V. Vinogradov openly stated that scientists continued to be apprehensive of semiotics.[29] As a matter of fact, V. V. Vinogradov was the first (or perhaps one of the first) who subsequently dared to give any credit to V. N. Vološinov. Until now, references to Vološinov's contribution have been rare. Even authors who approached the problems of semiotics as, for example, did A. G. Volkov in his *Language as a System of Signs* (*Jazyk kak sistema znakov*), published by the Moscow University Press in 1966, did not have the courage to mention Vološinov's name. This is also generally true about the majority of recent studies on semiotic in *Voprosy Filosofii* [Problems of Philosophy], an official journal of the Soviet Academy of Sciences. Also, the *First International Conference on Sign and the System of Language,* which took place in Germany in 1959, fully avoided mentioning Vološinov's name, although many Russian scholars and many Marxist and non-Marxist semioticians took part in the discussions. Vološinov's name was even avoided in V. Zvegincev's paper, "Man and Sign" (*Čelovek i znak*), published in 1967 in the "Festschrift," *To Honor Roman Jakobson* (The Hague: Mouton), although V. Zvegincev, a well-informed editor of Soviet Russian surveys of modern linguistics, must have been aware of the honorable credit Roman Jakobson had given to Vološinov's contribution to semiotics. Thus the daring, penetrating views of Valentin Vološinov have been only semiresurrected, and his *Marxism and the Philosophy of Language* continues to be a controversial book—which, indeed, it is. It is a controversial book but, at the same time, it is a book of brilliant observations about the paramount importance of sign for human community, for human consciousness, and for that which makes people human; it is a book about the miracle of language which, being a generative process, "can only be grasped with aid of another generative process."

---

29. See R. A. Budagov, V. V. Vinogradov, B. V. Gornung, M. M. Desnickaja, and B. A. Serebrenikov, "Teoretičeskie voprosy jazykoznanija," *Izvestija A. N.,* **XVII,** (1959), p. 216.

APPENDIX II

The Formal Method and the Sociological Method (M.M. Baxtin, P.N. Medvedev, V.N. Vološinov) in Russian Theory and Study of Literature

I. R. Titunik

During the 1920s, especially the latter half of the decade, massive attention in the world of Russian literary studies was focused on the work of the so-called *formal method* or *formalist school*. The contingent of brilliant young scholars of language and literature who came to be known as the formalists had begun operating about 1916, as *Opojaz*,[1] their primary unifying concern having been the establishment of an autonomous science of literature based on "concrete poetics," that is, on the specific, intrinsic characteristics of verbal art. Unquestionably, formalism was the most scientifically advanced, the most dynamic and influential movement in Russian literary thought of the time. Neutrality toward the challenge of the new school was a practical impossibility.

The situation that supervened around 1925 was, however, far from a simple marshaling of pro and con forces. The formalists had by that time attracted to their work hosts of disciples, partisans, and fellow travelers of various kinds and degrees. But among the new adherents were many "epigones" and "ecclectics" whose scholarship betrayed misconception of what the movement's scientific orientation was, and who created spurious brands of formalism from which the Opojazists, though repeatedly and outspokenly critical, found it difficult to disassociate themselves.[2]

1. *Opojaz* is the acronym for *Obščestvo izučenija poètičeskogo jazyka* [Society for the Study of Poetic Language]. It was one of the two groups comprising the formalist movement; the other group, the Moscow Linguistic Circle, ceased functioning as such in the early 1920s. A detailed account of the "history and doctrine" of Russian formalism, plus bibliography, is given in V. Erlich, *Russian Formalism* (The Hague, 1955). The anthology, *Readings in Russian Poetics (Formalist and Structuralist Views)* [hereafter *Readings*], edited by L. Matejka and K. Pomorska. MIT Press, Cambridge, Massachusetts, 1971, presents English translations of many of the most important formalist studies in literary theory and analysis. The book also includes essays on Russian formalism by the editors.

2. See B. Èjxenbaum, "The Theory of the Formal Method" in *Readings*, pp. 5 and 18.

On the other side were the movement's numerous opponents, no less mixed in character. Some opponents were uncompromising foes, out to discredit and demolish formalism at all costs, who did not hesitate to feature in their arguments against it the "formalism" espoused by the movement's misguided new enthusiasts. At the same time, there were many other critics of formalism who, while disagreeing on major principles, evinced admiration for certain aspects of the formalists' work and even a willingness to come to terms with them. In both these variants of opponent, Marxists of various stamps and standings were represented.

As the decade of the 1920s ended and that of the 1930s began, the formalist movement and the controversy in which it was embroiled came more and more under the effect of changes occurring in the political and governmental life of the Soviet Union. The interests of argument, of free-wheeling debate and polemics, were being gradually supplanted by the demands of dogma. Increasingly, formalism was put in the position of a "heresy," but the more sinister results of this trend were to become realities of Soviet life only somewhat later. In the interim, though loyalty to the stand taken by dogma was a prerequisite, it was still possible to contend with formalism in rational terms. During this period—the late 1920s and early '30s—a certain group of young, self-avowed Marxists (whose Marxism, however, was to prove other than the regulation kind, and who were to suffer dire consequences despite, or more likely on account of, their Marxism) were carrying out investigations in the theory of language and literature or, more broadly and accurately, in the field of semiology with particular emphasis on language and literature. The principal of this group was, apparently, M. M. Baxtin; the membership included P. N. Medvedev and V. N. Vološinov.[3]

What exactly the relationship of the Baxtin group with the formalists was is a question that allows of no easy answer, and perhaps can never be answered in full as regards the actual, historical situation. True, all three of the scholars named did, to one degree or another, articulate antiformalist positions, and did

3. It was not until fairly recently that the very existence of this group became a matter of published information. Brief mentions of a Baxtin "group," "circle," "school" appeared in two books on psycholinguistics by A. A. Leont'ev (*Psixolingvistika*, Leningrad, 1967, pp. 86-88; and *Jazyk, reč', rečevaja dejatel'nost'*, Moscow, 1969, p. 79). Curiously enough, all quotations representing the Baxtin point of view in Leont'ev's books are from Vološinov's *Marksizm i filosofija jazyka*. The fullest account of the Baxtin group to date is the report of a meeting held at Moscow University in honor of M. M. Baxtin's 75th birthday, published in *Voprosy jazykoznanija*, 2, 1971, pp. 160-162. The report summarizes the contents of four speeches given at that meeting. Included in the remarks of the second speaker was the following identification of the Baxtin group: "M. M. Baxtin's immediate entourage consisted of such people as his student, follower, and collaborator, V. N. Vološinov, the literary scholars P. N. Medvedev and L. V. Pumpjanskij, the indologist M. I. Tubjanskij, the biologist I. I. Kanaev, the writer K. Vaginov, the musicologist I. I. Sollertinskij." The relation of Baxtin to the *Opojaz* is also briefly discussed there.

so purportedly as Marxist opponents of formalism for whom no compromise was possible. At the same time, completely defensible claims to another effect can be made: that the Baxtin group and the formalists shared a number of crucial concerns in common; that formalist theories had nurtured and stimulated the thinking of the Baxtin group—and not only by way of reaction; that in certain respects, specifically and concretely within the domain of poetics, the Baxtin group was operating with concepts very close to ones that were still being formulated, qualified, and further developed by the formal method as it continued to evolve; finally, that the two lines were bound to converge, and did in fact converge, but only elsewhere and under different auspices—in the structuralism of the Prague School and especially in the work of Jan Mukařovský.

However, the conclusion that the Baxtin group were really formalists or neoformalists operating under cover of Marxism and antiformalism for the sake of professional survival would not only be an exaggeration and distortion of the facts, but would also obscure the real main issue. Clearly, what the Baxtin group wanted was a fresh start on new premises—the premises of a Marxist semiology or, as they termed it, a Marxist study of ideologies (*nauka ob ideologijax*). In their view, only on the basis of such a study and within its overall context could a proper theory and study of literature be constructed. In contradistinction to the formal method, they declared theirs to be the *sociological method.* Acknowledgment of overlapping and parallelism between the two methods was neither circumstantially expedient nor really to the point. The point was *contradiction:* contradiction in basic outlook and orientation with all the consequences that issued therefrom. Thus the utility and necessity of contending with formalism arose, not as a matter of demolishing formalism, but of using it to set perspectives in which the "right" premises would be shown in concrete contradiction with the "wrong" ones.

This task—specifically, the adumbration of a Marxist theory and study of literature via critical analysis of formalism—was carried out by P. N. Medvedev. In 1928 he produced a study under the title *Formal'nyj metod v literaturovedenii* [The formal method in literary scholarship], symptomatically subtitled *Kritičeskoe vvedenie v sociologičeskuju poètiku* [A critical introduction to sociological poetics].[4] The book was issued by the Institute for Comparative History of Occidental and Oriental Languages and Literatures in its series, "Problems of

4. Apparently this study did not sit too well with the authorities. A second version was published in 1934 under the new title, *Formalizm i formalisty* [Formalism and the formalists]. It is essentially the same study, but sandwiched in between virulently worded, outright condemnations of formalism. It did not, however, save Medvedev from being, as the *Kratkaja literaturnaja ènciklopedija* [Concise Literary Encyclopedia] (Vol. 4, Moscow, 1967, p. 723) puts it, "illegally repressed" soon thereafter. In the present essay, all quotations are from the 1928 version. For the sake of convenience, page numbers referring to that edition appear in brackets after quotations.

Methodology and Theory of Language and Literature," the very same series in which, the next year, V. N. Vološinov's *Marxism and the Philosophy of Language* appeared. The two books significantly complement each other, share complete identity of assumptions and outlook, concepts and terminology, and even closely coincide in the very wording of the argument in a number of passages. The nature and scope of concern with formalism was, of course, quite different. For Vološinov, criticism of the epistemological and methodological bases of formalism in general, what he termed "abstract objectivism," comprised one part of a twofold critical analysis out of which a new Marxist conception of language as the medium of ideological creativity par excellence was supposed to take shape. In Medvedev's case, the Russian formal method was the primary material whose treatment was meant to serve the purpose of delineating, by contrastive analysis, a Marxist sociological poetics, conceived, in full accord with Vološinov, as one of the branches of that vast, overall "study of ideologies. . .which encompasses, on the basis of unitary principle in conception of object of study and unitary method of study, all the domains of mankind's ideological creativity [p. 11]."

The key problem, both in the general study of ideologies and in the particular study of literature, was what Medvedev called the "problem of specification." As he saw it, the very bases for the study of ideologies and all its branches were already firmly grounded in the unitary, monistic philosophy of Marxism, which endowed all domains of ideology definitive meaning, function, and relationship in human society and history and, hence, constituted no problem. The problem lay instead in the specific properties of each of the domains, in the elucidation of that which distinguished one from the others. The urgency of this problem was attested to by the fact that between holistic (Marxist) theory and concrete analysis a perilous disjuncture had occurred and, as a result, any object under investigation inevitably either was divested of its specificity or had its specificity isolated from all social connections and treated as a value on its own. A way out of this dilemma was precisely what Medvedev sought:

> What is lacking is a properly worked out *sociological* study of the specific properties of the material, forms and goals belonging to each of the domains of ideological creativity.
> Each of them, after all, commands its own "language," with its own forms and operations, and its own specific laws for the refraction of the unitary reality of existence. The specificity of art, science, ethics, and religion must not, of course, obscure their ideological unity as superstructures over the one, common basis, each of them infused with unitary socioeconomic coherency; but neither ought their specificity be effaced for the sake of general formulations of that coherency [pp. 11-12].

In the field of literary study, the problem of specification became the vital point of contradiction between the formal and the sociological methods precisely because here different sets of premises confronted one another in pursuit of the same aims. The formalists, who, as Medvedev willingly declares, had "come forward precisely as specifiers" and had "succeeded in imparting to the problem of specification in literary science considerable acuity and theoretical bearing [p. 54]," represented a challenge which the Marxist sociological method could not afford either to ignore or dismiss. The accomplishments and/or pretensions of the formalists in "specification" had created an arena for vital, productive contradiction over one and the same object, an arena which afforded the Marxists the proving grounds for their own conceptions:

> Marxist study of literature makes contact with the formal method and comes into conflict with it on the grounds of the paramount and most urgent problem common to both—the problem of specification. Therefore, criticism of formalism can and should be "immanent" in the best sense of the word. Each of the formalists' arguments should be examined and disproved on its own proper grounds—the grounds of the distinctive characteristics of literary fact. The very object of study itself—literature in all its uniqueness—must abrogate and cast off the definitions of the formalists as definitions inadequate to it and its uniqueness [p. 55].

Or, as Medvedev asseverates in the final words of his study (an extraordinary and courageous tribute under the circumstances):

> We believe that Marxist science ought to be grateful to the formalists, grateful because the formalists' theory can stand it in good stead as an object for serious criticism in the process of which the bases for Marxist literary scholarship can be elucidated and should come out all the stronger.
> Every young science—and Marxist literary scholarship is very young—must much more highly prize a good foe than a poor ally [p. 232].

What, in the Medvedev—Vološinov Marxist view, made literature amenable to objective study, and what made that study necessarily sociological was, of course, literature's inalienable *social quality*. Social quality was predicated over the whole of ideological creativity. As Vološinov asserts, everything ideological is semiotic, and every sign, *as sign*, is a social phenomenon. It was precisely the social quality of all ideological products that other approaches and methods— positivistic, formalist, subjective-psychological, idealistic—had failed, indeed were unequipped, to appreciate, with the result that they inevitably misrepresented and misconstrued the objects of their study.

At the same, however, the social nature of literature was open to misinterpretation even from a sociological view. That is, literature could be seen merely in terms of social content and relationship, as a direct reflection of social life or as an agency for registering the effects of other ideological systems. Such indeed had been the point of view and practice of "social-minded" literary criticism and scholarship in Russia from the mid-19th century on. The consequences of this brand of "literary sociology" were a naive identification of literature with "real life" and a complete loss of contact with the specific, distinctive properties of literature itself. Even under Marxism this notion had survived in the doctrine that literature derives directly from the socioeconomic basis.[5]

Literature, Medvedev argued, not only participates in the social process, it is in and of itself a special social entity:

> Literature enters into the milieu of ideological activity as one of its autonomous branches, occupying a special place in it as a set of distinctively organized verbal productions with structure of a kind specific and peculiar to such productions alone. This structure, as any other ideological structure, refracts the generative process of socioeconomic existence, and does so in its own particular way. . . . In its content, literature reflects the ideological purview, i.e., other, nonartistic (ethical, cognitive, etc.) ideological formations. But in reflecting these other signs, literature itself creates new forms, new signs of ideological communication; and these signs—works of literature—become a functioning part of the surrounding social reality. At the same time as reflecting something outside of themselves, works of literature constitute in and of themselves phenomena of the ideological milieu with autonomous value and distinctive character. Their functionality does not amount merely to the auxilliary-technical role of reflecting other ideologies. They have an autonomous ideological role and a type of refraction of socioeconomic existence entirely their own [pp. 27-29].

Essentially, what Medvedev propounds is an elaborate and dynamic "system of systems" (to borrow a term from a context that will be brought into the discussion later on) wherein each ideological domain is an autonomous system of a specific kind in a complex (mediated) interrelationship and interaction with all other systems and in an equally complex, ultimate dependence on the one common "socioeconomic basis." Literature is to be regarded as just such a member-system. It is composed of works of literature—ideological productions with a structure peculiar and distinctive to themselves—operating within the immediate milieu of literary culture at some particular stage in the development (generative process) of some particular literature, the milieu of which is only one of a whole atmosphere of milieus, so to speak, governed by the unitary socioeconomic basis, likewise in process of generation, which "knows how to speak the language of literature just as it knows how to speak all other ideological languages [p. 43]." Thus this "system of systems" is permeated through and through with social quality, and all of it, from the smallest technical details to the most elaborate nexus of interrelationships, falls under the competence of sociological study.

What is needed for the construction of a proper science of literature is, according to Medvedev, a *sociological poetics* whose concern will be precisely to contend with the problem of specification in literature, to find the solution to such questions as:

> What is a literary work, and what is its structure? What are the elements of that structure, and what are the artistic functions of those elements? What is genre, style, plot,

5. See Vološinov's criticism of this doctrine, p. 18 of this book.

theme, motif, hero, meter, rhythm, melodics, etc.? How is the ideological purview
reflected in the content of a work, and what functions does that reflection have in the
whole of the work's artistic structure [p. 45]?

And coupled with sociological poetics, indeed, in necessary reliance on and
dialectical relationship with it, is a sociological history of literature that studies:

the concrete life of a work of art in the unity of the developing literary milieu; the
literary milieu within the process of generation of the ideological milieu with which it
is encompassed; and, finally, the ideological milieu in the process of generation of the
socioeconomic milieu with which it is permeated [p. 42].

Such is the general scheme for the construction of a theory and study of
literature presented by Medvedev.

Naturally, the contradiction between the formalist and sociological points of
view had to be expressed in categorical terms. There was no room for compromise in Medvedev's argument. The formalists' premises were either right or
wrong, and everything else depended on premises. Although the formalists themselves never propounded a unified "school theory" and indeed deliberately eschewed doing so, some fundamental position had to be postulated for them—and
not merely postulated but fixed and "galvanized."[6] The formalists' position was
declared to be basically that literature was an extrasocial phenomenon, or rather,
that that which constituted the "literariness" of literature—its specificity—was
something self-valuable, self-contained, and self-perpetuating that should and
must be isolated from the social surroundings in which it existed in order to be
made an object of knowledge; that while social forces and events could, and did,
sometimes even drastically, affect literature *from the outside,* the real, intrinsic
nature of literature remained immune, exclusively and forever true to itself
alone; that, therefore, proper and productive study of literature is possible only
in "immanent" terms.

This was held to be, of course, the basis for a program of literary specification, but a basis which hypostasized the problem, thereby contrasting and con-
flicting with the basic outlook of the sociological method on the same problem:

6. The problem was that the formal method was not a "methodology" or "doctrine"
properly speaking, as B. Èjxenbaum cogently explains in "The Theory of the Formal
Method." In order for the Marxist sociological doctrine to conflict with a formalist "doctrine," the latter had to be spelled out as such. To this end, Medvedev did not hesitate to
construe formalist working hypotheses as invariable principles and formalist focuses of attention as value judgments. Thus the history of the formal method was viewed, not in evolutionary terms, as Èjxenbaum had insisted it should be, but as the systematic filling in of a
preconceived program. Anything in formalist writings not consistent with this "program"
was taken as evidence of "betrayal" of their own doctrine on the part of this or that formalist. The picture of the formal method obtained by this procedure does not reflect the
way the formalists actually operated. They did, of course, have a general theory; only it was
a general theory in (to crib a phrase) a continuous process of generation.

The specificating trends of our formalists are diametrically opposite Marxist trends. The formalists conceive specification to be a matter of isolating a particular ideological domain and sealing it off from all the other forces and energies of ideological and social life. They conceive of specificity, of uniqueness, as a static force unto itself, hostile to everything else; i.e., they conceive uniqueness in nondialectical terms and, therefore, are incapable of incorporating it with the vital processes of interaction occurring in the concrete unity of social, historical life [p. 54].

Such, in Medvedev's presentation, was the nature of the essential contradiction between the basic stand of the formal method and that of the sociological method. The implications and consequences of the formalists' basic stand were already concretely represented by an elaborate set of theories and analyses produced over a period of a dozen years or so and covering virtually the entire range of issues within the domain of poetics. If those theories and analyses were to be subjected to criticism from the sociological point of view, it would presumably be possible to refute the formalist interpretation of the issues and, at the same time, to hammer out their sociological interpretation, i.e., construct a sociological poetics. And exactly that was the task Medvedev undertook to carry out via long, complex, detailed, point by point argument. To summarize that argument in the same manner would be a formidable task itself and a far greater burden than the present essay is designed to support. At the risk of depriving the argument of much of its real substance, attention will be focused here only on certain of its aspects—aspects which correlate with concepts advanced by V. N. Vološinov in *Marxism and the Philosophy of Language*, and which may be identified under the terms "utterance," "form of the whole" and "generative process."

The formalists, Medvedev argues, while correct in wanting to disclose the specificity of literature, made a fundamental error at the very outset of their investigations by seeking that specificity in the notion of "poetic language." [Henceforth, without further indication, this summary is presented from Medvedev's point of view.] The error stemmed from the formalists' reliance on linguistics and its categories (phonetics, morphology, syntax) and their adopting the tendency of linguistics to divorce form and meaning, appropriating the former as the proper object of study and relegating the latter to other disciplines. Meanwhile, the fact is that no such thing as poetic language really exists, either in the dialectological sense or as a matter of the opposition, postulated by the formalists, between "poetic language" and "practical language." Language cannot be said to break down into poetic and nonpoetic languages but can only be said to carry out different *functions*, the poetic function among them. What determines the poetic function of language is poetic context—works of literature:

"Poetic properties are acquired by language only in concrete poetic constructions. These properties belong not to language in its linguistic capacity but precisely to the construction, whatever kind of construction that might be [p. 117]."

Therefore, the proper point of departure for investigation into the specificity of literature is not poetic language (a fiction in any case) but poetic context, poetic construction—literary works of art themselves.

Once this is established, then the entire linguistic apparatus that the formalists applied to their study of literature is revealed to be irrelevant. The basic verbal components of poetic constructions cannot be, and are not, the units of linguistic analysis (phoneme, morpheme, syntagma) but must be, and are, the real units of speech—utterances. The literary work of art is a special kind of whole utterance or organization of utterances. And since the utterance by its very nature is ideological, the problem of meaning, instead of being relegated elsewhere, is made a central factor of poetic construction; and a wholly different conception of poetic construction than that held by the formalists is required.

The proper approach to the problem of poetic construction lies not in definition of its exclusivity (i.e., in terms of the poetic versus the ideological), but in disclosure of its integration:

> of that element in a poetic work which would be integral both with the material actuality of word and with word signification, which, as a medium, would unite depth and commonalty of meaning with the given actuality of uttered sound, [and therefore would] make possible coherent and consistent transition from the peripheries of a work to its inner meaning, from outer form to inner ideological significance [p. 162].

And that medium is "social evaluation," the historically generated, assumed, common code that defines the mentality and outlook, the choice, range, and hierarchy of interests, i.e., the ideological purview, of a given social group at some particular time in its existence. It is social evaluation that mediates between form and performance; it is social evaluation that endows every particular speech act—each and every utterance—with its real, here and now meaning, "defining its individual, class and epochal physiognomy [p. 165]."

The special character of the poetic utterance consists in the fact that, whereas utterances in all other ideological domains are organized for purposes lying outside verbal expression, in literature "social evaluation is wholly realized, achieves finalized structure, in the utterance itself. . . . The entity of the utterance here is not meant to serve any other entity. Social evaluation here is molded and fully structured in pure expression [p. 172]."

On this basis arises the problem of the "form of the whole," in which cardinal importance belongs to the concept of genre. The formalists had come to the problem of genre only after having worked out the components of literary construction on the grounds of poetic language and without reference to any notion of genre. Inevitably, they construed genre as a mechanical assemblage of devices —a fixed set of devices with some particular dominant. Thus the formalists entirely missed the real significance of genre.

Genre is not that which is determined and defined by the components of a literary work or by sets of literary works, but that which, in effect, determines and defines them. Genre is "an archetypal form of the whole of an utterance, the whole of a work. A work really exists only in the form of some particular genre. The constructional value of each and every element of a work can be understood only in connection with genre [p. 175]." It is genre that gives shape and meaning to a work of literature, as a whole entity, and to all the elements of which that entity is comprised. Genre is that area where construction and theme meet and fuse together, the area precisely where social evaluation generates forms of that finalized structuredness *[zaveršenie, zaveršimost']* which is the very *differentia specifica* of art.

Genres are definable in terms of specific combinations of features stemming from the double orientation in life, in reality, which each type of artistic "form of the whole" commands—an orientation at once from outside in and from inside out. What is at stake in the first instance is the actual status of a work as a social fact: its definition in real time and space; its means and mode of performance; the kind of audience presupposed and the relationship between author and audience established; its association with social institutions, social mores, and other ideological spheres; in short—its full "situational" definition.

On the other side, what is involved is the work's thematic orientation, its thematic unity. Each genre has the capacity to deal with only certain aspects of reality; to each belong certain principles of selection, certain manners of envisioning and conceptualizing reality; each operates within a certain scale of depth and range of treatment. These two kinds of orientation are inseparably linked and interdependent. Such a concept of genre offers a dynamic, creative principle for the interpretation and integration of all components of construction, including all those components which the formalists had featured in their studies but which they had deprived of all contental meaning and had reduced to ready-made entities with fixed functions capable of operating only within a conventional set of rules, thereby making literature, in effect, wholly analogous to a game of chess.

The formalist doctrine on the evolution of literature, on literary history, suffered from the same deficiency as their genre theory; indeed, that deficiency was in their very conception of literature and it manifested itself at every level of analysis. Thus the stages in the formation of their doctrine on literary history could be summarized in the following way: on the basis of investigation of poetic language the formalists arrived at the notion of the device as the basic component of literature; literary works were defined as assemblages of devices; specific types of such assemblages defined literary genres, schools, movements; the history of literature was, then, the history of the assembling, disassembling, and reassembling of devices (the same devices!).

To explain how this process of historical change came about, the formalists brought to bear their principles of "automatization" and "perceptibility." These principles, despite the formalists' avowed intent to study literature as an "entity external to consciousness," amounted in fact to a crude sort of techno-psychologistic notion of artistic perception. Instead of dispensing with the subjective consciousness, the formalists constructed a theory that presupposed a subjective consciousness which "feels" artistic effect and loss of effect. Moreover, by necessity, this "feeling" occurs within the confines of one individual consciousness or, at best, the individual consciousnesses of one and the same generation of persons, for "there can be absolutely no connection between automatization and perceptibility spread over two individuals following one another in time, just as there can be no connection between one man's nausea and another man's gluttony [p. 203]." Furthermore, the formalists' scheme of literary evolution, which issued from these principles and which was represented by them as a dialectical process, amounted to nothing more than the play of two forces that alternate as "junior" and "senior" lines, and must go on doing so ad infinitum. Thus it was not psychologism the formalists had rid themselves of, but history and ideology.

The real, objective solution of the problem of literary history lies in viewing literature as it really is in actual existence: a dynamic, generative process of a special kind within the dynamic, generative process of social interaction or communication. That is, the solution of the problem of literary history is to be sought in the "dialectics of the 'intrinsic' and the 'extrinsic'":

> The generative process of social communication conditions all aspects of literature and every single literary work with respect to its creation and reception. On the other hand, the generative process of communication is also conditioned by the generative process of literature, which is one of its factors. In generative process, it is not at all a matter of combinations of elements of a work changing, while the elements remain self-identical, but a matter of the elements themselves changing, and of their combinations together changing as well—of the whole configuration changing.
> The generation of literature and of an individual work can be understood only within the whole framework of the ideological purview. The further we remove a work from that context, the more certain the work will turn inert and lifeless within itself.
> The ideological purview, as we know, is incessantly in the process of generation. And this process of generation, just as any other such process, is dialectical in nature. Therefore, at any given moment of that process, we shall discover conflicts and inner contradictions within the ideological purview.
> Into those conflicts and contradictions the literary work of art, too, is drawn. The work absorbs and makes intrinsic to itself some elements of the ideological milieu, while rejecting other elements as extrinsic. Therefore the "intrinsic" and the "extrinsic" in the process of history dialectically change places, without, needless to say, remaining absolutely identical all the while. What appears today a fact extrinsic to literature—a piece of extraliterary reality—may tomorrow enter literature as one of its intrinsic structural factors. And conversely, what was literary today may become a piece of extraliterary reality tomorrow [p. 206]. . . . The dialectical conception of the "extrinsic" and the "intrinsic" of literature and of extraliterary reality (ideological and other) is the *conditio sine qua non* for the construction of a genuine Marxist history of literature [p. 208].

Such, in brief outline and with reference only to certain key points, is Medvedev's argument. In its own terms and for its own purposes, it declares the ultimate, total irreconcilability of the formal and sociological methods. However, from another perspective, this conclusion proves not altogether to be the case.

To begin with, the formalists actually never did deny that literature was a social fact, though, of course, they insisted that it was a social fact *sui generis*,[7] one with specificity and coherency peculiar to itself—a position identical with that of Medvedev's sociological poetics. However, it was not the problem of literature in its full social dimensions that interested the formalists at the outset. Their initial motivation was to redirect attention from what had been the main concerns of literary study—literature's cause and effect, its creators, its social associations, and functions, its philosophical or metaphysical significance—to that which had been obscured, minimized or totally neglected by those concerns: the real, proper object of study—the literary material itself. The formalists operated, as Boris Èjxenbaum states in his lucid summation of the formal method in 1925, with "theoretical principles drawn from the study of the concrete material with its specific characteristics" and adhered to those principles "to the extent they are proved tenable by the material. If the material requires their further elaboration or alteration, we go ahead and elaborate or alter them."[8]

What this amounted to was not a doctrine or even a "methodology," but a process of study describable as beginning from the beginning with working hypotheses and proceeding step by step—a process wherein each successive step requires the qualification and reassessment of the preceding ones, while the context of study itself becomes constantly more complex and comprehensive. Therein precisely consisted the "factor of evolution" in the formal method which Èjxenbaum justly underscored time and time and time again.

In contrast, Medvedev's sociological method may be described as a process of beginning from the end, which process requires a predetermined general theory that sets everything in its appointed place beforehand and whose overall, governing mode of operation must inevitably be *eclecticism*. And indeed, Medvedev does openly and explicitly declare eclecticism to be *the way* for the Marxist; it is Marxism itself, he claims, that guarantees success [p. 42]. The formalists were a great deal more cautious in this respect; they worked on the assumption, again in Èjxenbaum's words, "that there is a difference between theory and conviction."[9]

Thus the contradiction between sociological poetics and formalism can be stated in somewhat different terms that do not preclude a connection between

7. See "The Theory of the Formal Method," *Readings*, p. 33. Curiously enough, the most extreme and explicit separation between literature and society was made by the Marxist sociologist of literature, P. N. Sakulin, out of somewhat misguided admiration for formalist views. See Medvedev, *Formal'nyj Metod* pp. 48-50.

8. "The Theory of The Formal Method," pp. 3-4.

9. *Ibid.*, p. 4.

them: while sociological poetics, as conceived by Medvedev, must implement the social nature (as determined by Marxist concepts) of literary fact from the very start of investigation and on all levels of analysis, formalism maintained the position that literary fact had first to be studied *as such* before its full social nature could be understood properly. From this point of view, the evolution of the formal method can be said in fact to have been working, via the problem of specification, toward, if not sociological poetics strictly speaking, certainly toward a conception of literature in its dynamic relationship with social life.

In 1928, Roman Jakobson and Jurij Tynjanov, undoubtedly the two most profound thinkers associated with the formalist movement, produced a series of "theses" under the title "Problemy izučenija literatury i jazyka" [Problems in the Study of Literature and Language] which spelled out a program strikingly similar in crucial respects to Medvedev's, but without commitment to Marxist presuppositions. These "theses" represented not, of course, what the formalists had begun with and had already accomplished, but what all of that, under new qualification and reassessment, was leading to. In the interests of demonstrating the coincidences between Medvedev's sociological poetics and the stage that the formal method had reached by 1928, the liberty will be taken here of stringing together a set of excerpts from the document composed by Jakobson and Tynjanov:

> The history of literature. . .being simultaneous with other historical series, is characterized, as is each of those series, by an involved complex of specific structural laws. Without the elucidation of those laws, it is impossible to establish in a scientific manner the correlation between the literary series and other historical series. . . .
> The literary and extraliterary material used in literature may be introduced into the orbit of scientific investigation only when it is considered from a functional point of view. . . .
> The opposition between synchrony and diachrony was an opposition between the concept of system and the concept of evolution; thus it loses its importance in principle as soon as we recognize that every system necessarily exists as an evolution while, on the other hand, evolution is inescapably of a systemic nature. . . .
> An indifferent cataloging of coexisting phenomena is not sufficient; what is important is their hierarchical significance for the given epoch. . . .
> An analysis of the structural laws of language and literature and their evolution inevitably leads to the establishment of a limited series of actually existing structural types (types of structural evolution).
> A disclosure of the immanent laws of the history of literature allows us to determine the character of each specific change in literary systems. However, these laws do not allow us to explain the tempo of evolution or the chosen path of evolution when several theoretically possible evolutionary paths are given. This is owing to the fact that the immanent laws of literary evolution form an indeterminate equation; although they admit only a limited number of possible solutions, they do not necessarily specify a unique solution. The question of a specific choice of path, or at least of the dominant, can be solved only by means of an analysis of the correlation between the literary series and other historical series. This correlation (a system of systems) has its own

structural laws, which must be submitted to investigation. It would be methodologically fatal to consider the correlation of systems without taking into account the immanent laws of each system.[10]

As evidenced by the Jakobson-Tynjanov theses, certain concepts, coinciding
with points in Medvedev's program, were already in process of formulation and
development by the formal method. The idea of "function" with regard to poetic language had been advanced as early as 1923 by Jakobson. The functional
role of meaning, i.e., the meaning of words in poetic contexts, was subjected to
systematic investigation in Jurij Tynjanov's first major work, *Problema stixo-
tvornogo jazyka* [The Problem of Verse Language] (Leningrad, 1924).[11] Indeed,
functionality became a key qualification, which obliged the formalists to con-
vert gradually all static concepts of device, composition, genre, and literature itself into dynamic ones. The underlying principle had been clearly enunciated by
Tynjanov:

> The unity of a work [of literature] is not a closed symmetrical whole, but an unfold-
> ing dynamic integrity; between its elements stand, not the static sign of equation and
> addition, but always the dynamic sign of correlation and integration. The form of a
> literary work must be perceived as a dynamic entity.[12]

And along with the concepts of "function" and "dynamic integrity," the
essential historicity (diachronism) of literature was posited. In another article of
1924, Tynjanov had written:

> It is exclusively in terms of its evolution that we shall be able to arrive at an analytical
> "definition" of literature. Once we take that position, we discover that the properties
> of literature which seemed the basic, primary ones constantly change and do not char-
> acterize literature as such. To this category belong the concepts of "aesthetic quality,"
> in the sense of "the beautiful."
> What remains stable turns out to be what had always been taken for granted: litera-
> ture is a verbal construction which makes itself felt precisely as a construction, i.e.,
> literature is a *dynamic verbal construction.*
> The requirement of incessant dynamism is what brings evolution about, seeing that
> every dynamic system necessarily becomes automatized and a constructional princi-
> ple of an opposite kind dialectically comes into play.[13]

This train of reasoning required the consideration of issues deliberately de-
ferred at earlier stages in the development of the formal method. Theoretical

10. *Readings*, pp. 79-81.
11. Two chapters from this book are translated in *Readings:* "Rhythm as the Construc-
tive Factor of Verse," pp. 126-135, and "The Meaning of the Word in Verse," pp. 136-145.
The latter chapter shows certain remarkable resemblances with points advanced by V. N.
Vološinov in *Marxism and the Philosophy of Language.*
12. *Ibid.*, p. 128.
13. "Literaturnyj fakt" [Literary Fact], *Arxaisty i Novatory* (reprinted in Munich, 1967)
pp. 14-15.

cognizance of the dynamic, evolutive nature of literature necessarily posed the problem of the relationship between literature and extraliterary factors, or what in Medvedev's program would be the "dialectic of the 'intrinsic' and the 'extrinsic'."

Such posing of new problems not only advanced and expanded the formalists' context of study, but also, in the way highly characteristic of the formal method, required reconsideration and reevaluation of their theoretical apparatus. Having begun their work with a sharp opposition between "poetic" and "practical" languages, the formalists gradually reordered their perspectives until it became clear that language was itself the nexus of the relationship between literature and society, that language provided the way of access to the study of literature in its full social dimensions. The new perspectives were sketched out in Tynjanov's 1927 article, *O literaturnoj èvoljucii* [On literary evolution], from which the liberty once again will be taken of presenting a series of excerpts:

> In order to be able to investigate the basic problem [of literary evolution], one must agree in advance that a literary work is a system and that literature is a system. Only once this basic understanding is accepted can a literary science be constructed which does not review a chaos of manifold phenomena and orders of phenomena, but studies them. The issue involving the role of orders of phenomena contiguous with literature in literary evolution is by this very fact not cast aside but, on the contrary, posed. . . .
>
> Is the so-called "immanent" study of a work as a system possible outside its correlation with the system of literature? Such an isolated study of a literary work would be an abstraction no less than the abstraction of isolating elements and examining them outside the work in which they appear. Abstracting of that sort is constantly and effectively applied by literary criticism to contemporary works, since the correlation of a contemporary work with contemporary literature is a fact already assumed and merely not expressed. . . But even with respect to contemporary literature the procedure of isolated study is not really possible.
>
> The very existence of a fact as a *literary* fact depends on its differential quality, that is, on its correlation either with the literary or with an extraliterary order, in other words—on its function. What in one epoch is a literary fact would in another be a matter of general social communication, and vice versa, depending on the whole literary system within which the given fact operates. . . .
>
> The system of the literary order is first and foremost a *system of the functions of the literary order in incessant correlation with other orders*. Orders change with respect to their constitution, but the differentiatedness of human activities remains. . . .
>
> What constitutes the correlation of literature with contiguous orders? Moreover, what are the contiguous orders? We all have the answer ready at hand: social conventions [*byt*].
>
> But in order to solve the problem of the correlation of literature with social conventions we must ask: *how* and *in what respects* are social conventions correlated with literature? After all, social conventions are constitutively many-sided, multifaceted, with only the function of all their aspects being specific. *Social conventions correlate with literature first of all through their verbal aspect.* Exactly the same correlation

applies from literature to social conventions. The correlation of the literary order with the order of social conventions is realized along verbal lines; literature has a *verbal* function with respect to social conventions.[14]

Thus the formalists pointed the way to the study of a "system within a system" without recourse to the eclecticism upon which Medvedev is obliged to rely.

As for Medvedev's accusatory ascription of crude "techno-psychologistic" notions to the formalists' concept of literary evolution, it is a flagrant case of failure (or refusal) on his part to see his own principles in operation. "Automatization" and "perceptibility" belong, of course, to the realm of social experience and not to private "feeling"; they are not subjective, but "intersubjective responses."[15]

What is involved here is the immensely important problem of *norms*. It was the problem of norms, as suggested in the Jakobson-Tynjanov theses, that held the key to productive, comprehensive study of literary structure, to types of literary structures (genres), and to literary evolution. Jakobson had devoted an early article, "O xudožestvennom realizme" [On Realism in Art],[16] essentially to the topic of norms, drawing into his discussion the communicative processes of verbal art and the participants in those processes. Thus the foundations were laid for the bridge from the formal method to the semiological method of Czech structuralism. It was also in the work of the Prague school, which prominently featured, to borrow the title of one of Jan Mukařovský's major studies, "aesthetic function, norm, and value as social facts,"[17] that the formal and sociological methods may be said to have achieved their logical, inevitable synthesis.

14. *Readings*, pp. 67, 68-69, 72, 73 (translation somewhat reworded). The term *byt* (here rendered as "social conventions") defies precise translation into English; the closest to it is "culture" or "mores" as used in the field of anthropology. Different renderings of *byt* in English unfortunately tend to obscure the relatedness of the concept in different contexts. So, for instance, under Tynjanov's direct inspiration, Ėjxenbaum began investigation of what they jointly called *literaturnyj byt;* this was rendered as "literary environment" in *Readings* (pp. 56-65), since that seemed the most suitable term for the particular context. Tynjanov's concept of *byt,* moreover, comes very close to what Vološinov, in *Marxism and the Philosophy of Language,* calls "behavioral" or "life ideology" (*žiznennaja ideologija*). For instance, in "Literaturnyj fakt" (*Arxaisty i Novatory,* p. 19), Tynjanov writes: "*Byt* teems with the rudiments of various intellectual activities. By its very makeup, *byt* is rudimentary science, rudimentary art and technology. It differs from fully developed science, art, and technology by its mode of operation."

15. See V. Erlich, *Russian Formalism* (The Hague, 1955), p. 152.

16. Translated in *Readings*, pp. 38-46. As L. Matejka and K. Pomorska note (*ibid.,* p. vii), this article appeared in 1921 in Czech and probably did not come to the attention of Jakobson's Russian colleagues until around 1927.

17. Jan Mukařovský, *Estetická funkce, norma a hodnota jako sociální fakty* (Prague, 1936). The work is available in English translation: No. 3 in Michigan Slavic Contributions, Ann Arbor, 1970. On Russian formalism and the Prague school, see the chapter "Formalism Redefined" in V. Erlich, *Russian Formalism*, pp. 128-136.

The preceding sketch of the relationship between the formal and sociological methods was meant to provide a general basis for the contention that the Baxtin group, while operating with new and different premises and hence not deriving from the formalist school, nevertheless did share crucial concerns in common with the formalists and employed concepts of literature that significantly paralleled and overlapped with formalist concepts, thus making possible the eventual convergence of the two "methods."

In the meantime, however, there were certain particular areas of study where, with considerable justification, the claim can be made (and has been made) that members of the Baxtin group, especially M. M. Baxtin himself and V. N. Vološinov, were directly inspired by formalist investigations and did function as "followers" of the formal method ("followers" in the best spirit of the formal method itself, i.e., qualifiers, reassessors, developers). It was also precisely in these areas that Baxtin and Vološinov may be said to have made their most substantive concrete contributions to literary study. The general scope of the areas of study in question can be identified via Vološinov's definition of "reported speech":[18] "speech within speech, utterance within utterance, and at the same time speech about speech, utterance about utterance."

As early as 1918, the formalists had entered on the agenda of literary study the problems of parody, stylization, and *skaz*.[19] Consideration of these problems held promise of opening access to investigation of the vital stylistic operations of verbal art and the role of those operations in the construction of literary works and in literary evolution, particularly as regarded prose fiction. Such problems were in fact handled as counterparts to the problems of sound texture and rhythm in verse that were the formalists' primary concern. This was especially the case with *skaz* where intonation, tones of voice, verbal gestures, and pantomime were said to play crucial roles.

A further dimension of study was established via the concept of dialogue, thanks, in large measure, to L. Jakubinskij's 1923 article, "O dialogičeskoj *reči* [On Dialogic Speech]," in which the primacy of dialogue as the most "natural" form of speech (in both the senses of man's biological and social "nature") was posited.[20] To problems of monologue, viewed against the background of dialogue,

18. The Russian term *čužaja reč'* means both "reported speech" in the technical sense and, literally, "another's," or "other," or "alien speech." Thus, the Russian term itself includes the double frame of reference so vital to Vološinov and Baxtin's theories. That double reference could not be reproduced in English with any single term and had to be shared out between "reported speech" and "another's speech."

19. The Russian term *skaz*, as a technical literary term, has no English equivalent. Generally associated with oral speech or, rather, the illusion of oral speech in the narrative of a literary work, it perhaps can best be described as narration with marked speech event features. The Russian term is retained here and throughout.

20. Jakubinskij's article has not, to my knowledge, been translated into English. The Russian original appeared in *Russkaja reč'*, I (Petrograd, 1923).

as well as to the problems of parody, stylization, and *skaz*, V. V. Vinogradov devoted a whole series of illuminating theoretical and literary historical investigations, beginning in 1923.[21] All these pioneering, seminal studies on the formalists' part failed, however, to arrive at a comprehensive principle under which the interrelationship of the various issues involved could be fully recognized and made the basis for a unified field of investigation.

In 1926, V. N. Vološinov published an article entitled "Slovo v žizni i slovo v poèzii" [Word in Life and Word in Poetry].[22] While its main, immediate purpose was to sketch the preliminary theory for the construction of sociological poetics (in which capacity it is an important forerunner to Medvedev's book), it had the effect, in the course of its argument, of crystallizing a conceptual center for all questions involving monologue, dialogue, stylization, parody, *skaz*, and, in the strict sense, reported speech. In this way, it set the stage for Vološinov's own fundamental study of reported speech and Baxtin's magnum opus on "polyphonic structure."

Taking as his point of departure the idea that every instance of verbal intercourse operates within a system of assumed value judgments (the code of "social evaluation"), Vološinov describes the work of poetry as a "powerful condenser of unarticulated social value judgements" in which the vital roles are played by the three participants in the event of discourse, termed "author," "listener," and "hero":

> First and foremost, value judgements determine the author's selection of words and the reception of that selection (co-selection) by the listener. The poet, after all, selects words not from the dictionary but from the context of life, where words have been steeping in and become permeated with value judgements. Thus he selects the value judgements associated with the words, and does so, moreover, from the standpoint of the incarnated bearers of those value judgements. It can be said that the poet works constantly in conjunction with his listener's sympathy or antipathy, agreement or disagreement. Furthermore, evaluation is operative also with regard to the object of utterance—the hero. The simple selection of an epithet or metaphor is already an active evaluative act with orientation in both those directions: toward the listener and toward the hero. Listener and hero are constant participants in the creative event which does not for a single instant cease to be an event of living communication involving all three.[23]

---

21. None of the studies by Vinogradov relevant here has, to my knowledge, been translated into English. Their titles are included in the bibliography to V. Erlich, *Russian formalism*, p. 258.

22. *Zvezda*, 6 (1926), pp. 244-267. Vološinov is also the author of a lengthy, three-part essay entitled "Stilistika xudožestvennoj reči" [The Stylistics of Verbal Art], *Literaturnaja učeba*, 2 (1929), pp. 46-66; 3 pp. 65-87; 5 pp. 43-57. This essay essentially rehearses the basic ideas of *Marxism and the Philosophy of Language* for the particular purpose of instructing and guiding novice writers.

23. *Zvezda*, 6 (1926), p. 258.

In effect, the *principle* of dialogue has been predicated over all discourse, with particular and special meaning for verbal art. By "author," "listener," and "hero" with reference to verbal art, Vološinov clearly and explicitly means factors within the artistic structure of a literary work and not the actual, real-life writer, reference and reading public, which are factors of a different order. "Author," "listener," and "hero" are rather "the essential constitutive factors of a work of literature. . . the vital forces that shape form and style and are completely detectable by any competent scrutinizer."[24]

Each of the participants represents a context of discourse in active, dynamic relationship with the other two. The author's speech context is "dominant" in the sense that it coincides with the message as a whole, encompassing the other contexts and incorporating them within itself. But at the same time as presenting the context of hero, the author establishes a relationship with that context through which he affects that context in some way or by which his own, authorial, context is affected. Likewise, at the same time as positing a listener, the author enters into a relationship with the latter's assumed or anticipated context of response whereby effects on the hero's context (listener-hero relationship) and/or on the author's own (author-listener relationship) are produced. Thus, the communicative triad of the addresser of the message (speaker, author, sender, encoder, etc.); addressee (listener, reader, receiver, decoder, etc.), to whom the message is directed; and the message content (referent, object, "hero"), whom or what the message is about is registered as the prime organizing center of literary structure. The three are bound together by a complex network of highly variable evaluative interrelationships; and that network becomes a unifying focus of investigation for a very broad range of literary problems.

In the third, final, section of his *Marxism and the Philosophy of Language,* Vološinov focused attention on the fundamental principles governing the phenomena of reported speech. His concern was not strictly with verbal art, but it was in verbal art that Vološinov saw the fullest and most intricate expression of those principles in operation. Thus while presented as a study of a special, "pivotal" problem in syntax, Vološinov's investigation into the dynamic interrelationship of reporting and reported messages has definite bearings on literary problems as well. Indeed, Vološinov vividly demonstrates the vital interconnectedness of the studies of language and literature.

The literary implications of Vološinov's analysis have reference to at least two crucial areas, two dimensions, of literary study. First of all, the correlation between forms of reported speech (patterns and modifications) and the socioideological generation of language has direct bearing on literary history. In Vološinov's view: "It is the function of society to select and make grammatical (adapt to the the grammatical structure of its language) just those factors in the active and

24. *Ibid.,* p. 260.

evaluative reception of utterances that are socially vital and constant and, hence, are grounded in the economic being of the particular community of speakers [page 117 in this book]." The forms of reported speech, therefore, are important not as abstract grammatical categories but as language processes in dynamic interrelation with other social processes:

> We are far from claiming that syntactic forms—for instance, those of direct and indirect discourse—directly and unequivocally express the tendencies and forms of an active, evaluative reception of another's utterance. Our speech reception does not, of course, operate directly in the forms of indirect and direct discourse. These forms are only standardized patterns for reporting speech. But, on the one hand, these patterns and their modifications could have arisen and taken shape only in accordance with the governing tendencies of speech reception; on the other hand, once these patterns have assumed shape and function in the language, they in turn exert an influence, regulating or inhibiting in their development, on the tendencies of evaluative reception that operate within the channel prescribed by the existing forms [pages 117-118 in this book].

Therefore, the concrete implementations of reported speech forms (the modifications and variants of patterns) must be registered not only among the primary distinguishing characteristics that mark the epochal shifts in overall ideological development, and, hence, also the epochs of literary history, but also must figure among the primary distinguishing characteristics of all literary schools, trends, movements; i.e., they must be regarded as fundamental constituent features of the very process of literary evolution as such.

The essential point is that the patterns of reported speech change historically with respect to the weight, value, and the hierarchical status of reporting and reported messages in their interrelationship. Direct discourse in medieval literature is not the same as direct discourse in, say, the literature of the Renaissance or that of the second half of the 19th century. Furthermore, under the impact of developing literary and extraliterary tendencies, certain modifications and variants are advanced to a commanding, structure-organizing position. Such, for instance, is the role of forms of quasi-quoted speech in modern prose fiction, forms that underlie such things commonly referred to as "interior monologue" or "stream of consciousness." At the same time, such hard to define literary realities as classicism, romanticism, realism, symbolism, etc., are also susceptible to definition in terms of coordinates of the historical variables in the interrelationship of reporting and reported contexts. This possibility, firmly established in Vološinov's analysis of reported speech, has hardly even yet been recognized in literary scholarship.

With its distinction between the "linear" and "pictorial" tendencies in the dynamism of the reporting-reported interrelationship, its exposition of opposed "referent-" and "texture-analyzing" orientations in indirect discourse, and its presentation of a whole system of modifications and variants of direct discourse, including, importantly, quasi-direct discourse, Vološinov's treatment of reported speech also provides focal points for the concrete stylistic analysis of texts, primarily, but of course not exclusively, texts in the narrative genres. Every text represents a selection and concatenation of reporting-reported procedures. Analysis of the specific organization of these procedures in a literary work reveals its stylistic structure, not of course in the sense of an inventory of its stylistic ingredients, but precisely of its value-charged stylistic mode of operation. Thus, for instance, in connection with what he termed "anticipated and disseminated direct discourse," Vološinov took a story by Dostoevskij, *Skvernyj anekdot* [A Nasty Story]," and from analysis of it concluded:

> . . . almost every word in the narrative (as concerns its expressivity, its emotional coloring, its accentual position in the phrase) figures simultaneously in two intersecting contexts, two speech acts: in the speech of the author-narrator (ironic and mocking) and the speech of the hero (who is far removed from irony). This simultaneous participation of two speech acts, each differently oriented in its expressivity, also explains the curious sentence structure, the twists and turns of syntax, the highly original style of the story. If only one of the speech acts had been used, the sentences would have been structured otherwise; the style would have been different [page 136 in this book].

The range of procedures extends from the relatively straightforward, sharply and mutually delimited relations of reporting and reported contexts to extremely complex, even highly ambiguous, "mixed" forms in which the key role is played by the phenomenon of "speech interference." Needless to say, all procedures involve evaluative processes, the simpler forms no less than the complex ones. Every literary work operates in one or more registers of this range; many literary works, modern novels especially, are characterized by systems of registers with varied and often subtly nuanced transitions from one to another. To fail to take account of this interrelation and interplay of reporting and reported contexts, as do many discussions about "showing and telling," the dramatic or objective mode of narration, point-of-view narration, "reliable" and "unreliable" authors and narrators, "stream of consciousness" technique and other, similar topics, is to miss the central integrity of the text.[25]

25. Vološinov's ideas regarding reported speech (indeed, the ideas of the Baxtin group in general) have found fresh and vital reintroduction into Russian literary scholarship via the semiotic studies of the extraordinary, recently developing "Tartu" or "Lotman" school. (On this school, see the English introduction to the Brown University reprint of Ju. M. Lotman, *Lektsii po strukturaľnoj poètike* [Lectures on Structural Poetics], Providence, Rhode Island, 1968, pp. vii-x.) A concrete case in point is B. A. Uspenskij, *Poètika kompozicii* [The Poetics of Composition] (Moscow, 1970). Uspenskij not only applies Vološinov's theories throughout his study, but also, virtually for the first time in Russian literary scholarship, gives Vološinov full credit for them. Symptomatically enough, the new Russian semiotics of art makes explicit its debt not only to the Baxtin group but also to formalist theorists, especially Tynjanov, Jakobson, and Vinogradov.

In his preface to *Marxism and the Philosophy of Language,* Vološinov himself noted that the object of study in Part III of the book

> "the problem of utterance within utterance, has a broad significance extending beyond the confines of syntax. The fact is that a number of paramount literary phenomena—character speech (the construction of character in general), *skaz*, stylization, and parody—are nothing else than different varieties of refraction of 'another's speech.' An understanding of this kind of speech and its sociological governance is an essential condition for the productive treatment of all the literary phenomena mentioned [*Marksizm i filosofija jazyka*, Leningrad, 1930, pp. 11-12].

However, Vološinov's own efforts did not, and could not (considering that syntax was the primary focus of his attention), include full treatment of the implications of his theory for the study of literature. Indeed, stylization, parody, and *skaz* are not dealt with at all. It was not Vološinov but rather M. M. Baxtin who fully and systematically elaborated the literary theory and analysis of "another's speech." Treatment of this topic forms the theoretical basis for Baxtin's extraordinary treatise on the art of the polyphonic novel as exemplified by the works of its great creator, Fedor Dostoevskij.[26]

Baxtin argues that recognition of duplexity in such phenomena as stylization, parody, *skaz*, and any one utterance in a dialogic exchange, i.e., recognition that "in all of them discourse maintains a double focus, aimed at the referential object of speech, as in ordinary discourse, and simultaneously at a second context of discourse, a second speech act by another addresser [p. 176]," already reveals the inadequacy of traditional stylistics, with its exclusive "monologic" frame of reference, and calls for an entirely new approach which takes the principle of duplexity into fundamental account.

The new approach is established through a system of analysis based on the interrelation of the contexts of "author's speech" and "another's speech." Author's speech is defined as speech having direct and immediate reference to its object and expressing the "ultimate conceptual authority." It is

> "handled stylistically as speech aimed at its direct referential denotation: it must be adequate to its object (of whatever nature, poetic or other); it must be expressive, forceful, pithy, elegant and so forth, from the point of view of its direct referential mission—to denote, express, convey, or depict something; and its stylistic treatment is oriented toward the concurring comprehension of its referent [p. 178]."

26. *Problemy tvorčestva Dostoevskogo* [Problems of Dostoevskij's Creative Art] (Leningrad, 1929). In 1963, after Baxtin was "rehabilitated," a new, expanded edition of this book came out under the title *Problemy poetiki Dostoevskogo* [Problems of Dostoevskij's Poetics]. To my knowledge, no translation of the full text of either edition has yet appeared in English. One chapter, having to do with *Notes from Underground*, was translated for the Crowell Critical Library edition of *Notes from Underground*, edited by R. G. Durgy, pp. 203-216 (Crowell, New York, 1969). The basic, theoretical chapter, also from the 1929 edition, "Discourse Typology in Prose," appears in *Readings*. Page numbers in brackets after quotations in the present essay refer to *Readings*.

To just such a context of speech Baxtin assigns the term "monologue." The direct speech of another—the speech of the heroes, the characters in a work—while also having direct, referential meaning, occupies a different position, "lies on a different plane," than the author's direct speech. It is in fact included in and subordinated to the author's context and is therefore subject to different stylistic treatment:

> The hero's utterance is handled precisely as the words of another addresser—as words belonging to a personage of a certain specific individuality or type, that is, it is handled as an object of the author's intentions, and not at all in terms of its own referential aim [p. 178].

This type of utterance Baxtin calls "represented" or "objectified" utterance.

Monologic utterance (author's direct speech) and objectified utterance (character's direct speech) are the first two degrees of distinction in Baxtin's theory of speech forms. They are both, in his classification, "single-voiced" utterances:

> The unmediated, intentional utterance is focused on its referential object, and it constitutes the ultimate conceptual authority within the given context. The objectified utterance is likewise focused only on its referential object, but at the same time it is itself the object of another, the author's, intention, Still, this other intention does not penetrate the objectified utterance; it takes that utterance as a whole and, without altering its meaning or tone, subordinates it to its own purposes. It does not impose upon the objectified utterance a different referential meaning. An utterance which becomes objectified does so, as it were, without knowing it, like a man who goes about his business unaware that he is being watched. An objectified utterance sounds just as if it were a direct, intentional utterance. Utterances both of the first and the second type of discourse each have one intention, each one voice: they are single-voiced utterances [p. 180].

From these basic "single-voiced" utterances, Baxtin proceeds to "double-voiced" utterances:

> An author may utilize the speech act of another in pursuit of his own aims and in such a way as to impose a new intention on the utterance, which nevertheless retains its own proper referential intention. Under these circumstances and in keeping with the author's purpose, such an utterance must be recognized as originating from another addresser. Thus, within a single utterance, there may occur two intentions, two voices [p. 180].

Among such double-voiced utterances are included stylization, parody and *skaz*.

Between stylization and parody, a crucial difference in double-voicedness occurs. "Stylization presupposes style; it presupposes that the set of stylistic devices it reproduces had at one time a direct and immediate intentionality and expressed the ultimate conceptual authority [p. 181]." The effect of stylization is to "conventionalize" any such style. Therefore, stylization implies a certain concurrence, an agreement between the two voices involved: "The author's intention, having penetrated the other speech act and having become embedded in it, does not clash with the other intention; it follows that intention in the latter's own direction, only making that direction conventional [p. 185]." Such a double-voiced utterance is at the same time "unidirectional." Parody, in contrast, involves the presence within one utterance of two not only different but *opposed*, clashing intentions: "The second voice, having lodged in the other speech, clashes antagonistically with the original, host voice and forces it to serve directly opposite aims. Speech becomes a battlefield for opposing intentions [p. 185]." Baxtin designates such a double-voiced utterance "varidirectional." *Skaz*, identified simply as "narrator's narration," occupies the same range as both stylization and parody; it is either unidirectional (stylized *skaz*) or varidirectional (parodic *skaz*).

What unites the unidirectional and varidirectional variants of this third, double-voiced type of discourse is the passivity of the "other voice": ". . . in stylization, narrator's narration and parody the other speech act is completely passive in the hands of the author who avails himself of it. He, so to speak, takes someone else's speech act, which is defenceless and submissive, and implants his own intentions in it, making it serve his new aims [p. 190]." In this respect, they contrast with another set of variants of the same third type where the relationship between the two speech acts is *active*. Here are found such forms as hidden polemic and hidden dialogue, indeed the forms of dialogue itself and all forms of speech affected by "awareness of another speech act." In these variants, "the other speech act remains outside the bounds of the author's speech, but is implied or alluded to in that speech. The other speech act is not reproduced with a new intention, but shapes the author's speech while remaining outside its boundaries [p. 187]." These active variants of the third type of discourse play particularly important roles in creating polyphonic structure.

Polyphonic structure takes its special shape and meaning against the background of, and in contrast to, "homophonic" structure. They contrast precisely as monologic and dialogic structures in the sense the terms "monologue" and "dialogue" acquire in Baxtin's system of analysis. In homophonic structure, "whatever the types of discourse employed by the author-monologist and whatever their compositional deployment, the author's intentions must dominate and must constitute a compact, unequivocal whole."[27] The author's voice, as the bearer of the ultimate conceptual authority, constantly regulates and ultimately resolves any interplay of other voices in the text; indeed, it is from its unitary position that all other voices are meant to be perceived and judged (Tolstoj can be cited as a particularly egregious case). In polyphonic structure, the other voices in the text come into their own, as it were; they acquire the status of full-fledged verbal and conceptual centers whose relationship, both among themselves

27. *Problemy tvorčestva Dostoevskogo*, p. 134.

and with the author's voice, becomes intensely dialogic and not susceptible to subordination to "the verbal-conceptual dictatorship of monologic unity of style and tone."[28]

The theory of discourse and system of analysis elaborated by Baxtin have a meaning far broader, of course, than that as instruments for the exposition of Dostoevskij's polyphonic art (although Baxtin's immense achievement in that regard ought not be overlooked). Together with Vološinov, Baxtin fundamentally reoriented the whole field of stylistic inquiry from componential, taxonomic description to systematic disclosure of speech formations in the dynamic terms of "speech within speech and speech about speech," for only in those terms can the actual *structure* of such formations be grasped. Therein, too, of course, consists the essential sociological dimension to the study. As Baxtin states it:

> The problem of the orientation of speech toward another utterance has a sociological significance of the highest order. The speech act by its nature is social. The word is not a tangible object, but an always shifting, always changing means of social communication. It never rests with one consciousness, one voice. Its dynamism consists in movement from speaker to speaker, from one context to another, from one generation to another. Through it all, the word does not forget its path of transfer and cannot completely free itself from the power of those concrete contexts into which it has entered. By no means does each member of the community apprehend the word as a neutral medium of the language system, free from intentions and untenanted by the voices of its previous users. Instead, he receives the word from another voice, a word full of that other voice. The word enters his context from another context, permeated with the intentions of other speakers. His own intention finds the word already occupied. Thus the orientation of word among words, the various perceptions of other speech acts, and the various means of reacting to them are perhaps the most crucial problems in the sociology of language usage, any kind of language usage, including the artistic [p. 195].

Baxtin called his study of polyphonic structure an "immanent-sociological analysis," the immanent-sociological character of literature residing, as indicated, in language usage. Unmistakably, this point of view and the point of view, mentioned above, arrived at by Jurij Tynjanov fundamentally coincide. Furthermore, nothing even remotely suggesting the necessity for eclecticism appears in Baxtin's argument. While admitting that his study does not even begin to constitute a sociological explanation of the literary phenomenon in question, Baxtin insisted that it is an indispensable prerequisite for such an explanation:

> "The very material to be made the subject of sociological explanation must first be identified and elucidated as an intrinsic social phenomenon, for only in that case can sociological explanation be in accord with the structure of the fact it attempts to explain."[29]

28. *Ibid.*
29. *Ibid.*, p. 213.

With its symptomatic difference in terminology, indicating a difference not so much of basic principles as of basic emphases, this statement of Baxtin's fully correlates with the Jakobson-Tynjanov theses and further substantiates the claim that the sociological poetics of the Baxtin group (minus Medvedev's eclecticism; that is, minus Marxist presuppositions) and the formal method, both of them en route to complex, comprehensive study of literature as a system of signs within a system of signs, represented parallel, overlapping, interdependent, and ultimately completely reconcilable methods.

Index